Dedicated to my wife Dolly,
my love for almost fifty years; and
our children, Opher, Guy, and Hila,
now located on three continents;
and to our seven grandchildren.
They are the ones who led me down
the yellow brick road to where
futures are formed.

Acknowledgments

The idea of writing about product form germinated ten years ago from a series of lectures on forecasting the future, which I presented to my industrial design students. I felt then that envisioning future products using product semantics methods underscored the form part but ignored the wider scope of semantics. As I was preoccupied then with academic management at the Holon Institute of Technology in Israel, my research work was kept on a prolonged hold.

Only when taking an extended sabbatical leave to the Bay Area was I able to go on with my research interests. At the invitation of my colleague and good friend, Professor Ricardo Gomes, then the Chair of the Department of Design and Industry (DAI) at San Francisco State University, I had at last the time, place, and means to make this book a reality. I should also thank Dr. Marilyn Jackson, and Professor Jane Veeder, the current Chair, for helping me out while at DAI.

The early airings of my theories were before the DesignX group at the Center for Design Research (CDR) at Stanford University. Research discussions and critique by the DesignX group, headed by Professor Larry Leifer, made me attentive to the complexities of qualitative vs. quantitative research in design. I should also thank my Israeli colleague Professor Gabriela Goldschmidt for introducing me to the CDR and for her advice regarding publishing my book.

Rudolf van Wezel, the director of BIS Publishers was enthusiastic from the beginning about a book on product form, a topic for which he was looking for quite some time. His enthusiasm converted a manuscript into reality. Professor Paul Hekkert, Head of the Industrial Design Department of Delft Technical University (TUDelft) was the editor of my manuscript. Paul's deep knowledge of the cognitive sciences and their role in design helped me much in articulating (the better word nowadays is "framing") the scientific base of my hypotheses.

On behalf of BIS Publishers, John Loughlin did an excellent job of language editing. I enjoyed his arguing with some of my assumptions. And finally, a book about both design and form depends much on the quality of book design: putting together text, diagrams, photos, and other images into a gorgeous and coherent layout. I am much indebted to Sandra van der Putten for realizing my vision.

Contents

PREFACE
A Firearm with a Moustache

Form (n)

(Philosophy) (in the philosophy of Plato) An ideal archetype existing independently of those individuals which fall under it, supposedly explaining their common properties and serving as the only objects of true knowledge as opposed to the mere opinion obtainable of matters of fact. Also called Idea.

Collins English Dictionary

Twenty year ago, I visited the Doge's Palace Armory Museum in Venice, Italy. The museum was crammed with military artifacts attesting to the long history of the Venetian Republic. Next to the so-called cold weapons (swords, battle axes, bows and arrows) was an almost anonymous display of very early handguns. To my surprise, several handguns had a small metal Salvador Dali moustache attached horizontally to the tip of the barrel, exactly where the front sight is on modern guns. What was the military purpose of it? Suddenly it hit me; if I were out there in the Middle Ages and somebody were to point that newly introduced weapon at me, how could I be intimidated by it if I had never seen it before? That moustache-like shape was actually a minia-turized replica of the crossbow, the primary hand held weapon of the time. That was an intimidating cue, carried over to a new object in order to visually classify it. I later discovered that there existed an earlier gun-cum-crossbow combination, both func-tioning on the same wooden stock.

Several years afterwards, one of my industrial design students was working on a small hand gun specifically intended to be used by women for their personal protection. The barrel on her design had an external wavy shape; internally, of course, the gun bore was drilled straight. She rationalized that the wave gave the gun a softer, feminine look. On seeing the wavy barrel for the first time, we instructors and students alike concurred that the bullet undoubtedly had to come out of the barrel jumping like a Kangaroo. Such is the immense power of visual cues.

This book is probably the first all-encompassing book about the visual language of man-made products. The language of mass-produced objects has hidden visual cues based on the way our cognitive faculties interpret what we see ("the mind's eye"). Increasingly, recent research in the cognitive sciences shows that the mind is subconscious "primed" by prior experience. When we see an object, we compare it to an internal model previously established in our mind in order to determine what it is. But it does not just produce an image; it is as if we have in our mind some sort of a mental dictionary that correlates images to words. It seems that the mind associates images with words and words with images. When we hear common or specific object names, such as chair, tennis racket, or lightsaber, we see in our mind's eye an icon or archetypal image of that object in our mind. And it is then that our previous experience of the world comes to bear. A powerful harbinger of form is inherently cultural; we understand what falls in context with our shared traditions and patterns of behavior. If we are introduced to an object we have not seen before, we will try our best to classify it ("It looks like a…") by using verbal or visual metaphors. We are adept at relating images to words in our mental dictionary. As spoken languages and culture continually evolve and change, so does the language of form and, therefore, our understanding and classification of objects we see.

This book explains how mass-produced objects evolve over time and what made them change. Form evolution behaves in a similar way to language evolution and, in certain ways even similar to natural evolution. In a way, the book deals with meta-design, suggesting a birds-eye-view explanation of product evolution. It is expressly directed at a wide audience of prac-ticing designers, educators, historians, and the layman interested in visual culture. As it is the first book that looks at product form development in a comprehensive way, I hope it will be seen on library shelves in design schools. Visual language is better explained by visual examples. Therefore, the book is highly visual (but also textual), explaining fundamental ideas through exten-sive use of computer-generated images, photos, and diagrams showing the evolution of products families.

This book is not a historical review of thousands of years of evolution of man-made tools, artifacts, and objects, nor is it a book about the history of style. This book focuses on relatively recent history and on present and future trends.

I had hesitations as to the name of this book—*Form of Design* or *Design of Form*? Both words happen to have several dictionary meanings, from the metaphysical to the practical. The definition of the word "design" is notoriously disputed, with as many definitions as there are designers. "Form" can be understood as the shape and structure of an object, but also as the essence of something (just two of many dictionary definitions. Collins Dictionary has twenty-four separate meanings of the noun "form"). Therefore, I feel more comfortable with the book's subtitle: *Deciphering the Language of Mass-Produced Objects*.

Though form was, and very much is, a mainstay of product design, it was often played down or even neglected, being considered as merely skin deep. The design field came of age; it is no longer an applied technical profession but a respected body of knowledge. Design studies now cover weighty topics such as ethics, problem solving, design thinking, and design research methodology. It is understandable that during a period of academic formation, form as a legitimate research subject was set aside in preference to more academic studies. As design research has come of age and design thinking is an acknowledged management method causing D-schools to compete with B-schools, it is time to overcome that uneasiness of dealing just with the visual nature of design. Form is presently still an under-treated area of design research, even though the first research community focusing on form, DeSForM, has been active since 2005, signifying a growing interest in the visual language of man-made products.

At the end of the day, whatever the process they go through, most designers—product designers in particular—create a physical entity: a form. Throughout undergraduate studies in design, student's form development is analyzed and criticized (albeit not in isolation, usually in concurrence with problem solving, innovation, and the user in mind). We should openly recognize that form development and aesthetic considerations are indispensable essentials of the design profession.

Product designers, who are so attentive to form development in their practical work, are often not sufficiently knowledgeable of how the human mind reads visual forms as a coherent language. It may be because product designers are concerned with the particular physical object at the expense of theoretical nuances. I am often surprised at the lack of inquiry into form archetypes in product development. The commonplace explanation is that designers traditionally gaze into the future rather than the past, interested in where design goes to rather than where design came from.

Graphic designers, though not well versed in Jungian psychology, are by far more familiar with form perception than are product designers. Graphic designers often have to translate complex textual knowledge into visual form (especially those designers who deal with infographics), so that they become appreciative of visual abstraction in their training. No wonder that archetypes of man-made products are often described by graphic icons.

I emphasize here that form recognition studies should not be the exclusive domain of the cognitive sciences. From the early toolmakers to the latest technological innovations, form is an acknowledged expression of the human species. Form is the cultural constituent of design.

For four hundred years, these form aesthetics were the sole domain of art historians. Art historians tend to capitalize on the individual creative genius, and to focus on art movements in historical context, thus requiring time perspective, stopping short of recent times. Industrial design is still a young profession; history of design is even younger. So far, the writings of design historian have a tendency to follow art history methodology, albeit with an enhanced understanding of technology and materials and with lesser bias against style and function. Still, it is so easy to fall into the "Form follows Function" trap, as if form will arise by itself from the functional solution to the problem. This is a classic Deus ex machina approach. This traditional approach gives incentive for a book that points out what affects form other than function alone.

The purpose of this book is three-fold: to find order in man-made things (a theory), to develop an analytical tool (a method), and to assist in forecasting future product form (application). I spell out the governing rules of form evolution and use case studies to demonstrate this evolution over (recent) times of diversity of product families such as smartphones and bicycles, accompanied by numerous illustrations, in order to assist in identifying the visual evolutionary processes involved.

Part 1 of the book sums up the current natural and social sciences knowledge on how the mind interprets what it sees (the mind's eye), and is followed by a summary of design research on the visual language of products.

Part 2 outlines the theory of product form evolution and sets a number of governing rules that define such form evolution.

Part 3, presents actual applications of ideas discussed in Parts 1 and 2, and occupies about two thirds of the book. Fourteen case studies investigate the evolution of form of contemporary product families over time, trying to gain insight into why product form changed the way it did (and it is not just due to technological advancement). Here I tried to be as visual as possible with diagrams of form development explained by text and image.

If he or she wishes, the reader may go directly to Part 3 and then back to the previous Parts, or read from the beginning and jump every now and then to a case study. It is easy to do since each case study stands on its own.

The question left largely unanswered in this book is the last of the three purposes I have mentioned earlier: forecasting the future of product form by investigating the past. Can we identify trends and predict where will they lead design into the future? I assume that none of us believe that the future will be visually sterile, as was suggested by the Star Trek television series environment (I still give the series credit for envisioning future smartphones, stun guns, and non-intrusive medical analyzers).

Can we extrapolate into the future in the design fields as engineers often do? In the age of increased disruptive innovation as a management method should we also expect disruptive design? In my mind I foresee the increased importance of the designer's role as an interpreter, making the new understood and accepted.

PART 1
The Nature of Man-Made Artifacts

INTRODUCTION
What we "read" between the lines

What is it...?

Reading between the lines is a common human trait and a familiar literary technique. The title of this introduction refers of course to visual lines rather than the printed ones, and to what we may infer from "reading" what is hidden behind them. The image is strictly visual, what we read there may be also verbal.

The following is a little quiz in which we will try to get some hints about the nature of understanding the language of man-made objects. I will show several pictures of unfamiliar objects and ask you to record the thought process that you go through in trying to understand what you see. I am aware that different people think differently and rely on different visual cues, but it is reasonable to assume that if we reach the same conclusion we may have a corresponding thought process. Here we go:

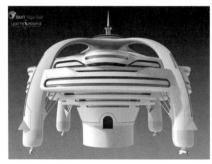

1.

That seems to be very futuristic—a Star Trek-variety of a space ship? Because of the perspective, I realize that it is quite big, so maybe an architectural structure? So the horizontal bands are probably floors or decks. Those four arches remind me of the famous Los Angeles Airport landmark. So, something to do with travel? Only now I notice the four propellers at the bottom of each arch. Transportation! Travel, decks, propellers; oh, It is a futuristic cruise ship! Just add water and it all falls in place (fig. 3).

2.

Something circular. A wheel. But how do you ride this thing? By the size of the screws it is small, not a bike. It is a tool. The elongated thing is probably a handle. Now I notice the stylized image of a lion, its front paws grabbing the disc. These teeth on the disc—they are a reference to cutting. Lion grabs its food, cutting. It is a food-cutting tool (close, it is a pizza cutter).

3. A CRUISE SHIP

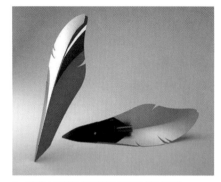

4.

Wheels again...and a flowing body—a futuristic motorcycle? The configuration and wheels location make no sense of it. That tip on the right reminds me of something. I still don't know what it is.

5. TWO VIEWS OF THE SAME OBJECT

This one is easy: obviously a metallic feather. The tip looks important. There's a black box hidden at the tip, a short tube. I get it: it is a quill pen. You have to recall history for that.

Back to figure 4—it is a ballpoint pen. We hardly see it even after the pen in figure 5. Yes, we see the tip, but we also see so many distracting elements associated with totally different images. Even in our hand we may not understand it (to clarify, one wheel is a pen clip, the other the clicking lever).

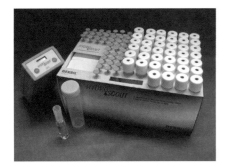

6.

Obviously, this is a piece of lab equipment. Maybe from a medical lab? Since we have seen so many CSI programs, this must be a DNA analyzer. The sealed test tube next to it is a definite clue. (Actually, it is a water-testing device, but what's the difference?)

7.

One cannot be mistaken in guessing the object in figure 7. We recognize the hammer and we recognize the flame. Obviously it is a whimsical lighter, in spite of the unusual mixture.

8.

Is it a bar's fancy beer-tap? No, it is a modern bathroom's sink faucet with a long lever. But where does the water come out? Wait, I have seen these tiny holes on the handle before, as on a microphone. It's much smaller than I thought, and so now I recognize the earlobe shape. It is a portable, behind-the-ear Bluetooth telephone headset.

9.

However strange the form or the materials, we always recognize a couch for what it is.

10.

Kids' games? Bottles? One definite visual hint and we know that it is a USB drive.

11.

The Sony logo is a clear giveaway for an electronic gadget with a color display. But why does it not have the usual flat shape? What is the cylindrical thing in the middle? A battery case? The whole concept looks more like a bracelet with a hinge. Look at figure 14 on the next page.

12.

It is a machine of sorts. I have not seen it before and I do not pretend to know what it is or what it does, but certainly it is an industrial machine.

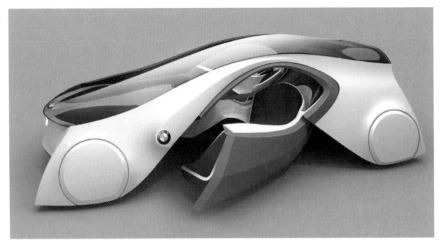

13.

Quite strange…sculptural…futuristic…. If not for the minimal indication that it has wheels hidden behind the skin I may have missed that it is a concept car. Now I even see the BMW emblem.

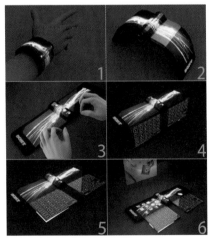

14. A WEARABLE COMPUTER CONCEPT

It is a wearable folding computer concept. We were really close in our guess.

15.

This thing cannot have any use. It must be a sculpture, a work of art. I can even guess the artist could have named it something like "Revelation No. 29" or "Mona Lisa revisited."

This man-made objects identification quiz was just a sampler. Every day we use our accumulated visual knowledge (actually a visual language) as cues, analogies, or references in order to make the unfamiliar familiar. If several clues fit together, we know that we are on the right track to understanding what it is.

From here on I will spend less time asking, "What is it?" but rather deal with "Why does it look the way it does?" Let's go on to an overview of scientific and design-based knowledge in the next two chapters.

The mind's eye

The focus of our inquiry

In Shakespeare's time the phrase "mind's eye" was assigned to what appears only in our imagination. Nowadays—perhaps popularized by Oliver Sacks' book using the phrase in its title—"mind's eye" refers to overall human ability for visualization, the experience of mental imagery and our ability to "see" things with the mind. We recognize now that seeing is not a simple, straightforward process; it is affected by what we think and believe, and is tinted by our prior experience. Policemen will tell you how often witnesses may differ in identifying the model and color of a car that escaped from a crime scene. It is enough that the word "blue" will be pronounced nearby and the witness will recall a blue car.

Researching and plotting the various case studies in Part 3 of this book, I came to recognize that there is a gripping inter-action between how we classify related objects in lingual terms (for example:

telephone, walkie-talkie, Walkman, smart-phone, tablet, laptop, and so on) and how we visually classify images of the same objects. Moreover, when we see a photograph of a chair, the word chair appears as if out of nowhere on the tip of our tongue. When we say merry-go-round we see in our mind's eye images of a revolving merry-go-round and horses. Some may even hear a pipe organ and children may indicate a spinning motion with their hand. In a less scientific language I may say that there must be a language-to-image dictionary in our brain. The previous chapter, *What we "read" between the lines*, reflects our anxiety when we do not understand what we see or if we do not find the right word to define an object. Therefore, I will focus my discussion in this chapter on cognitive processes specific to image and language and their interaction and then expand briefly into culturally related concepts. I will begin with the cognitive sciences, move briefly through the life sciences, and end this swift journey in the social sciences ant the humanities. I am not going to probe deeply into the cognitive sciences except as required to support this book's hypothesis.

For further reading, I suggest exploring the following references:

- Pinker, Steven, *How the Mind Works* (Norton, 1997)—a very readable general reference on the cognitive sciences.

- Weinschenk, Susan M., *100 Things Every Designer Needs to Know About People* (New Rider, 2011)—practical and to the point. Look up the chapter on how people see.

- Ware, Colin, *Visual Thinking for Design*, Morgan Kaufmann, 2008—an informa-tive and ample-illustrated book.

- Ware, Colin, *Information Visualization: Perception for Design* (3rd ed. Morgan Kaufmann, 2012)—this is the authorita-tive book on the subject.

Mental processing of images

With no hesitation, the sight faculty is considered to be the human species' most developed sense. The eye's actual acquired information about the world is quite rudimentary; most of the visual processing is done in the brain. A good demonstration of our brain's capacity to intervene in what we see is the famous "Did you notice the gorilla passing through a basketball game?" short video you can find on the internet (though the title is already a rude spoiler).

1. WHO IS THE FAMOUS PERSON IN THE CROWD?

Early Man, the hunter-gatherer roaming the savannas of Africa, had to rely on keen visual comprehension of the environment in order to survive. The present Social Man uses sight in order to easily identify faces and interpret facial gestures. We, today, are so adept in visual recognition that we swiftly locate a familiar face in the crowd, as though we skip analyzing the rest. Psychology textbooks used to demon-strate this almost instantaneous ability for people to identify faces with this photograph of President John F. Kennedy in the crowd (fig. 1).

These qualities are the results of millions of years of Man's evolutionary adaptation. As this book deals with recent man-made objects—a very recent phenomenon in historical terms, a blink of an eye in evolutionary terms—we should look into several aspects of the mind's eye in order to gain insights into our mind's dealing in object recognition.

Gestalt, Geons, and More: theories of object recognition

The human visual system recovers 3-dimensional form of what we observe from inherently ambiguous 2-dimensional retinal images. How this feat is accomplished is perhaps the most fundamental problem faced by the science of cognition. Despite the impression that vision seems effortless, a vast volume of processing is involved in the construction of an internal representation of the visible scene outside.

Though science does not yet have a verified definitive explanation, there are several theories about object perception. Each offers an incomplete explanation and each is partly inadequate, though in different ways. It is quite likely that the brain form-processing could involve aspects of more than just one of these theories, depending on the particular problem to be solved by the brain.

2. FIGURE-GROUND EFFECT APPLIED TO LOGOS

3. EXAMPLES OF THE LAW OF CLOSURE (LEFT, CENTER) AND THE LAW OF PROXIMITY (RIGHT)

Gestalt theory

Perception is not a passive recording of all that is in front of the eyes, but is a continuous judgment of contents, shapes, and scale and color relationships. We are ever fascinated by visual illusions that show our sense of sight to be operating selectively and that it is sometimes misled by its own interpretation. Designers are familiar with the figure-ground effect, where the sense of sight tries to extricate a figure from its background. In the well-known illusion we may see either a silhouette of a wine cup in white or silhouettes of two opposing faces in black, but we cannot see both of them at once, because each of them belongs to a different gestalt judgment. Graphic designers add substance to images by using the figure-ground effect (fig. 2)

The perception of a shape requires the grasping of the essential structural features in order to produce a "whole," or Gestalt. The theory of the Gestalt, or laws of perceptual organization, was proposed by Christian von Ehrenfels in 1890. He pointed out that a melody is still recognizable when played in different keys and argued that the whole is not simply the sum of its parts but a total structure. For example, motion pictures are based on the Gestalt principle, with a series of still images appearing in rapid succession to form a seamless visual experience.

As stated by Gestalt psychology, the whole is different from the sum of its parts. Based upon this belief, Gestalt psychologists developed a set of principles to explain perceptual organization.

These principles are often referred to as the laws of perceptual organization:

- Law of Similarity—items that are similar tend to be grouped together. The American flag is grouped into *stars and stripes*, as the wording implies.

- Law of Simplicity, or Law of *Pragnanz* (clarity or good figure in German)—reality is reduced to its simplest form. We see the Olympics logo as five identical circles rather than compute their complex overlapping.

- Law of Proximity—things that are near each other seem to be grouped together. The Unilever logo is perceived as the letter U rather than an intricate set of shapes (fig. 3, right).

- Law of Continuity or Alignment—points that our mind connects by imaginary straight or curving lines are seen in a way that follows the smoothest path.

- Law of Closure—things are grouped together if they seem to complete some entity. Our brains often ignore contradictory information and fill in missing information (fig. 3, left and center). Take a face for example. It is a combination of shapes: eyes, nose, ears, mouth. One may recognize a face even if it is partially hidden because our mind closes the image and supplies the parts that are missing.

These intrinsic abilities of our brains demonstrate how the mind is essentially seeking unifying patterns and simple whole shapes. These abilities were developed over millions of years of human

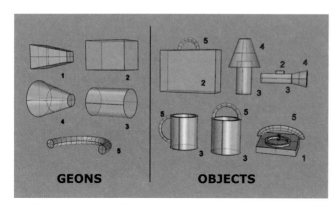

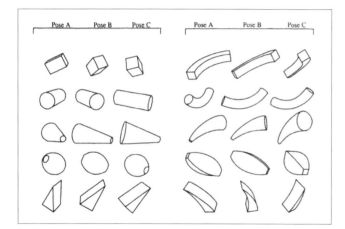

4. SEVERAL BASIC GEONS (LEFT) AND GEON-DEFINED OBJECTS (RIGHT)

5. GEONS ARE READILY RECOGNIZED IN SPITE OF DIFFERENT SPATIAL POSITIONING

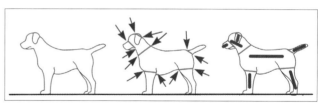

6. FROM FORM TO CONCAVE LOCATION SUBDIVISION TO STRUCTURE

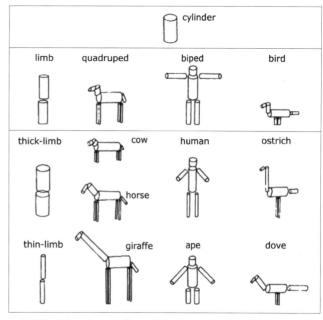

7. MARR AND NISHIHARA'S STRUCTURAL ANALYSIS OF OBJECTS BASED ON HIERARCHY OF CYLINDERS

brain development in order to maximize cognition by creating processing shortcuts in our mind from the rudimentary information our eyes provide.

3D form recognition

Form cognition theories that deal with three-dimensional objects can be divided roughly into two approaches: the image-based and the structure-based. Image-based theories, such as Gestalt, treat what we see as if it is a photograph. Thus, for example, an upside-down face is much harder to recognize than a right-side-up face. Structure-based theories claim that object recognition is done by way of extracting the 3D structure of objects and

are therefore less dependent on viewing angle distortion (what we call parallax). Accordingly, recognition is possible from any viewpoint as individual parts of an object can be rotated to fit any particular view.

Neuropsychological evidence suggests that there are several stages in the process of object recognition. First comes processing of basic object components, such as color, depth, and form. Then these basic components are grouped into a unified Gestalt figure and figure-ground separation takes place. Then the visual representation is matched with existing structural descriptions in memory. Finally,

semantic attributes are applied to the visual representation, providing meaning, and thereby recognition.

Geon theory is the most familiar Structure-based theory, though controversial and often contested. The geon theory was first proposed by Irving Biederman in order to explain object recognition. In his theory, our minds use a perceptual set of geometric 3D primitives or geons (short for geometrical ions). Biederman proposed a set of thirty-six basic 3-dimensional geons or shapes, such as cylinder, cube, cone, sphere, etc. (fig. 4, left) that can be assembled in various arrangements to form a virtually unlimited number of objects. Different connections of the same geons can lead to different objects as a cup or a bucket (fig. 4, right).

Object identification involves finding the relationships between the separate geon components of the object, thus leading to a geon structural description (GSD) that lists the geons, their attributes, and their relations with adjacent geons. It is this structural description that provides a solution to viewpoint invariance: if two different spatial views of an object result in a similar GSD, they should be treated as equivalent by the object recognition system (fig. 5).

We designers feel at ease with the geon theory. Is it not the same approach as we are used to in building objects in 3D design software: using essentially the same basic primitives and then combining them together, manipulating them and then adding a layer of details? But it is not so simple, unfortunately. The geon theory is still inadequate to most cognitive scientists since it does not explain how the brain deconstructs an object into its geon primitives.

Marr and Nishihara (1978) suggested a higher-level approach to structure-based object recognition that resolves the geon theory weakness. They suggested that concave sections of the silhouette contour are critical in defining how different solid parts are perceptually defined (fig.6). A roughly drawn animal can readily be segment into generalized cones representing the head body, neck, legs, etc. Based on the resulting segmentation the brain reads a simplified form made from skeletal cylinders. Recognition is acquired when the observed object viewpoint is mentally rotated to match the stored archetypal description in the brain (fig. 7).

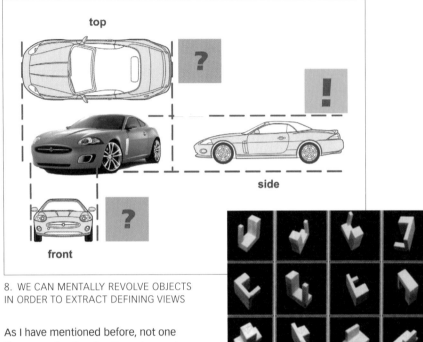

8. WE CAN MENTALLY REVOLVE OBJECTS IN ORDER TO EXTRACT DEFINING VIEWS

As I have mentioned before, not one theory carries the day. Recent experiments suggest the brain employs a combination of the geon theory and the Marr and Nishihara model.

View-dependent theory: Children tend to draw objects on the basis of the most form-defining silhouettes. Many objects have defining silhouettes that are easily recognizable—a house, a teapot, a person, or a car (fig. 8, left). These canonical

9. WE FEEL AT HOME WITH CONTOUR BASED OBJECT RECOGNITION (BOTTOM IMAGES)

silhouettes are often based on a particular view of an object, often from a point at right angles to a major plane of symmetry. Thus the researchers consider silhouettes to be especially important in determining how we perceive the structure of objects. They argue that buried in our brain are mechanisms that determine how silhouette information is interpreted.

Contour-propagation theory: (Tse, 2002) This theory is based on the fact that we can easily read 3D shapes even if drawn in silhouette and/or line drawings, such as comic strips (fig. 9). This capability is amazing, given both the scarcity of information in such images and the fact that no object in the world looks like a line drawing, or like contours without any surface information. The word propagation in this theory means that mental processing may involve not only the contour information but also considers information residing away from edges and inside the flat surfaces.

Neuroscience Research: insights into perception

Until the 21st century, science and medicine were restricted in performing invasive investigations of the brain. Therefore, our knowledge of the mind was based on behavioral and cognitive changes that appear in patients following a stroke or brain injury. Visual agnosia is the neuropsychology term for the inability of the brain to recognize or understand visual images. This impairment is usually seen in older people as a result of damage to the visual association cortex of the brain. An individual with visual agnosia has otherwise normal visual functioning and can see, but is unable to interpret or recognize what he sees, be it human faces or objects. Judging from the effect of localized brain injuries, researchers found that object memory tends to be grouped and located in the cortex corresponding to the nature of the images—faces, animals, man-made objects, etc. Strangely, animal recognition and object recognition are located in the same cortex area. This and other evidence led to the conclusion that image grouping is based mainly on the frequency and strength of memory acquisition. (A popular portrayal of visual agnosia is presented in Oliver Sacks' popular book, *The Man Who Mistook His Wife for a Hat*, as the title implies).

A classic experiment by Palmer, published in 1975, investigated whether the context in which an object is seen affects the perception of that object. Participants were most likely to identify objects correctly after previously seeing an appropriate context (for example, a photo of a kitchen table and then a photo of a bread loaf) and less likely to do so after seeing an inappropriate context (for example, a photo of a dilapidated house followed by a photo of a Rolls Royce in the garage). Furthermore, identification was worse when objects were in conflicting contexts even when compared to when there was no context at all. Palmer established the concept of schema—the way we perceive is affected by what we already know. A schema is a mental structure that holds our knowledge about a particular type of object, event, or group of people (fig. 10). It seems that our mind habitually searches for meaning—when presented with a random series of images or statements, the mind tries to put them together in a way that tells a meaningful, coherent story.

10. (LEFT) VISUAL PRIMING: THE FIGURE IN THE MIDDLE YOU SEE AS EITHER 13 OR B DEPENDING ON SCHEMA; (RIGHT) YOU READ "EIGHT" BECAUSE THE LETTERS ARE DRAWN FROM THE NUMERAL 8

Lupyan and Ward (2013) at the University of Wisconsin-Madison showed in a series of experiments that Language seems to enhance or block our visual perception. Students were presented with images of familiar objects in one eye and strong light flashes in the other eye that suppressed the perception of these objects. Hearing the name of the object prior to the flashes made them overcome that suppression and identify the object faster than with no cue at all. On the other hand, hearing a wrong name worsened their performance. Lupyan and ward concluded that language can enhance the sensitivity of visual awareness. It seems that, often, visual perception involves making inferences from incomplete information, and the brain is used to filling the gaps to make the best guess about what we see. The right word may prime our guess in the right direction. In the words of the authors, here are the implications:

... if we consider that the real purpose of perceptual systems is to help guide behavior according to incomplete and underdetermined inputs, and that perception is at its core an inferential process, then perception needs all of the help it can get. If tuning the visual system can make it more sensitive to a class of stimuli or a perceptual dimension that is currently task-relevant, then having a highly permeable perceptual system that allows for influences outside vision, including language, can be viewed as highly adaptive. Indeed it is perhaps this power of language to modulate processing on demand—from perception onward—that makes it so effective in guiding behavior.

The majority of brain researchers in the first half of the twentieth century believed that cognitive processing in the brain is carried out in separate streams that do not influence each other. For example language and vision are distinct and separate processes. New neuroscience research reveals the existence of complex neural networking in the brain. Thanks to the emergence of new non-invasive real-time brain imaging technologies such as Positron Emission Tomography (PET) and Functional Magnetic Resonance Imaging (fMRI), which measures brain activity by detecting changes in oxygenated blood flow in the brain (fig. 11), researchers can follow patterns of brain activation in real time, while their test subjects respond to given experiments. The researchers can detect which areas of the brain are activated and to what degree. As it turns out, often several brain centers and cortex areas are highlighted concurrently during tasks.

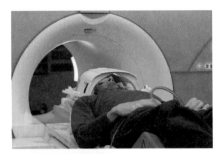

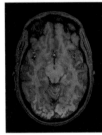

11. FMRI MACHINE (TOP) AND AN IMAGE OF HIGHLIGHTED VISUAL AND AUDITORY CENTERS

Bannert and Bartels from the University of Tübingen devised a very clever experiment in order to investigate prior knowledge influence on what we see. In an aptly named paper, *Decoding the Yellow of a Gray Banana* (2013), they describe an experiment in which participants were given the task of checking the movement of objects on a black-and-white screen while undergoing an fMRI scan. The task was actually irrelevant because the researchers were looking for something else: the activation of brain areas known to define color. The black-and-white pictures were of a banana, broccoli, strawberries, a tennis ball, a can of Coke, and other objects with a strongly associated color. Though concentrating on the task at hand and nothing else, the participants' brains showed activation of the yellow, green, and red areas in the cortex, according to the black-and-white image, as if the brain encoded or added the color of what the object should be. From this, and a growing body of similar research, it looks as if vision is heavily influenced by prior knowledge about object in our environment. In the words of the researchers, "The present findings have implications beyond color vision, as they show how object knowledge can serve as a prior to constrain

the inferences the visual system makes at earliest processing stages about the appearance of complex natural scenes."

As this book is focused on language and image presentation in the brain and their interaction, we should not forget that mental visual imagery and language are the two leading types of representation used by humans. These two modes of mental representations are not exclusive from each other. In fact, the importance of mental imagery in human cognition comes in part from the interactions between mental image and language. Several cognitive neuroimaging studies have attempted to unravel the neural bases of these interactions. Mental images generated from verbal description elicit activations in both visual and language areas of the cortex. The activations follow two different routes, depending on whether the trigger is verbal, visual, or both in conjunction. These findings provide a neural proof to the dual coding theory.

The Symbolic Mind: reading combines form-recognition and meaning

The invention of writing is one of the greatest human accomplishments that led Man from vanished prehistory into recorded time and accumulated knowledge. Our particular interest in writing lies in two areas; one has to do with Man's exceptional ability to symbolize, be it a full alphabet or with pictogram writing (such as Chinese), which demonstrates the human brain's capacity to reduce a sometimes complex image to a simpler recognized sign (I use the term archetype in later chapters). The other is our capacity to read fluently—actually converting separate images of letters and words into meaningful language. Is there a similarity between our amazing ability to combine

12. WE READ THE TEXT, NOT THE DESIGN

letter signs into words and meaning? Being aware that reading is a very recent cultural development, and the processes of face recognition and environment visual recognition, honed by millions of years of evolution, we might be amazed at our ability to read text fluently even if it comes in dissimilar fonts (fig. 12), or even upside down, or a non-standard concoction of capitals and lower case letters.

Stanislas Dehaene, the French neuroscientist, is probably the leading expert on the cognitive neuroscience of language. His book, *Reading in the Brain: The Science and Evolution of a Human Invention* (2009), sums up the current knowledge on that subject.
Dehaene has used medical brain imaging to study language processing and to explain the neural basis of reading. Dehaene and his colleagues identified a region they called the "visual word form area" (VWFA) that was consistently activated during reading, and also found that when this region was surgically removed to treat a patient with intractable epilepsy, reading abilities were severely impaired. Dehaene demonstrated that rather than being a single area, the VWFA is the highest stage in a hierarchy of visual feature extraction for letter and word recognition. It's a complex and surprising circuitry, in that it is housed in several interconnected parts of the cortex that perform specific processing tasks and yet still perform puzzlingly abstract articulations.

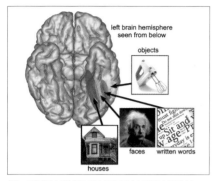

13. PATCHWORK OF SPECIALIZES VISUAL DETECTORS IN THE LEFT HEMISPHERE. DETECTION OF WRITTEN WORDS IS TAKEN FROM OBJECT DETECTION (BASED ON DEHAENE, ISAHI, PUCE)

More recently, Dehaene's group has turned its attention to how learning to read may depend on a process of "neuronal recycling" that causes brain circuits originally evolved for object recognition to become tuned to recognize recurrent letters, pairs of letters and words (fig. 13). They tested these ideas by examining brain responses in a group of adults who did not learn to read due to social and cultural constraints, assuming that these adults were using these cortex locations for their original pre-reading purpose.

An important question arises here: our cortex is the creation of millions of years of evolution in a world still without writing, so how did the cortex adapt so fast to recognize words? Moreover, for five thousand years, reading and writing were solely the domain of the very few, namely scribes and priests. Reading as an essential element of human education is very recent. Obviously, genetic change was not involved in just two centuries. A new biological structure just for reading couldn't have been created so quickly. Moreover, writing arose concurrently but independently in several remote geographical areas—the chance for special mutations specific to reading in all those places is pretty slim. Dehaene has concluded is that we "recycle" parts of the brain that were evolved to do other

things. By learning to read, part of the higher-level visual cortex dedicated itself to letter and word recognition.

To me, the ability of the mind to acquire visual elements of language by specializing in processing the codes of written and printed signs is particularly thought provoking. It suggests that we are very adept in analyzing man-made visual artifacts and comparing or relating them to our memory, visual language, and even written and spoken language. If printed language signs make sense to us, why not objects' appearance?

The symbolic man: semiotics

No sooner is a form seen than it must resemble something: humanity seems doomed to analogy.

Roland Barthes, French literary theorist, philosopher, linguist, critic, and semiotician

Semiotics is the branch of knowledge dedicated to the study of signs and sign processes. Designers are likely to assume that the word *sign* has to do with what we professionally call signage systems. Actually, directional signs are just narrow constituents of semiotics. Semiotics is by far wider in scope, having to do with philosophy, linguistics, cultural studies, and the gamut of psychological, biological, and sociological phenomena that occur in understanding signs. Semiotics also deals with terms such as indication, designation, likeness, analogy, metaphor, symbolism, signification, and communication. Semiotics is frequently seen as having important anthropological dimensions too.

14. MEANING MAY BE CONVEYED BY BODY LANGUAGE

15. ALFRED HITCHCOCK—A MASTER OF FILM SYMBOLISM

Visual contents are an important area of analysis for semioticians and particularly for scholars working with visually intensive forms such as advertising and television because images are such a central part of our mass communication sign system. The broadening importance of visual semiotics encourages additional research into how visual communication creates meaning. It is claimed now that at the heart of semiotics is the realization that the whole of human experience, without exception, is an interpretive structure mediated and sustained by signs (fig. 14).

Semioticians classify signs or sign systems in relation to the way they are transmitted. In order to illuminate one way in which semioticians look at things, let us peek at stage and film semiotics, which study the various codes and signs on stage and in the movies, and how they are interpreted by the viewer In spite of their artificiality. In film, the actors often stand one behind the other, facing the audience and not each other; recalling the past is indicated by switching to black and white or via a wiggly picture; squeaky doors and shadows moving on stairways are associated with horror, and so on (fig. 15). Pamela Smith's book, *Symbols, Images, Codes: The Secret Language of Meaning in Film, TV, Games and Visual Media,* provides many examples.

Designers are quite familiar with product semantics, which is a branch of semiology (Semioticians prefer the terms Design Semiotics or Product Semiotics) that studies of the use of signs in the design of physical products. Product designers frequently resort to metaphors to exhibit original and aesthetic solutions to design problems. They may use metaphors as a tool or method in the design process, which help to identify, frame, and solve design problems. I will elaborate on product semantics and product metaphors in the next chapter.

16. WE USE OUTDATED PRODUCTS AS SYMBOLS BECAUSE THEY ARE INGRAINED IN OUR MIND'S DICTIONARY

Familiar products may also be used to express ideas or words. If you closely inspect the latest iPhone screen icons (fig. 16), you will be surprised by signs still represented by objects that we barely see any longer, especially not anywhere else in the iPhone itself: a 35mm reflex camera represents digital photography, time is represented by an analog clock, an

envelope stands for e-mail, zebra striped film-board represents video, old telephone handset stands for telephone. Probably most anachronistic are mechanical cogwheels representing computer setting. Symbolic icons tend to last.

Semiotics is closely related to the field of linguistics, which studies the structure and meaning of language. But semiotics differs from linguistics in that it generalizes the definition of a sign to encompass signs in any medium or sensory mean and not only the spoken and written language. To coin a word to refer to a thing, society must agree on a clear meaning within its language. That agreed word can transmit that meaning only within the language's grammatical structures and codes. Cultural and literary semiotics examines the literary world, the visual media, the mass media, and advertising, as defined in the work of Roland Barthes. Codes also represent the values of the culture and may add new shades of connotation to every aspect of life.

Closely associated with semiotics is cognitive linguistics: the branch of linguistics that interprets language in terms of the concepts, sometimes universal, sometimes specific to a particular tongue, that underlie its forms. And so, let us draw our attention now to language.

Insights we may gather from linguistics

The limits of my language mean the limits of my world.

Ludwig Wittgenstein, Tractatus Logico-Philosophicus, 1921

In 1975 the linguist Eleanor Rosch asked 200 American college students to rate, on a scale of one to seven, whether they regarded the following items as a good example of the category "furniture." These items ranged from chair and sofa (which scored the highest score) to a love seat (which ranked tenth), to a lamp (thirty-one), all the way to a telephone (ranked sixtieth). This was the beginning of the prototype theory that explains how the brain employs cognitive category classification. Classification may be quite complex, depending on what classification category we employ. A somewhat parallel linguistic classification approach, called Semantic Feature Comparison Model obeys the familiar saying "If it looks like a duck, walks like a duck, quack like a duck, and flies like a duck, it is a duck." The features define the object we observe (fig. 17).

The philosopher Ludwig Wittgenstein, in his second book, Philosophical Investigations (1953), compared the various uses of the term "games" (board games, card games, ball games, Olympic games, and so on) and came to the conclusion that they do not have a common denominator, but rather possessed what he called family resemblance. The notion of family resemblance is better expressed today by another notion—conceptual distance.

These three examples or approaches are different but still related explanations of how our brain uses language in order to classify and relate man-made objects.

In later chapters, I will discuss the evolution of the visual language intrinsic to the form of man-made objects; therefore, we will briefly investigate the nature of language by raising questions of particular interest to us—questions that arise when associating spoken language with the language of form. Let me begin by asking whether the language we speak influences our culture and thence the products of our culture.

The philosophers Friedrich Nietzsche and (to a greater degree) Ludwig Wittgenstein considered language to have an important bearing on thought and reasoning. The American linguist Benjamin Whorf advocated a theory that due to linguistic differences in grammar and usage, speakers of different languages conceptualize and experience the world differently. His theory, known as the Sapir-Whorf Hypothesis (also known as linguistic relativity) states that language and culture are so closely connected that one defines the other. To illustrate, the anthropologist Margaret Mead found that some of the South Pacific people who she studied did not have a word for "war" in their vocabularies. Evidently, these people did not participate in war of any kind. The hypothesis says that we must be able to think or conceive of a phenomenon before we can name it or experience it. Whorf claimed Eskimos have many different words for snow, describing it in ways that would probably be meaningless to us. They verbally differentiate myriad types of snow, while people living in the desert do not have even a single word for snow.

Some linguists, specifically Noam Chomsky and his followers, who adhere to Universalist principles, often criticize the Sapir-Whorf hypothesis. They believe,

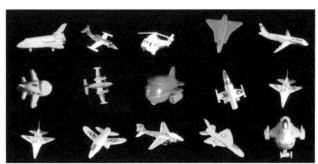

17. WE IDENTIFY FEATURES OF AIRPLANES IN SPITE OF DIFFERENT CONFIGURATIONS, ORIENTATIONS, OR COLORS (MOKHTARIAN & ABBASI, 2000)

in particular, that the human mind is pre-rigged for language. If a language has no word for the number "four" it does not mean that the concept of four is not perceived. Steven Pinker argues in his book *The Language Instinct* that thought exists prior to and independently from language. Following that criticism, the Sapir-Whorf hypothesis fell out of favor for quite a while, but recent work by several linguists has led to a revival of the relativistic linguistic theory, albeit in a somewhat modified way.

The Sapir-Whorf hypothesis is significant to designers, not only in the context of design for global markets. It was already suggested that a novel product is not entirely understood until it is given a proper name and that name turns familiar. The early cars were called "horseless carriage"—a good description before the word automobile (move on its own) was invented. More recent, the Japanese word Kawaii (cute) has taken on the additional meanings of "cool," "groovy," "acceptable," "desirable," "charming," and "non-threatening." This awareness brought about a whole class of kawaii products exclusive to Japan—almost a culture in itself, from cupcakes to Hello Kitty figures, even to cute small cars (fig. 18).

Recent evidence suggests that culture and language can influence perception; for example, there is evidence that people tend to perceive things in ways that are influenced by the manner in which

18. A KAWAII (CUTE) SUZUKI

they have learned to think in order to function efficiently in their ecological setting. In English we call the device that records incoming telephone messages "answering machine" (a genderless mechanical device). In Hebrew the term used is "electronic secretary" (a humanized feminine electronic gadget). From these different terms we may infer that the visual expressions of that telephone device in these two languages may differ. The English-speaking design student may envision an electronic gadget, maybe with a reference to the telephone. The Hebrew speaking design student may envision a product with feminine features with an earphone-microphone device or a short-hand writing pad.

Years ago I attended a lecture by a French industrial designer who complained about the status of his profession in France. In France, the word design was commonly associated with the word *dessin* (to draw), which lacks the significant planning connotations the word design has in English. In France, dessin industriel may imply just drafting.

Ever-changing language

All living languages change. They have to. Languages have no existence apart from the people who use them.
And because people are changing all the time, their language changes too, to keep up with them.

David Crystal, A little book of language, Yale 2010

A question designers may ask linguists has to do with how language changes over time. If language changes so much as the linguist David Crystal states in the box above, we can rationalize that the language of man-made products may evolve and change even faster as it is influenced not only by culture but also by the ever-increasing rate of technological innovation. Can language provide any insight to this question? Let us examine part of a short article on the nature of language change written by the American National Science Foundation:

In some ways, it is surprising that languages change. After all, they are passed down through the generations reliably enough for parents and children to communicate with each other. Yet linguists find that all languages change over time—albeit at different rates. For example, while Japanese has changed relatively little over 1,000 years, English evolved rapidly in just a few centuries. Many present-day speakers find Shakespeare's sixteenth century texts difficult and Chaucer's fourteenth century Canterbury Tales nearly impossible to read.

Languages change for a variety of reasons. Large-scale shifts often occur in response to social, economic and political pressures. History records many examples of language change fueled by invasions, colonization and migration. Even without these kinds of influences, a language can change dramatically if enough users alter the way they speak it.

Frequently, the needs of speakers drive language change. New technologies, industries, products and experiences simply require new words. Plastic, cell phones and the Internet didn't exist in Shakespeare's time, for example. By using new and emerging terms, we all drive language change. But the unique way that individuals speak also fuels language change. That's because no two individuals use a language in exactly the same way. The vocabulary and phrases people use depend on where they live, their age, education level, social status and other factors. Through our interactions, we pick up new words and sayings and integrate them into our speech. Teens and young adults, for example, often use different words and phrases from their parents. Some of them spread through the population and slowly change the language.

Well, it seems that continual change is a given cultural norm. If language constantly changes because people and

19. LANGUAGES AND DICTIONARIES CHANGE CONTINUALLY

their culture evolve, why should the more visual aspects of language not follow suit, including the language of man-made objects (fig. 19)?

Visual language

Language is not just verbal or written. Speech as a means of communication cannot strictly be separated from the whole of human communicative activity, which also includes the visual. The word "imagination" definitely suggests that we can also think in images. Visual language is defined as a system of communication using visual elements. The term visual language in relation to vision describes the perception, comprehension, and production of visible signs. Just as people can verbalize their thinking, they can visualize it. A diagram, a map, and a painting are all examples of uses of visual language. Its structural units include line, shape, color, form, motion, texture, pattern, direction, orientation, scale, angle, space, and proportion. The elements in an image represent concepts in a spatial context, rather than the time-based linear progression used in talking and reading. Speech and visual communication are parallel and often interdependent means by which humans exchange information.

What we have in our minds in a waking state and what we imagine in dreams is very much of the same nature. Dream images might be with or without spoken words, sounds, or colors. Classical Greek philosophers believed that a replica of an object enters the eye and remains in the soul as a memory as a complete image. It is amazing that such an insight originated more than two thousand years before the workings of the brain were unraveled.

Visual thinking

Designers are trained to solve problems, frequently in a visual way (fig. 20). Designers can form images in their mind's

20. VISUAL THINKING BY DESIGNERS

21. VISUAL INSTRUCTION FOR COFFEE MAKING

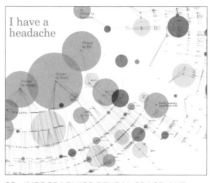

22. INFOGRAPHICS REVEAL SPACE AND SIZE RELATIONSHIPS—PART OF "I HAVE A HEADACHE" INFORMATICS THAT DEMONSTRATES WIDE AVAILABILITY OF PAIN KILLERS. DESIGNED BY HELP REMEDIES

eye, manipulating and evaluating ideas before, during, and after putting them on paper or on the computer screen. Visual thinking used by designers institutes a cognitive system equivalent with, but different from, the verbal language system. And not just trained designers. It seems that human beings have an innate capacity for cognitive modeling and its expression through sketching, drawing, construction, acting out, and so on, that is fundamental to human thought.

Graphicacy

Literacy (communicating in words by means of writing and reading) and numeracy (communicating information by means of numbers) are already well-developed achievements of the human species. The development of the visual aspect of human communications as a parallel discipline to literacy and numeracy has been referred to as graphicacy, still far from being a familiar term. The ability to think and communicate in visual terms—both the understanding and conception of the visual—becomes of equal importance with that of literacy and numeracy in today's learning process.

For a long time the visual aspects of communication were the domain solely of artists. Not detracting from the cultural importance of art, we should bear in mind that the artist is a special kind of visual exploiter whose purpose is often beyond universal visual communication.

Our society is becoming increasingly reliant on graphics to communicate information. Until recently, words and numbers were the main vehicles for communication—compared with graphics, they have long been relatively easy to produce and distribute. However, advances in information and communications technology and visualization techniques now mean that graphics are far more readily available and widely used than ever before (fig. 21). The Twenty-first century is an age in which graphic communication is becoming essential for comprehending knowledge by reading infographics—again a new term, but one that is becoming increasingly common (fig 22). The form and spatial arrangement of items that visually

represent data and contents are used as the basis for the graphic entities and structure that are displayed in the graphic representation. This is not the case with written text in which the words and their arrangement bear no resemblance to the represented subject matter. Because of these and other fundamental differences between text and graphics, it is appropriate that the mental processes involved in comprehension and production of graphics may differ from those involved in comprehension and production of text because they involve additional brain areas involved in mathematical and spatial analysis.

Natural vs. technological evolution

As this book deals with the evolution of product families over time we should clarify what the term evolution means. Evolution usually brings to mind natural, Darwinian evolutionary processes. On the other hand we are aware that man-made objects evolve due to invention and tireless improvement, and the introduction of new materials and technologies. These are largely technological evolutionary processes. Man-made objects also evolve, in use and in form, due to continual cultural change. I will discuss the latter in the next section. In this section I will compare natural or biological evolutionary processes and technological evolutionary processes, and clarify the differences between them.

The science dictionary defines natural evolution as the process by which species of organisms arise from earlier life forms and undergo change over time through natural selection. The modern understanding of the origins of species is based on the theories of Charles Darwin combined with a modern knowledge of genetics based on the work of Gregor

Mendel. Darwin observed that there is definite variation of traits or characteristics among the different individuals belonging to a population. Some of these traits confer fitness—they allow the individual organism that possesses them to survive in their environment better than other individuals who do not possess them and to leave more offspring, what we call survival of the fittest. The offspring then inherit the beneficial traits, and over time the adaptive trait spreads through the population. In the twentieth century, the development of the science of genetics helped to explain the origin of the variation of the traits between individual organisms and the way in which they are passed from generation to generation.

Natural evolution deals with change through random mutations. There is no leading hand. But seeing how cleverly birds are built for flying, Colin Tudge writes the following.

> It seems it is politically incorrect to suggest that evolutionary change over time brings about improvement. Such an idea is deemed to be "teleological," implying that evolution has some goal in mind; whereas, as some moderns insist, evolutionary change over time should be seen as a random walk, liable at any stage to go this way or that. We cannot speak of "improvement" because there are no objective criteria to measure improvement by. Natural selection does not strive for technical perfection.
>
> **Colin Tudge**, the Bird, Crown, 2008

Adrian Bejan, a professor of Mechanical engineering at Duke University, observes the same phenomena but offers a logical explanation. Bejan claims that a technical perfection in natural evolution exists and demonstrates that there is a physics basis for such an improvement over time:

> It seems it is politically incorrect to "Evolution" means design modifications over time. How these changes are happening are mechanisms, which should not be confused with the principle, the constructal law [Bejan's term]. In the evolution of biological design, the mechanism is mutations, biological selection, and survival. In geophysical design, the mechanism is soil erosion, rock dynamics, water-vegetation interaction, and wind drag. In sports evolution, the mechanism is training, selection, rewards, and the changes in the rules of sports competitions. In technology evolution, the mechanism is innovation, technology transfer, copying, theft, and education.
>
> **Adrian Bejan & J. Zane**, Design in Nature p. 199-201

Bejan continues to say that the constructal law reveals the broad patterns that abound in nature. Despite their great diversity, flow systems, from tree roots and branches to river drainage systems, are faced with similar challenges and constraints so they tend to acquire similar designs. Rivers are not living things, but trees are and blood vessel distribution in the lungs is. Inanimate and animate designs evolve as if they are "intelligent," because they appear to come up with the same answer to the problem of how to flow more easily. That is why their designs are predictable. Moreover, Bejan applies the same efficiency principles ultimately to explain the design of Man (fig. 23).

Technological evolution

Technological evolution is the name of a theory in science and technology studies, which describes the underlying process of technological development. The theory was first articulated by the Czech philosopher, Radovan Richta. It concentrates on the history of social impact of technology in the different ages of technology, from a manual-labor society to a machine-assisted society and now to the knowledge society.

Technological evolution does not work in random as mutations in natural evolution do. The process of technological evolution focuses on the ability to achieve all the material values technologically possible

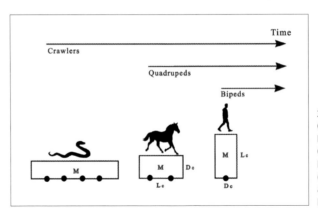

23. DESIGN IN NATURE—CONSTRUCTAL LAW DEFINES RELATIONSHIP OF BODY LENGTH TO MODE OF LOCOMOTION (BASED ON BEJAN & ZANE, DESIGN IN NATURE)

and desirable by mental effort of the engineer available at that specific moment in time. Of course the solution to a given problem will be very different in different ages. Technology is unquestionably purpose- and goal-oriented—engineers often use the term optimization for this.

Such intentionality represents a gulf between technological evolution and natural evolution. Samuel Butler was the first to discuss the issue in an article titled *Darwin Among the Machines* (1863). George Dyson, a historian of technology, tries to forecast where technology we lead us. He also sees a positive relationship between natural evolution and technological evolution. In his book, named after Butler's article, *Darwin Among the Machines* (1997), he challenges the assumption that nature and machine are opposing forces. Dyson believes them to be allies. Observing the beginnings of miniaturization, self-reproduction, and telecommunication among machines, Butler predicted that nature's intelligence, only temporarily subservient to technology, would resurface to claim our creations as its own. Dyson has distilled the historical record to chronicle the origins of digital telecommunications and the evolution of digital computers, beginning long before the time of Darwin and exploring the limits of Darwinian evolution to suggest what lies beyond. Dyson concludes that we are in the midst of an experiment that echoes the prehistory of human intelligence and the origins of life. Just as the exchange of coded molecular instructions brought life as we know it to the early Earth's primordial soup, and just as language and mind combined to form the culture in which we live, so too, in the digital universe, are computer programs and worldwide networks combining to produce an evolutionary theater in which the distinctions between nature and technology are increasingly obscured. Nature, believes Dyson, is on the side of the machines.

24. FUSION OF MAN AND MACHINE?

I find it stimulating to follow the gradual obliteration of the boundaries between the natural and the artificial. As we say: it must be in our DNA (fig. 24).

Scientific evolution

Progress in science, and subsequently in the practical application of science (engineering), is often seen as gradual and evolutionary. Even when scientific theories are replaced by newer theories, the change was often seen as seamless and rational. This was the prevailing view of the Logical Empiricists, who dominated philosophical thinking about science from the late 19th to the mid-20th centuries. The philosopher Thomas Kuhn famously challenged such prevailing views of science and scientific endeavor by arguing that change in scientific theory is not incremental, but rather is a revolutionary process that inevitably results in a complete change of worldview. You will find that the term paradigm change, often used in scientific evolution, will also appear in Part 2 of this book, when dealing with product form evolution.

Cultural evolutionary processes

Evolution in design

Philip Steadman, a professor of Urban Studies and Built Form Studies at University College London (UCL), wrote in 1979 what was probably the first compilation of evolutionary thinking in design: the evolution of designs—biological analogy in architecture and the applied arts. Steadman surveyed the history of various biological analogies. He examined the effects of these analogies on architectural and design theory and considered how biological thinking of his time were relevant for design. Though Steadman has confined his study to a literature survey and criticism focused on the history of ideas, the book, by the sheer juxtaposition of these ideas, metamorphosed into a concept of evolutionary processes in design. Interestingly, most of the literature Steadman surveyed dealt with products rather than with buildings, for example, the evolution of the boomerang in aboriginal Australia; the evolution of military helmet in medieval Europe; and the evolution of car form in the early 19th century, based on Le Corbusier writings.

In a chapter titled How to speed up craft evolution? Steadman deals with the ever-accelerating product evolution of recent times. Steadman even points the way for planning ahead in the face of future evolution, for example, in a purist approach suggested by Le Corbusier, where clean form, intentionally devoid of short-term stylistic vogues, will have a better chance of survival over time.

The 2008-revised edition of Steadman's classic work adds an extensive afterword covering recent developments such as the introduction of computer methods in design that have made possible a new kind of 'biomorphic' architecture and the implications of Richard Dawkins' cultural concept of meme.

Meme

Richard Dawkins, in his 1976 book, *The Selfish Gene*, coined the term meme. Dawkins, a well-known British evolutionary biologist, defined the meme as a unit of cultural transmission, or a unit of imitation and replication. Dawkins used the term to refer to any cultural entity that an observer might consider a replicator. He hypothesized that one could view many cultural entities as replicators, and pointed to melodies, fashions, and learned skills as examples. Memes generally replicate through exposure to humans, who have evolved as efficient copiers of information and behavior. Because humans do not always copy memes perfectly, and because they may refine, combine or otherwise modify some memes with others to create new memes, memes can change over time.

Note that meme sounds like gene. This is purposeful. There is an evolutionary similarity. Memes may evolve by natural selection in a manner analogous to that of biological evolution. Memes do this through the processes of variation, mutation, competition, and inheritance, each of which influences a meme's reproductive success. Memes spread through the behaviors that they generate in their hosts. Memes that propagate less prolifically may become extinct, while others may survive, spread and (for better or for worse) mutate. Memes that replicate most effectively enjoy more success, and some may even replicate effectively even when they prove to be detrimental to the welfare of their hosts.

A field of study called Memetics arose in the 1990s to explore the concepts and transmission of memes in terms of an evolutionary model. Since meme is a cultural, social sciences idea, unsurprisingly there is more than one way to look at it. The following excerpts may shed some light what memes are about:

Examples of memes (following memes.org)

- Jingles: advertising slogans set to an engaging melody.
- Earworms: songs that one can't stop humming or thinking about.
- Proverbs and aphorisms: for example: "You can't keep a good man down," "The early bird gets the worm," or "Waste not, want not."
- Snippets of gossip. (He's a "player.") (She's a "gold-digger.")
- Children's culture: games, activities, and chants (such as taunts) typical for different age-groups.
- Santa Claus as a meme. And his symbolizing the principle of abundance, generosity.
- Conspiracy theories, superstitions, UFO aliens, Martians.
- Fashions, neckties, skirts, colors, brands.
- Medical and safety advice: "Don't swim for an hour after eating" or "Steer in the direction of a skid."
- Popular concepts: these include Freedom, Justice, Ownership, Open Source, Egoism, or Altruism
- Group-based biases: everything from anti-Semitism and racism to cargo cults.
- Longstanding political memes such as "mob rule," national identity, "republic, not a democracy," and Yes, Minister.
- Internet phenomena: Internet slang. "Internet memes" propagate quickly among users of email, websites, blogs, discussion boards, and other Internet communications as a medium.

- "A contagious information pattern that replicates by parasitically infecting human minds and altering their behavior, causing them to propagate the pattern." (Glenn Grant) This definition seems to come out of a health organization warning. Let me remind you that we often say things like, "this clip went viral on youtube"—this is exactly the meme behavior implanted in this particular definition.

- "Memes, like genes, vary in their fitness to survive in the environment of human intellect. Some reproduce like bunnies, but are very short-lived (fashions), while others are slow to reproduce, but hang around for eons (religions, perhaps?). Note that the fitness of the meme is not necessarily related to the fitness that it confers upon the human being who holds it. The most obvious example of this is the "Smoking is Cool" meme, which does very well for itself while killing off its hosts at a great rate." (Lee Borkman).

"It is important to note here that, in contrast to genes, memes are not encoded in any universal code within our brains or in human culture. The meme for vanishing point perspective in two-dimensional art, for example, which first appeared in the sixteenth century, can be encoded and transmitted in German, English or Chinese; it can be described in words, or in algebraic equations, or in line drawings. Nonetheless, in any of these

25. AN EXAMPLE OF MEME MAP

forms, the meme can be transmitted, resulting in a certain recognizable element of realism which appears only in art works executed by artists infected with this meme." (Peter J. Vajk)

The philosopher and cognitive scientist, Daniel Dennett, in an essay named *The Evolution of Culture*, claims that one of the most persistent sources of discomfort about memes is the suspicion that the human mind, seen in terms of brain parasitized by memes, will undermine human creativity. He refutes this suspicion by claiming that looking at creativity in terms of memes gives us ways to identify with the products of our own mind. As a designer, I welcome the association of products, memes and creativity.

Architectural memes

As Philip Steadman pointed out, there is in many ways a parallel between the two areas of design: architecture and product design. Therefore, there is a good reason to follow Nikos Salingaros. In his book *A Theory of Architecture*, Salingaros speaks of memes in architecture. He states that the most successful memes come with a great psychological appeal. "Images portrayed in architectural magazines representing buildings that could not possibly accommodate everyday uses

become fixed in our memory, so we reproduce them unconsciously." Apparently, product designers are as much influenced by design magazines, internet design sites, and prize-winning products as is everyone else.

Meme maps

Meme mapping represents the evolution and transmission of a meme across time and space. Such meme maps are without scale (fig. 25). As you will see, I will often use my own version of meme mapping to demonstrate the evolution of product families.

The grand view: the ecology of artifacts

Product designers are intensely aware of user interface (UX) to the point that interaction design and experience design are considered to be evolving areas expanding from product design. To my disappointment, until very recently not much was published on interaction between man and his artifacts from the social studies point of view. I am not talking here about tool making in archeology and paleontology or about tool making by tribes deep in the Amazon or in New Guinea as observed by ethnographers, but rather about studies of modern tool making by urban anthropologists.

It might be because the word artifact in the social sciences has a too-broad meaning as it stands for anything created by humans. What I am looking for are discussions on objects of popular culture from the cultural point of view, about physical manifestations of popular culture, about objects of desire. Only in recent times has attention been given unambiguously by social scientists to man-made everyday objects—what is sometimes called material culture. (I find this term to have somewhat negative connotations.) Mind you, I do not mean books about interiors, cars, airplanes, ships, or gadgets since there are quite a few of these on any bookstore shelf. A distinct exception in focusing on contemporary artifacts, though not a social scientist by training, is Henry Petroski, an American civil engineer who, not surprisingly, also teaches history at Duke University. Petrosky wrote quite a few books about common objects such as pencils, toothpicks, library bookshelves, and other everyday mundane objects. (I suggest reading *The Evolution of Useful Things*.)

Deyan Sudjic, in his undeniably authoritative position as the director of the Design Museum in London, dealt with most of the cultural issues of product design and the interaction between art, design, and commerce in a lovely book, *The Language of Things: Understanding the World of Desirable Objects*. Virginia Postrel, an American journalist, columnist, and editor, wrote in *The Substance of Style* about the rise of aesthetic values in present day society. The book is a fluent portrait of the democratization of taste and fashion in our current culture. Industrial designers were seldom interested in the cultural aspects of products. An exception here is Prasad Boradkar; his book, *Designing Things: A Critical Introduction to the Culture of Objects*, offers an accessible and critical overview of the cultural meanings of things.

The various concepts of cultural and technological evolution presented in this chapter almost call for one overall encompassing view, a contemporary successor of Philip Steadman's book. This is a monumental task, out of the scope of this book. Others did try to tackle this issue, at least in part.

For example, Sjostrom and Donnellan, in a paper presented in 2012, *Design Research Practice: A Product Semantics Interpretation*, talk about the meaning of an ecology of artifacts on the basis of Krippendorff's proposal that designers need to recognize the meaning of ecology of artifacts (see the next chapter). They write, "Designers who can handle the ecological meaning of their proposals have a better chance of keeping their designs alive." People attach meaning to artifacts in relation to other artifacts. This relationship can span a number of dimensions such as cooperation, competition, interdependence, reproduction, and retirement (death) of artifacts in specific contexts. The most obvious example from a technical perspective is that artifacts depend on infrastructure. However, there are other relations in ecology of artifacts, such as competing artifacts, or artifacts that 'thrive' through the existence of other artifacts. The point stressed in that paper is that the meaning of a single artifact is based on its place within a larger ecology.

Bruce Sterling, a science fiction author and futurist, wrote a highly original manifest in a small book called *Shaping Things*. Sterling offers a brilliant, often hilarious, history of shaped things. He analyses how the tools that designers deliver change society, and how that changes us, and that leads again to design changes. Sterling traces the history of tools from artifacts (farmers' tools) to machines (customers' devices) to products (customers' purchases) to current gizmos (end-users' platforms) and to the future, which is defined by what

Sterling calls spimes. A spime is a location-aware, environment-aware, self-logging, self-documenting, uniquely identified object that throws off data about itself and its environment in great quantities. A universe of spimes is an informational universe, and it is the use of this information that informs the most exciting part of Sterling's argument.

Reviewing the designed form

Design and form

To design is much more than simply to assemble, to order, or even to edit; it is to add value and meaning, to illuminate, to simplify, to clarify, to modify, to dignify, to dramatize, to persuade, and perhaps even to amuse.

Paul Rand, noted American graphic designer, 1914-1996

In this chapter we will investigate how designers considered form and form evolution of products. Understandably, in the century that industrial design existed as an established profession, the way designers studied form has changed considerably, from mere visual description of style to establishing theories based on scientific investigation methods, not to forget evidence gathered from other fields. This chapter will deal with several aspects of the accumulated theory. In the next chapter, *In Context 1: Aesthetics of form*, I will further elaborate on that specific topic.

As I have stated in the preface to this book, though physical form has always been a mainstay of product design, it was often played down or even neglected, being popularly labeled as only skin deep or as pure "styling." At the end of the day, whatever the method they use, product designers create a physical entity—a form. We should openly recognize that form and aesthetics are indispensable elements not only of the design profession, but of our "object oriented" contemporary culture.

For a good illustration of how our attitude-by-language has changed, moving from the physical, through the emotional, and into the realm of our zeitgeist, follow Donald Norman's series of books on products: *The Design of Everyday Things* (1998), *Emotional Design: Why We Love (or Hate) Everyday Things* (2004), and his recent *Living with Complexity* (2010).

Early inquiry of form

As I stated in the preface, discussion about aesthetics and form for at least four hundred years was the exclusive territory of art historians. Art historians tend to embrace the creative genius, the personal contribution of the individual to art and art history. Historians also emphasize the chronology of art movements, separated into modes of presentation: architecture, painting, and sculpture. Unfortunately, design as a creative discipline was considered by art historians as a minor art and not as significant as other artistic modes.

Historical research calls for substantial time perspective in order to grasp and describe an objective picture of the period. Industrial design of man-made products is still a very young profession. As a discipline, history of design is by far even younger. Though substantial research was already carried out, design history, even by design historians, often follows the established art history tradi-

tion, albeit with improved understanding of tool-making and technological development and with lesser bias against style and form decoration. Still, celebrating landmark works by known designers, admittedly often being trendsetters, counted much more than did recording overall design trends perceived from the glut of everyday manufactured articles. The founding of serious design-research journals, design societies, and conferences dedicated to the study of man-made products and their interaction with users brought about interest in form-centered research, a glimpse into it will be given later in this chapter.

On the nature of form

In 1896, the American architect Louis Sullivan coined his famous principle *Form Follows Function*. It was a turning point in the history of art and design. The Sullivan design principle entails the belief that the form of tangible products would emerge naturally from a clear understanding of the function they are to serve. This design principle was the beacon, and in its light, modernism followed. Nowadays, we may understand Sullivan's dictum as merely a disapproval of the prevalent overly ornate style of the Victorian Era as culminated in the Crystal Palace of 1871 (fig. 1).

1. VICTORIAN TASTE IN FURNITURE DESIGN

In the 1960s, David Pye, a professor of furniture and design at the Royal College of Arts, investigated design as being a union of both art and technology. His observations are so crystal clear that I prefer to bring them in verbatim.

Pye then endeavored to seek a basic design theory by investigating what functionality means. In a later chapter of his book he states:

> It seems that the work we call purely utilitarian is not more useful than its more ornamental counterpart. It is merely more economical.

David Pye, the Nature of design, Reinhold, 1964, p.85

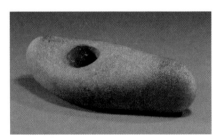

2. A NEOLITHIC BATTLEAXE, SCANDINAVIA

3. MEDIEVAL BATTLEAXES

As an example to illustrate what Pye means, we tend to think that weapons must be purely utilitarian, as the warrior's life depends on them since they factor largely in determining life or death in battle. Yet if we follow the history of weapons through the ages it is surprising how significant is the ceremonial identity of weapons. The Nordic Neolithic battleaxe (fig. 2) seems to be plain and practical, but imagine how many days were invested in polishing the stone by hand; on top of it we know nothing of the beauty of the missing wooden handle it had.

We may speculate about the decorative qualities of the prehistoric axe, but we may have no doubt about the decorative qualities of medieval steel battleaxes

4. VATICAN SWISS GUARD'S CEREMONIAL LANCE

The thing which sharply distinguishes useful design from such arts as painting and sculpture is that the practitioner of design has limits set upon his freedom of choice. A painter can choose any imaginable shape. A designer cannot. If the designer is designing a bread knife it must have a cutting edge and a handle; if he is designing a car it must have wheels and a floor.

These are the sort of limitations which arise, as anyone can tell, from the 'function' of the thing being designed.

Little is ever said which touches on the fundamental principles of useful design, and what is said is often nonsense. Most of the nonsense probably starts at the point where people begin talking about function though it were something objective: something of which it could be said that it belonged to a thing (....)

Now plenty of people do really believe that form can follow function; that if you thoroughly analyze the activity proper to the thing you are designing, then your analysis will provide all the information needed, and the

design can be derived logically from the function. Plenty of people still believe that 'purely functional' designs are possible, and believe that they themselves produce them, what is more! But none of them has yet divulged what an analysis of a function looks like and what logical steps lead from it to the design. All you will get from them is talk about the purpose of the thing, which, as we shall see, is a statement of opinion and can never be anything else.

David Pye, The Nature of Design, Reinhold, 1964, p.7-9

(fig. 3). Furthermore, we may realize that the purely decorative ceremonial axes of the Vatican Swiss guards of today (fig. 4) are mere symbolic weapons that cannot cut into anything. It is not unexpected then to agree with Klaus Krippendorff's statement, "Humans do not see and act on the physical qualities of things, but on what they mean to them."

Tracking the evolution of product form

The architect Le Corbusier, a prime mover of the international movement, showed a keen interest in the development of modern car form. He demonstrated this in writings such as *Towards an Architecture* (1923), and later in *The Radiant City*

(1935), and also in one issue of *L'Esprit Nouveau,* where he published a double page spread, *Evolution des Formes de l'Automobile 1900–1921.* He demonstrated in his drawings that the automobile body design gradually, but consistently, embraced aerodynamic principles. He demonstrated this specifically in an accompanying diagram under the caption "In search of a standard," which consists of a series of shapes compared for their air resistance: for example, an ovoid body or cone, which he claims gives the best penetration, confirmed by examination of natural creations such as fish and birds, but also, as he points out, comparisons to a man-made equivalent: the dirigible.

Raymond Loewy, the well-known pioneer of industrial design and a chief proponent of the streamlined style, included in his

professional biography, *Industrial Design* (1979), a chart that analyzed product shape evolution that he drew in 1925 (fig. 5). It is obviously a whimsical chart to some degree; notice the buildings. His approach is even more light-hearted when he draws the shape of the feminine body as becoming slimmer by design (not shown here). We can gather from Loewy's chart that progress culminates in streamlined forms. This is well in line with Loewy's philosophy of *Never Leave Well-Enough Alone,* which is the title of his renowned 1951 book.

A definitely more analytical exploration of form evolution appeared in a 1960s issue of the long gone *Industrial Design* (ID) magazine by Gifford Jackson, a New Zealand designer working in the USA (fig. 6). Though the analysis is limited

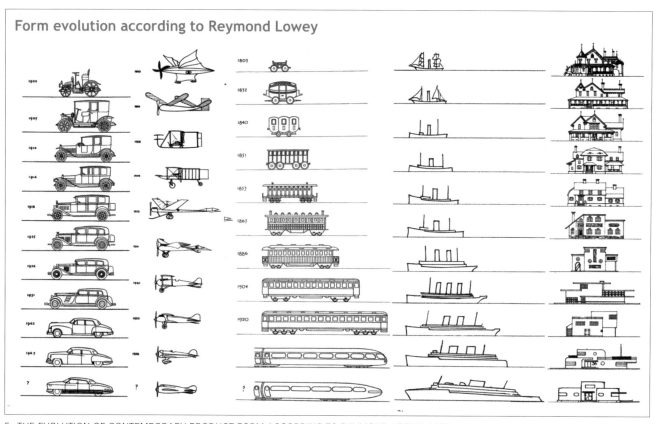

Form evolution according to Reymond Lowey

5. THE EVOLUTION OF CONTEMPORARY PRODUCT FORM ACCORDING TO RAYMOND LOEWY, 1925

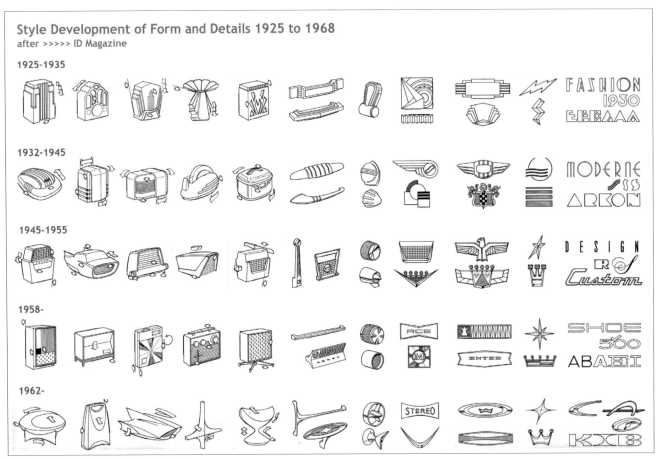

Style Development of Form and Details 1925 to 1968
after >>>>> ID Magazine

1925-1935

1932-1945

1945-1955

1958-

1962-

6. TRENDS IN STYLING OF INDUSTRIALLY DESIGNED PRODUCTS, BY GIFFORD JACKSON, IN INDUSTRIAL DESIGN MAGAZINE, 1960S

to the application of design styles to American products from 1925 to the mid-1960s, the chart defines overall design and form principles in each style period, including specific details such as knobs and handles, logo emblems, and product graphics. Looking at the chart, we may glean three important observations:

First, styles tend to overlap and coexist. A new style does not wipe out the older one; there is a gradual transition while the older one phases out. The second observation is that though the products shown in the chart are not real products, rather more something like form sculptures, each period had a definitive association to a well-recognized entity

of the period (what I will term in a later chapter a "technology leader"). Notice the skyscraper in 1925, the wing in 1932 (flying), the early jet plane in 1945, and space futurism from 1962.

The third observation is that some form conventions continue from one style period to another without failing. Notice the 3-step "rule" in early products or the use of textural materials from 1945 onwards.

Regrettably, in spite of the recent explosion of *infographics*—pictorial tools to visualize and explain processes—when it comes to investigate product evolution there is a tendency to deal with the

historical axis (timeline) rather than to express ideas, processes, or context. On top of it is the tendency to focus only on one company's product line (figs. 7 and 8) rather than on an overall development of a complete product family.

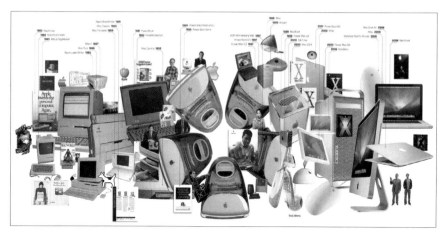

7. AN EXAMPLE—ONE OF MANY—OF APPLE'S PRODUCTS TIMELINE

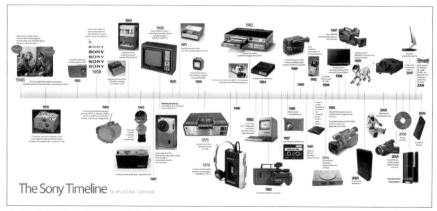

8. AN EXAMPLE OF SONY'S PRODUCTS TIMELINE

Research into product language

As I have briefly mentioned in the previous chapter, Philip Steadman devoted in his book a full chapter titled *How to Speed Up Craft Evolution?* to the problem of continually accelerating product evolution of recent times. He used Le Corbusier's examples of racing cars evolution to advocate ways of pre-planning, ahead of future evolution. He suggests a *purist approach*, where clean form may have a better chance of survival over time. The principal idea behind the purist theory was that certain simple universal geometrical forms were capable of inducing in the spectator correspondingly universal primary sensations, which would be relatively untainted by culture or by the individual's particular background; and that these forms could therefore provide the basis for a *universal plastic language* – a sort of visual Esperanto (an artificial international language invented by L. Zamenhof in 1887), which would transcend narrow cultural or historical limitations. Steadman concedes that even the purists recognized that any form, however pure and simple, would inevitably come to have attached to it a particular culture or other secondary associations of an incidental or 'literary' character. Interestingly, Steadman came to the conclusion that differences in architectural style and form are not due to the inventiveness or creativity of designers, but are rather a response to the social conditions and utilitarian needs imposed by the environment around them. Solution selection criteria are established during the design process and are a direct result of the needs and conditions of the users, critics, and clients. If we accept Steadman's observation at face value it should be imperative for designers to take heed of what cultural studies have to offer. Designers currently employ ethnographic research methods in design but there are many more ideas and observations relevant to the design process.

The beginning of interest in product semantics was regrettably not the domain of product designers. In fact, semiotics became a popular topic in cultural studies already in the late 1960s, partly as a result of the work of Roland Barthes, the French linguist, philosopher and keen critic of popular culture. In *Elements of Semiology* (1970), Barthes argued that an *object* can be considered a *sign*. It is a sign of what it does, and what it does grants it a signification. The three elements that play a role in such signification are the subject (interpretant), the signified thing (object), and the representative or signifier (sign). In another book, *Mythologies* (1967), Barthes analyzed advertisement and media and showed how seemingly familiar things signify all kinds of ideas about the world. Barthes' essay about the *Citroen DS* car (see *case study 6—the Automobile*) is a forerunner of early design semiotics.

Marshal McLuhan, in his influential book, *Understanding Media: The Extensions of Man* (1964), proposed that the medium itself, not the content it carries, should be the focus of study. The well-known maxim, "The medium is the message" was coined by Marshall McLuhan, meaning that the form of a medium embeds itself in the message, creating a symbiotic relationship by which the medium influences how the message is perceived. A medium affects the society in which it plays a role, not only by the content delivered over the medium, but also by the characteristics of the medium itself.

How do we relate message and media to our discussion of man-made artifacts? We incline to associate media with printed material, billboards, television, and film. How is media linked to man-made objects? It turns out that McLuhan understood "medium" in a broader sense than just print and image. He suggested the light bulb as a clear demonstration of the concept of "the medium is the message." A light bulb does not have content in the way that a newspaper has articles or a television has programs, yet it is a medium that has a social effect since a light bulb enables people to create space during nighttime that would otherwise be defined by darkness. In this case the light bulb is a medium without any content. McLuhan claimed that "a light bulb creates an environment by its mere presence."

When it was time for designers to theorize about the meaning of products, an early attempt took place in the Hochschule für Gestaltung Offenbach in Germany with the aim to develop what was called then a *Theory of Product Language*. The theory of product language originated as a reaction to a much too narrow functional approach of the 1960s and 1970s. Its beginnings can be traced back to earlier dialogues in the early 1960s at the Ulm School of Design, often thought to be the postwar successor of the Bauhaus. When the Ulm school closed, Jochen Gros carried the topic to the Hochschule für Gestaltung Offenbach. His 1973 dissertation on *Extended Functionalism and Empirical Aesthetics* laid the foundation of the theoretical discussion, which came to be known as the "Offenbach Approach."

The goal of the "Offenbach Approach" as a practice-oriented theory of product language was to integrate more non-material, emotional functions such as a sense of security, self-expression, emotional attachment, as well as cognitive needs into the creative process and to take these into consideration when conceiving design solutions. The product language approach directs focus from the object to the human-object-relationship, in which the semantic and symbolic dimension plays an important role.

Product semantics

> The early work on product semantics showed that meaning matters more than function, leading to the axiom that: Humans do not see and act on the physical qualities of things, but on what they mean to them.
>
> **Klaus Krippendorff**, the Semantic Turn; A New Foundation for Design, CRC Press, 2006

A good historical summation of product semantics development is an overview report by Sara Ilstedt Hjelm: *Semantics in Product Design* (2002).

> **Product metaphor:**
>
> Any kind of product that is shaped to reference the physical properties (e.g., form, sound, movement, smell, and so on) of another distinct entity for particular expressive purposes.
>
> **Nazli Cila**, Metaphors We Design By: The Use of Metaphors in Product Design, PhD thesis, 2013

Product Semantics culminated the early ideas developed at Ulm and Offenbach. The term itself was coined by Klaus Kripendorff, a communications professor at the University of Pennsylvania, who previously studied product design at Ulm, and who worked with Reinhardt Butter, who, himself, was a design professor at the Ohio State University. The term first appeared in an article they both wrote in the Industrial Designers Society of America (IDSA) journal *Innovation* in 1984. Kripendorff and Butter defined product semantics as both an inquiry into the symbolic qualities of objects and as a design tool to enhance these cultural qualities. They chose the word "semantic," (meaning "meaning") to emphasize this aspect of communication. They introduced the idea of a product as a text with several levels of meaning and criticized the blank design of modernism. In 1989 Kripendorff and Butter edited an issue of *Design Issues*, which has since become a standard reference in the product semantics literature, elaborating of the definition of product semantics as both

■ A systematic inquiry into how people attribute meanings to artifacts and interact with them accordingly.

■ A vocabulary and methodology for designing artifacts in view of the meanings they could acquire for their users and the communities of their stakeholders.

Later on, Kripendorff advanced these ideas in a book, *The Semantic Turn; A New Foundation for Design* (2006). While retaining the emphasis on meaning and on the importance of both theory and practice, *The Semantic Turn* extends the concerns of designers to the new challenges of design, including the design of ever increasing intangible artifacts such as services, identities, interfaces, multi-user systems, projects, and discourses; while at the same time it considers the meaning of artifacts in use: in language, in the complete life cycle of an artifact, and in the ecology of artifacts.

The semantics of artifacts concept became central in courses taught at leading design schools such as the Cranbrook Academy of Arts; The Ohio State University; the University of the Arts in Philadelphia; the Hochschule für Gestaltung Offenbach in Germany; the University of Art and Design in Helsinki, Finland; and others. The semantic approach at Cranbrook Academy, led by Michael and Katherine McCoy, who

9. CRANBROOK'S SEMANTIC DESIGN—THE PC AS A BOOKSHELF OF KNOWLEDGE

co-chaired of the graduate design program there, was fresh, innovative, and often whimsical (fig. 9). Their approach influenced other design schools and even industries, notably the Dutch concern *Philips*, to use product semantics as a tool that uses visual and linguistic metaphors in order to come out with novel form ideas leading to exciting and expressive appearance.

Nazli Cila, a design researcher at the Delft University of Technology, focuses her research on product metaphors as exemplified in her PhD thesis, *Metaphors We Design By: The Use of Metaphors in Product Design* (2013). Several chapters from the thesis have already been published in design periodicals and conference proceedings. Cila describes product designers as a group of creative artists who frequently resort to metaphors to exhibit original and aesthetic solutions to design problems. They may use metaphors as tools or methods in the design process, which help to identify, frame, and solve design problems. Metaphors facilitate translating abstract concepts into concrete product properties. Cila states that investigating product metaphors is a challenging problem because metaphors are mainly discussed in the context of language. According to Cila there are several types of associations between the source (existing) and target (proposed) products:

Pragmatic intentions
This type of metaphor aims to reduce the cognitive workload of the users in their reasoning about the function, use, and meaning of a product. The main goal is to turn a complex product into a clear and comprehensible one.

■ **Identification** refers to communicating the product type and product category to users. Metaphors generated with identification intentions assist the user in recognizing the product and

understanding the category to which it belongs. In this way, users can infer what the product is for. This is especially important to attain when launching a new product type. For instance, when the first e-books were launched on the market, they simulated actual books with the same size and cover that real books have.

■ **Use and Operation** refers to directing users how to approach the product and interact with it. Metaphors generated with this intention clarify the way the product is used or operated, and entail design attributes that make the product function smoothly and easily. An example might be the gestural controls of iPhone or iPad, such as making the gesture of turning a page to go to the next screen or dragging items to move them. The selection and application of these familiar gestures allow users to comprehend new or complex use situations because they rely on existing knowledge from everyday life.

Experiential intentions
Rather than being merely utilitarian tools, products are means for pleasurable and meaningful experiences. Metaphors can also be used with this intention, in promoting rich sensorial and emotional product experiences. This can be attained by telling a story through the product, giving an ethical/moral message, or creating a witty product.

■ **Prose and poetry** refers to assigning an abstract symbolic meaning to the product (such as a personality) to tell a story through the product.

■ **Ideology** refers to promoting (or criticizing) an ideology and giving an ethical, social, or moral message through the product by using metaphors.

■ **Fun/Wit** refers to creating a product that makes users smile. This is attained by building a surprising, unexpected, and incongruent relationship between target and source products. A certain degree of cleverness is involved in such products.

My particular interpretation of using semantic metaphors in product semantics differs somewhat from Cila's classifications. Evidently there is more than one way to cluster and classify meta-

13. AN EXPOSED WAY OF LOOKING AT SHOES

14. MOVING LAMP "HEAD" ANALOGOUS TO A BIRD'S HEAD

15. GARDENING TOOLS OR CUTLERY?

16. THE DISTINCT LANGUAGE OF AQUATIC PRODUCTS: RUBBER, GLASS, AND HYDRODYNAMICS

10. STUDIES OF A MOUSE DESIGN BY IDEO

11. MIRROR, MIRROR ON THE WALL...

12. PHILIPS COFFEE MAKER AND LEGENDARY METAPHOR

phors. I suggest these families of visual metaphors:

Functional semantics. The product's visual language should inform how it is meant to be handled and used. This metaphor type has always been in the core of industrial design in order to create a good user interface. This metaphor family is exemplified in IDEO's studies for a computer mouse (fig. 10). The grasping human hand is visually integrated in the mouse's form.

Symbolic semantics. This is an approach that promotes an appreciation for and the forming of relationships with the product through the use of cultural metaphors. Some cultural metaphors are universal, based on mythology and Jungian psychology principles, as stated in Carl Jung's book *Man and His Symbols*. Other cultural metaphors tend to be specific to one culture and are often misunderstood by others. A makeup mirror (fig. 11) has two symbolic metaphors complementing

each other. It may be understood as a mandala, reflecting the beholder's soul. In addition, the small light bulbs around the mirror are associated in western culture with movie theater marquee, catering to the mirror owner's vanity.

A decidedly cultural use of symbolic semantics is a Philips coffee maker (fig. 12). Sophisticated Europeans will quickly associate the "belly" and the leaning cups with the legend of Remus and Romulus, the founders of ancient Rome, who according to legend were reared by a female wolf (see insert).

Linguistic semantics. If we use words to define and describe artifacts, why not use our language skills to play with metaphors as poets regularly do? We can play back and forth between verbal language and visual language. This family of semantic metaphors is particularly open to creative lingual interpretations. Take, for example, when the literary saying, "The pen is mightier than the sword," is literally translated into a senior executive's ceremonial double-pen desk accessory on his desk as a clear sign of commanding power. As an embellishment, sometimes a globe is added to the pen accessory. Playing with language need not be restricted only to interchange with the verbal. Strictly visual metaphors work splendidly, too. What do we see in figure 13? Is it a shoe or a foot in flip-flops?

In the next example we are encouraged to associate an adjustable table lamp with the long neck of a pecking bird (fig. 14). A few will be reminded of the childhood toy of the drinking bird.

Evolutionary semantics: In a few words, this is what this book is all about. Man-made artifacts do not appear one day out of the blue. Public acceptance of the new depends on recognition and association with previous artifacts or with an established class of products (figs. 15 and 16). Something old, something new…

17. SONICUM LOUDSPEAKERS PLAY ON THE LOUDSPEAKER SYMBOL

The Sonicum loudspeaker (fig. 17) describes itself as a loudspeaker by relying in a whimsical way on a loud-speaker icon common in media elec-tronics. Here symbolic semantics is used as a means to denote evolutionary semantics.

Unfortunately, product semantics did not find its place as a key design theory, but instead remained largely a design tool. Industrial designers took the concept of product semantics as just one design method out of a range of methods intended to facilitate the creative process of idea generation. As a mere tool, product semantics lost some of its initial appeal and did not get the attention it may have deserved.

The progress of user-centered design

True, this book focuses on the outward appearance of product design, and on the ways the ordinary user recognizes what he sees. But form does not exist in isolation; form is just a facet of the way we under-stand and appreciate product design. Product design itself has come a long way in the past fifty years by establishing a serious body of knowledge in general, and, in particular, by considering the end user. My personal interest in semantics led me to realize that the language commonly used by designers has a role in deter-mining the nature of interaction between designer and user. Linguistic connotations often form our attitude towards and perception of objects.

Half a century ago, in the process of designing a new product, the designer considered the user habitually by his physiological attributes. Henry Dreyfuss' landmark book, *The Measure of Man,* was mainly about dimensions and percentiles. Its evolving science of "human engi-neering" focused on fitting the task to the user. To my mind human engineering is an unbearably inhumane term; I cannot avoid associating it with assembling androids. No wonder the Europeans preferred the term ergonomics (from Greek, meaning the laws of work), and the Americans preferred the somewhat milder *human factors*. After all, design was still much subjected to the industrial realm. Luckily, form had its place in the artistic contribu-tion of the designers.

Human factors specialists, wither from the behavioral sciences (e.g. cognitive psychology) or with an engineering background, combined forces with the computer scientists in developing Graphic User Interface (GUI), and later expanded their knowledge to Human-Computer Interaction (HCI), a term quite popular today. A parallel development occurred in the industrial design profession, leading to Interaction Design (not to be confused with interactive design), which represented a wider scope of reciprocal relationship between product and user. Graphic designers preferred a different but quite analogous term: Experience Design. The currently accepted cross-dis-ciplinary term is User Experience Design (UX). Designers included culture in the design process by suggesting that each designed product, be it 2D, 3D, tangible, or virtual, should tell a meaningful story or narrative. This gradual shift and expansion of the designer's role—a multi-faceted humanization of technology—leads us to the topic of this book: how we recognize, understand, and react to what we see in man-made objects around us.

Recent form-centered design research

The last twenty years or so have witnessed significant interest in under-standing and enabling visual object recog-nition. Such research has been carried out by the combined efforts of scientists from different fields, predominantly computer scientists and brain researchers engaged in artificial intelligence (AI). The practical applications of AI research were focused on developing machine learning, face recognition, and object recognition. Regrettably, designers did not participate in such research, except for a small number of designers. Paul Hekkert, a professor of form theory at the Delft University of Technology, and a trained psychologist, is one of the few who did participate. He currently leads a research group studying sense perception and emotional experience of products (see the next two chapters). It is not only individual research by these designers that gradually changes our understanding of form. The critical mass essential to progress in object recognition may be achieved through formation of international design forums dedicated to the study of form. One forum is the Design and Emotion Society, established in 1999 as an international network of researchers, in which designers and companies share an interest in experience-driven design. The network exchanges insights, research, tools, and methods that support the involvement of emotional experience in product design. The emotional experience of a product naturally includes its aesthetics and symbolism.

Another forum is the Conference on Design and Semantics of Form and Movement (DeSForM), founded in 2005, and specifically focused on form research. Additionally, the International Journal of Design (accessible at www.ijdesign.org), established in 2007, is often a venue for publishing research dedicated to form, emotion, and meaning. Recent design research on the visual form has concentrated mainly on how product form is accepted by the user. Such research concurs with marketing research examining what makes products successful.

I dare to predict that the increasingly accumulated body of knowledge in design research will not lead to a single inclusive theory of design. The Design Research Society is even careful not to suggest such an outcome. Designers, by the nature of being creative individuals, will not accept one all-encompassing paradigm if it seen to establish boundaries to creative freedom. Designers habitually keep disagreeing about how to model what they do. If you search the

....We believe that DesForM is the first international conference seeking to present current research into the nature, character and behaviour of emerging new typologies of co-designed, content rich, connected and intelligent objects within adaptive systems. It aims to bring together researchers in the many related fields of design to assess the outcomes of this research and begin to identify issues and territories for future investigation and exploration.

Our original working premise for this research was that forms, either concrete or abstract, always carry or mediate meanings. It is the responsibility of designers to make good use of these meanings, for example, to make products beautiful, to stress the importance of certain values, or to improve a product's ease of use. Further, it should promote or negotiate enriched experiences between people (communities) and people, people and objects, and in time between objects (systems of objects) and objects. Design uses its own languages for this purpose, just as poets, painters, journalists, sculptures,

filmmakers and other artists do. Objects, whether hard, soft or digital, are still being designed using a mono-sensorial approach rather than a multi-sensorial approach.

Design has long since practiced and developed its ideas on a cultural platform, rather than merely on a technological, marketing or a financial and business base. Understanding people, not as a single intellectual or physiological entity, but rather as a member of a cultural expression within a socio-political paradigm or 'world-view' is the essence of this cultural platform....

If we explore this new complexity in objects, we believe that we need to know how to read the objects and how to design them to be read in the way we intend, irrespective of additional readings or meanings which people might add and re-appropriate. Tomorrow's objects, which we expect, are in a continual state of becoming.

Quoted from the DeSForM manifest

literature for an explanation of the design process—finally no longer accepted to be a magical black box—you will find a deluge of diagrams representing design process models in different ways. Designers are creative even in charting the design process. After all, design thinking is a multifaceted process and a rule-breaker by nature. The way I see it, design research will advance in explaining the why rather than the *how*.

Aesthetics of imagination

Mads Nygaard Folkmann, who teaches at the Institute for Design and Communication, University of Southern Denmark, presents a fresh approach to the questions of what design is and how it works. In his recent book, *The Aesthetics of Imagination in Design* (2013), Folkmann investigates the nature of design from philosophical and cultural viewpoints.

Though his theory frames an upper hierarchy in design thinking, what I prefer to call Meta-design, many of his findings corroborate key concepts of language and evolution of form that we deal with here.

Drawing on formal theories of aesthetics and the phenomenology of imagination, Folkmann seeks to answer fundamental questions about what design is and how it works that are often ignored in academic research. He defines three conditions in design: the possible, the aesthetic, and the imagination. As you would expect, aesthetics and imagination have much to do with form. Imagination is a central formative power behind the creation and the life of design objects, and aesthetics describes the sensual, conceptual, and contextual codes through which design objects communicate. Even the concept of the possible—the enabling of new uses, conceptions, and perceptions—lies behind imagination and aesthetics. Imagination in design executes processes of abstraction (in my terminology, creating *archetypes*), negation, transfiguration (in my terminology, paradigm shift), and the envisioning of objects and their meaning. Seen in this light, the purpose of his book is to seek ways for using design as an aesthetic medium for creating new meaning through the process of imagination. He sees design as a strategy of renewing things whereby design objects become comparative objects; they are always dependent on previous objects (in my terminology, *evolution*).

Discussing semantics, Folkmann uses the term *symbolic coding*. The exploration of symbolic meaning in design is a never-ending venture. People attribute symbolic meaning to objects in different ways, and design objects afford symbolic meaning in a variety of dimensions. Semantics allows us to speak of a "language of products," as design objects not only carry functions but also information.

In terms of culture, Folkmann investigates the ways, impacts, and consequences of design as it assists us in seeing, perceiving, and understanding contemporary culture. He claims that design is an essential medium for the articulation and transformation of our late modern culture, constantly on the verge of developing new perspectives on and responses to the cultural, societal, and environmental challenges of the future.

A novel theory to explain form

Grey Holland, a practicing industrial designer, suggested a rather personal but ingenious theory of product form in a 2009 article labeled *A Periodic Table of Form: The Secret Language of Surface and Meaning in Product Design* in the design site *Core77*. Holland asserts that human evolution assigns priority to visual interpretation of form in nature and this innate priority continues in interpreting man-made products today. Holland suggests a model of empirical understanding of three-dimensional forms comprising a three-level definition of surface continuity, using terms borrowed from computer-aided design (fig. 18).

Positional continuity refers to the hard edge created when two surfaces intersect. The Positional forms suggest such notions as precision, accuracy, danger, structure, and fidelity.

Tangential continuity is defined by a circular arc (fillet) creating a smooth transition between surfaces. Tangential forms, seldom seen in nature, notably maintain a sense of utility, function, efficiency, practicality, or purpose, for example.

Curvature continuity is a continuous curvature for which one cannot tell where one surface ends and another begins. The Curvature surfaces intimate concepts like

18. POSITIONAL, TANGENTIAL, AND CURVATURE

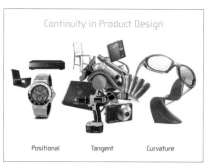

19. CONTINUITY IN PRODUCT DESIGN

20. CONTINUITY IN TRANSPORTATION DESIGN

sophistication, elegance, fluidity, grace, and refinement.

Examples of such forms are shown in figure 19 and figure 20. Holland goes on to build a 3-tier "periodic table" of form to further explain form and its visual and emotional meanings.

Does technology govern form?

Is form predominantly technology driven?

As I explained earlier, it is quite understandable why "form-follows-function" was an accepted paradigm of modernism for such a long time. It entails that form may arise almost by itself from a direct functional solution of a problem. This is a typical *Deus ex machina* approach. Many engineers are quite convinced that the visual outcome of a product that fulfills a specific utility, not just a decorative one, should be the direct end result of rigorous engineering design involving considerations of optimized functional performance and economic concerns (with the unfortunate interference of time-to-market considerations). This deep-rooted approach slowly begins to change. James Adams, an engineering professor of Stanford, in his book *Good Products, Bad Products* talks about the notion of quality. It may still be somewhat an elusive term since Adams states that quality encompasses considerations such as elegance and sophistication, which are not yet common in engineering parlance.

Perhaps the best case in point to convince the unconvinced about the myth of form-follows-function is a single image presented by a key lecturer in a recent design conference in the United States,

21. RUSSIAN AND AMERICAN DESIGN INTERPRETATIONS OF EXTREMELY FUNCTIONAL FORM

depicting two very different solutions to one of the utmost technological endeavors of the time, the space race (fig. 21). The American *Apollo* and the Russian *Soyuz* were both cutting-edge engineering solutions; but when seen one next to the other, it is astonishing how different they look. The Soyuz spacecraft may seem to most of us as having an archaic form language, in the spirit of 1940s science fiction magazine covers. Apparently both nations dealt with the same mission constraints but the way sophistication manifests itself visually is undoubtedly culturally biased.

That borrowed demonstration is conclusive enough that I could have ended the earlier paragraph with, "I rest my case." Still, I would like to present one additional example.

Face-to-face combat weapons of the past, such as swords and lances, had to be as efficient as possible since they were tasked with helping the user stay alive through the end of the battle. But this is not entirely true. Such weapons reflect the varying meaning different cultures

22. ARMOR AS PRIDE AND BEAUTY

23. ARMOR MOVES TO FANTASY

assign to bravery and fighting, leading to appropriate decorative overlay, often generously (see figs. 3 and 4 above). The same attitude could be perceived in body armor (fig 22). The helmet is an ultimate

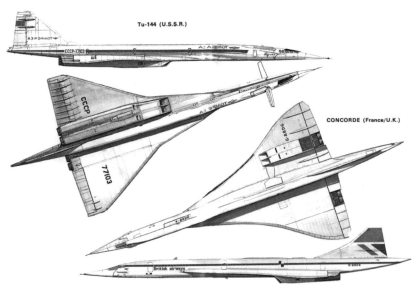

24. CONCORD VS. TU-144 COMPARISONS

example, undoubtedly replacing facial war painting of the distant past. The strong visual appeal of the armor (at least to some) is still echoed in popular contemporary hero fantasy films and in computer games (fig. 23).

In the present, when the military assigns specification for the next fighter plane, it may surprise us how the proposals of the competing aircraft companies may differ in their appearances. The same flight envelope allows for several engineering and, certainly, form solutions. It demonstrates that there may exist more than one form manifestation to a specified function. No wonder then, when the Soviet Union presented its own version of a supersonic passenger plane, the Tupolev Tu-144, it looked so similar to the earlier British-French *Concord* that the Russians were accused of blatant copying in form and spirit. The Soviet airplane was even nicknamed *Concordski* (fig. 24).

Bearing in mind that since form does not emanate squarely from function, it is sometimes tough to identify technology's contribution to the visual outcome. Both have their share in the way the product looks. The recent Apple vs. Samsung court battles over patent infringement are essentially about design patents—the way their smartphones looked, more than about any technological innovation.

There are instances when a novel functional solution suggests a new way of looking at form. When the first American stealth bomber, the Northrop Grumman B-2 (fig. 25) was exposed in 1997, it looked very different from any previous aircraft. Its shape was an integration of two conflicting constraints: an aerodynamic body had to live together with stealth ray-deflecting surfaces. Michael Erlhoff, the German design historian and educator, wrote then that the stealth bomber signified the dawn of new design aesthetics.

25. NORTHROP GRUMMAN B-2 STEALTH BOMBER

The function vs. form conflict may even shift from "Form follows Function" to "Function follows Form," as suggested in the following excerpt.

During the previous decades, Sullivan's dictum has been paraphrased many times. Postmodern semioticians claimed that "Form follows fiction", playful Italians came up with "Form follows fun" while frustrated architects countered with "Form follows anything". Perhaps it is time for a complete change in perspective. We find ourselves today at a point where technology and science are as complex and strained as aesthetics was a hundred years ago. Perhaps it is time to see how aesthetics could guide technology. Function follows form: design as a way of creating meaning and comprehensibility in a world of over-functional chaos.

Hjelm, Sara Ilstedt, Semiotics in product design (report), CID, Centre for User Oriented IT Design Universitat Stokholm, 2002, p. 25

Automation of form generation

In light of how challenging it is for machine learning to imitate that at which our brain excels, it is reasonable to predict that machine creativity will not take hold in the artificial intelligence domain, at least in the near future. It took IBM's *Blue* and later *Watson* super computers quite a few years to beat human chess masters. Face recognition programs often go haywire when faces are perceived not frontally but in oblique angles and in non-optimal environments. As creativity has to do with envisioning the non-existent, pre-loaded with emotions, and cultural contents—areas that computers have not much to offer—will artificial intelligence ever be able to accomplish form design?

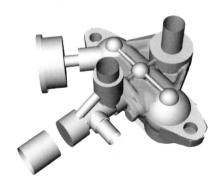

26. COMPUTER-ASSEMBLED MACHINE PARTS (LI, YANGYAN, ET AL, 2011)

27. COMPUTER-GENERATED VASES. PRIMITIVES INDICATED BY DIFFERENT COLORS (XU, KAI, ET AL, 2012)

28. COMPUTER-GENERATED CHAIRS BASED ON A VOCABULARY OF COMMON DESIGNS (XU, KAI, ET AL, 2012)

29. ALIENS COULD BE ASSEMBLED TOO (XU, KAI, ET AL, 2012)

We view 3D shape modeling as a creative task, whether for product design or scene modeling. Creativity has always been a trait bestowed to humans but not machines. An interesting question is whether a machine can assist humans in being creative and inspire a user during 3D modeling. One possible means to achieve this is through a design gallery which presents a variety of suggestive designs from which the user can pick the ones he or she likes the best…. The ensuing challenge is how to come up with intriguing suggestions which inspire creativity, rather than banal suggestions which stall the creative process.

Xu, Kai, et al, Fit and Diverse: Set Evolution for Inspiring 3D Shape Galleries, in ACM Transactions on Graphics (TOG)—SIGGRAPH 2012 Conference Proceedings

It may be quite a shock to designers to learn that there are promising advances in machine learning of form development. If we take into account that aesthetics rules are often mathematical (e.g. golden mean) or based on established conventions of stylistic details, and if we consider that sketching at the ideation phase of design often involves visual brainstorming—the more the better, even silly ideas, without criticism—then maybe the machine can take some of the early ideation labor.

A team of computer sciences researchers from China, Israel, and Europe investigated machine processing of commonplace and often tedious routines of combining basic machine parts in engineering design (fig. 26). Several members of the research team moved to disciplines other than engineering and into creative form generation (fig. 27). In a paper named *Fit and Diverse: Set Evolution for Inspiring 3D Shape Galleries*, they suggested the following (see text frame).

The researchers fed the computer 3-dimentional details of common products in certain product families such as chairs, lamps, candelabras, and even far-out forms such as fictional aliens. The computer analyzed the rules of combining product elements and inherent structure and offered an amazing variety of novel recombinations. The research results are quite intriguing and promising, as you can see in two examples from their paper (figs. 28 and 29). Evidently the process they suggest in creating new forms endorses this book's proclamation about product form evolution, continuation and change (see chapter Temporal aspects of form evolution). As you would expect, the selection of the more promising designs is still the territory of human designers.

A post-object society?

During a recent conference, I heard a talk by Dr. Kun-Pyo Lee, the head of design at the Korean giant LG Electronics. He often used the term "design behind the glass," noting that recent media gadgets such as smartphones and tablets, not to forget laptops and TV screens, provide less and less space for physical form design while most of design content lies behind the glass surface, relegated to virtual design. In the hottest market of media gadgets, almost all gadgets look the same (a boring sameness, unfortunately). This course of things may suggest that sometimes in the future the only physical entities to be left will be the tips of electrodes implanted in our brain—the embodiment of man-machine interface.

Is physical form gradually but persistently vanishing from our environment? I strongly believe it is not. We may assume future austerity of resources. We may assume that many daily operations will be assigned to unseen electronic agents. We are quite accustomed to science fiction movies showing empty, white, futuristic living spaces almost devoid of furniture and objects, something quite inhumane; is that a hint to the timeless purist approach suggested by Philip Steadman?

David Rose, an entrepreneur and educator at the MIT Media Lab, likewise shows his disdain to what he calls "glass slabs and painted pixels," which he refers to as a "terminal world" future, a future steered by some of the largest technology-driven firms. In his recent must-read book, Enchanted Objects: Design, Human Desire, and the Internet of Things (2014), Rose investigate four possible futures of advanced-technology objects that may take place in the next fifty years— Terminal world: the domination of glass slabs; Prosthetics: the new bionic you; Animism: living with bionic robots; and

a fourth possible future of enchanted everyday objects. You can gather from the word "enchanted" in the title of his book where he believes the future of our objects will be, and he explains in length why. Gladly, Rose's future vision is pro-object and decidedly humanistic.

Yes, I accept that several highly physical families of products will completely disappear from our life but I am certain that other objects will rise in their place. We may even invent objects just to keep us company. We will not be left with nothing to look at: with nothing to touch, feel, or smell. Our hand's dexterity evolved over millions of years in order to grasp and use tools. It is part of our being. After all, we should bear in mind that human propensity for adornment is almost as ceaseless as is our tool making. We will continue our affair with man-made objects, though the nature and form of these objects may change profoundly.

IN CONTEXT 1
Aesthetics of Form

Good form

> Pay attention only to the form; emotion will come spontaneously to inhabit it. A perfect dwelling always finds an inhabitant.

Andre Gide, French author, winner of Nobel Prize for literature

This book intentionally does not deal with beauty, with judgments about design quality and with what is often termed, somewhat vaguely, "good design." The investigation of the development of industrial products' form in the following chapters and in the case studies in Part 3 capitalize on comprehension of form without any reference to quality, beauty, or design ethics. Only when I discuss design classics will I include any discussion of quality.

Aesthetics

> What is especially striking and remarkable is that in fundamental physics a beautiful or elegant theory is more likely to be right than a theory that is inelegant.

Murray Gell-Mann, American physicist. Nobel Prize in physics 1969

Aesthetics is defined by the dictionary as a branch of philosophy dealing with the nature of beauty, art, and taste, and with the creation and appreciation of beauty. We will encounter later in this chapter that science sees aesthetics as the study of sensory or sensory-emotional values, sometimes called judgments of sentiment and taste.

According to Kant, beauty is objective and universal. Thus, certain things are beautiful to everyone. Beauty and Truth have often been argued to be nearly synonymous. Symmetry and simplicity are considered as universals of beauty and as such are used in mathematics and cosmology in order to help define truth. Scientists often consider the beauty of a theory or the beauty of a mathematical statement as indicative of truth. Occam's Razor is a principle attributed to the 14th century friar William of Ockham that still holds today. The Occam's Razor principle states that "when you have two competing theories that make exactly the same predictions, the simpler one is the better."

In real life, and contrary to Kant, aesthetic preference is something that ultimately varies from person to person, whether it is culturally taught or etched into our genetic makeup. Some theorists believe that the foundation of Man's preferred aesthetics is tied to evolution; we developed our taste in looks to accommodate survival and promote the wellbeing of our species. Therefore things like color preference, preferred mate body proportions, shapes, emotional ties with objects, and many other aspects of the aesthetic experience can be tied with how we evolved.

I remind you that understanding and appreciating beauty may also involve taste. Taste is a result of an education process and an awareness of so-called "elite cultural values," brought about by diffusion of such values to the culture of the masses. The contemporary view of beauty is less based on innate qualities, but rather on cultural specifics and individual interpretations. Bourdieu examined how the elite in society define the aesthetic values like taste and how varying levels of exposure to these values can result in variations by class, cultural background, and education. Aesthetic judgments may be culturally conditioned. For example, the international style in the urban landscape was considered to epitomize modernism but was later considered to be aloof and boring, giving way to sculptural experimentation and play by "breaking the rules."

Looking at beauty through another prism, the evaluations of beauty may well be linked to desirability, perhaps even to sexual desirability. Furthermore, judgments of aesthetic value can become linked to judgments of economic, political, or moral value. In a current context, one might judge a corporate jet plane or a Ferrari to be beautiful partly because it is desirable as a status symbol, or we might judge them to be repulsive partly because they signify for us over-consumption and offend our political or moral values.

The philosopher Denis Dutton identified six universal signatures in human aesthetics:

- Expertise or virtuosity. Humans cultivate, recognize, and admire technical artistic skills.

- Non-utilitarian pleasure. People enjoy art for art's sake, and don't demand that it keep them warm or put food on the table.

- Style. Artistic objects and performances satisfy rules of composition that place them in a recognizable style.

- Criticism. People make a point of judging, appreciating, and interpreting works of art.

- Imitation. With a few important exceptions like abstract painting, works of art simulate experiences of the world.

- Special focus. Art is set aside from ordinary life and makes a dramatic focus of experience.

Understandably, there are rather too many exceptions to Dutton's categories. Increasingly, academics in both the sciences and the humanities look to evolutionary psychology and cognitive science in an effort to understand the connection between psychology and aesthetics.

If we sum up the foundation for aesthetic judgment, it might be based on many variables such as the senses, emotions, intellectual opinions, will, desires, culture, preferences, values, subconscious behavior, conscious decision, training, instinct, sociological institutions, or some complex combination of these. Not surprising, aesthetic judgments can often be contradictory. No wonder I prefer to overlook aesthetic considerations in the following case studies, though I accept that there is sometimes a collective agreement on beauty, which is the outcome of a socially negotiated and agreed-on phenomenon. We agree on classic products but we can rarely predict them ahead of time.

Geometric rules of form

Almost every basic design course deals with what we call principles of design. Graphic designers will of course concentrate on two dimensional shapes and page layout, product designers will deal with sculptural qualities, and architects will also negotiate space. Most design occupations, in particular fashion design, will relate also to the human body's form and proportions.

There is no use in detailing here and elaborating on the principles of design. Terms such as golden mean (fig. 1) and Fibonacci numbers, and elements' spatial relationships such as composition, harmony, symmetry, proportions, balance, movements, rhythm, and focal point are the daily staple of designers (fig. 2).

It seems that designers are the modern bearers of the ancient Greek love affair with geometry. It probably has to do with

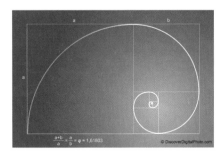

1. THE GOLDEN RATIO BASED ON FIBONACCI GROWTH IN NATURE— A MATHEMATICAL RULE

3. BRAUN SK55 STEREO RADIOGRAMME BY DIETER RAMS AND HANS GUGELOT FOR BRAUN, 1956

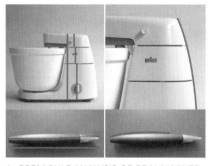

4. FORM RULE ANALYSIS OF BRAUN MIXER AND LAMY PEN, BOTH DESIGNED BY GERD MÜLLER

our tool of the trade, drafting, which is based on geometric conventions. It may also be the prolonged effect of the international style, a modern interpretation of classic rules of proportion and beauty. And of course it may appropriate our brain's perception of aesthetics. Either way, form composition is regularly contingent on geometric rules. Just look at any graphic design book on the grid.

2. GEOMETRY IS INTRINSIC IN MOST DESIGNS

5. THE COMPASS AS A TOOL FOR RATIONING—KIMBERLY ELAN'S BOOK COVER

In the field of industrial design we are still heavily indebted to Dieter Rams, the designer synonymous with the German firm Braun. Wolfgang Schmittel's book, Design, Concept, Realization (1975), dedicates a lengthy chapter to the design culture of Braun (figs. 3 and 4).
Rams' geometric principles and vocabulary of simplicity is not forgotten history. It was revived in Apple's iPhone line, based on a dieter Rams 1987 calculator. Rams stated that Apple is one of the few companies designing products according to his principles.

Kimberly Elam dedicated a full book to the art of product geometry. In Geometry of Design: Studies in Proportion and Composition (2001) (fig. 5), she offers a mathematical explanation as to how art works. Elam performs a visual analysis of a broad range of twentieth-century examples of design, architecture, and illustration, from the Barcelona chair to the Musica Viva poster, from the Braun hand blender to the Conico kettle, revealing underlying geometric structures in their compositions.

Object aesthetics

Simplicity is about subtracting the obvious and adding the meaningful

John Maeda, The Laws of Simplicity, MIT Press, 2006

Years ago, when I was a young industrial design graduate student at UCLA, one of my professors, who had an additional degree in psychology, inquired into the possibility of measuring pupil dilation that occurs in response to viewing images of products. Pupil dilation is a known sign of sexual interest. It was a very promising idea then but also quite complex in the pre-computer area. Such measurement of dilation and gaze is comparatively easy now, but analyzing data and establishing universal rules as to what makes a product accepted as beautiful is still quite intricate.

Helmut Leder, a professor of psychology at the University of Vienna in Austria, in Thinking by Design: the Science of Everyday Beauty Reveals What People Really Like—and Why (Scientific American Mind, July 2011), and Paul Hekkert, a professor of form theory at the Delft University of Technology, in Design Aesthetics: Principles of Pleasure in Product Design (Psychology Science, 2006), summarize cognitive science's knowledge about human aesthetic preferences. Both researchers and their teams sought to unravel the patterns and principles behind people's emotional reactions to objects. Understandably, and as I have suggested earlier, we have to take into account that each person's aesthetic taste seems distinct. In spite of that, their experiments suggest a large body of shared preferences.

The following is an abridged list of universals based of Ledder's and Hekkert's separate research on what people like and dislike, based on their perception of objects.

- Seeing something repeatedly—be it a couch, a car, or a coffeepot—boosts its attractiveness. Not surprisingly, with too much repetition comes boredom.

- People prefer large objects to small ones, although no one is quite sure why.

- People tend to choose rounded forms over sharper shapes, perhaps because angular objects such as thorns and knives signal danger in the brain.

- People are attracted to symmetry in faces and in products. People are known to prefer symmetrical faces, whose shape may suggest good health and reproductive fitness.

- An object's complexity can amplify visual appeal. We often find complex things prettier than simple ones, with complexity defined as the number of individual elements that make up a picture or shape. Complex symmetrical patterns were judged the prettiest. Simple symmetrical patterns received the next highest ratings, revealing that symmetry is more important to our impressions of beauty than complexity is. Combining symmetry and complexity gets higher beauty ratings. Some researchers have theorized that, as with symmetrical faces, archetypes are pleasing because they exhibit no gross irregularities—an extension of our preference for people and animals that appear to be in good health. But cognitive psychologists suggest another explanation, namely, that more typical faces or objects are easier to recognize, providing an efficiency advantage that may stimulate the brain's reward centers.

6. A BICYCLE CONCEPT THAT APPEALS TO DESIGNERS (DESIGNER: CHRIS BOARDMAN)

■ Experience affects our fondness for complexity. Overexposure to complexity creates a contrast effect. After repeated exposure to complex patterns, participants judged simple ones to be prettier. In contrast, substantial exposure to simple patterns rendered people partial to complexity, making it the overriding factor in their judgment of attractiveness. Symmetry, on the other hand, turns out to be resistant to exposure repetition.

■ A more subtle factor influencing aesthetic judgment is man's ingrained appreciation for the beauty of the archetype (Leder uses the term prototype), which is the statistical average of all examples of that product or item. Because an archetype resembles many different examples of a type, it seems familiar even if it is in fact new. Thus, people are attracted to "average" faces (see fig. 10).

■ The power of archetypes may depend on context because shapes can play with one's emotions. For example, if familiarity offers comfort and feelings of safety, then it ought to be particularly appealing when someone is feeling down. But cheerful people ought to react differently. They neither preferred the patterns they recognized nor displayed positive emotional responses.

■ Studies have shown that people tend to like the culturally accepted aesthetic norm in general including its appearance in furniture, works of art, and even meaningless patterns of dots.

■ "Something Old, Something New": Paul Hekkert asked volunteers to evaluate various designs of electric sanders, teakettles, telephones and cars on their originality and beauty, as well as on how typical they looked. The participants rated the most conventional models as the least attractive, with only slightly warmer reactions to objects with such unusual shapes that their purpose was unclear. The top scores went to designs that coupled originality with classic forms—for instance, archetypes (prototypes) bearing one unusual feature. In other words, the most popular products look innovative while retaining a sense of the known,

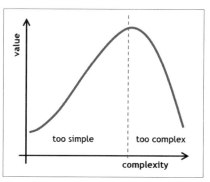

8. PRODUCT ACCEPTANCE VS. COMPLEXITY OF FORM (ACCORDING TO MIKE BAXTER / SHLOMO MAITAL)

a principle that American designer Raymond Loewy called "most advanced yet acceptable." That is why car manufacturers often try to maintain some continuity of design for the purposes of brand recognition.

■ Experts can handle more originality than non-specialists can. Hekkert and his colleagues have shown that those who know a lot about cars tend to favor unusually original designs. The more innovative a model, the more beautiful the experts judged it (fig. 6). The expert effect could result primarily from repeatedly seeing and evaluating a certain class of items. For consumers, these findings suggest that a well-informed buyer should spend some time with a product before committing, perhaps by test-driving a new car a couple times.

■ Contrary to the main focus of designers, looks are not always paramount. In a 2010 study, Hekkert and his group (Fenko et al, 2010) asked students to report their experiences with a recently purchased product (a pair of shoes, a printer, or a coffee machine) while buying it and then after the first week, the first month, and the first year of owning and using it. The students reported how much each of their senses contributed to their interactions with the product (fig 7). The

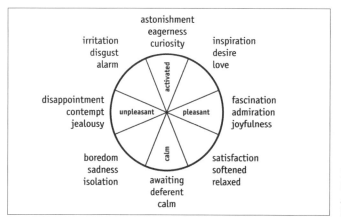

7. PRODUCT EMOTIONS ACCORDING TO DESMET (2007)

investigators found that an object's visual impact was strongest at the moment of purchase. After a month of using the product, however, how it felt to the touch became more important than its appearance, and after a year the look, feel, and sound of the product were valued equally. Of course, the role of the different senses varies with the product. After a year, the sense of hearing dominated the experience for users of high-tech products, whereas for shoes the senses of touch and sight were equally important.

Mike Baxter, in Product Design: Practical Methods for the Systematic Development of New Products (1995), suggest a fluctuating relationship between beauty and complexity of product that seems to me to make sense: simple is typically boring, and adding complexity is exciting, but over-complexity is misunderstood and thus less attractive (fig. 8).

Can beauty be quantified?

My guess is that mathematicians will answer yes, since beauty is truth, in line with the way beauty is understood in mathematics. Artificial intelligence scientists, who use mathematical models, will dare to analyze millions of faces and come with an ideal face based on the relationship of detailed features of the human face (fig. 9). On the other hand, social scientists and artists will point at the cultural complexity involved in defining beauty and are likely to state that "beauty is in the eye of the beholder."

The case for measuring beauty, both in humans and in nature, is based upon a ratio. Plants, animals and humans grow according to precise mathematical laws. Flowers don't unfold in "beautiful" patterns by chance. Rather, their development is based upon our familiar

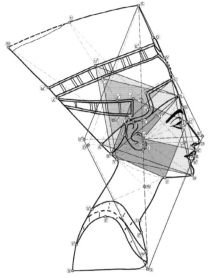

9. MEASUREMENT OF BEAUTY. THE EGYPTIAN QUEEN NEFERTITI

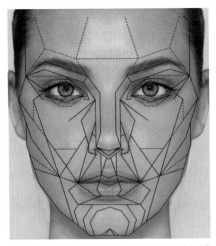

10. GEOMETRY OF IDEAL AVERAGE FEMALE FACE BASED ON PHI MASK DEVISED BY THE COSMETIC SURGEON DR. STEPHEN MARQUARDT

Golden Ratio, 1:1.618. In his search for practical rules for facial beauty, Dr. Stephen Marquardt, a plastic surgeon from California, has constructed a mask based upon this Golden Ratio (fig. 10). The proportion is seen everywhere on the beautiful face: the length of the nose, the positioning of the eyes, even in the teeth. And not only does this mask conform to beautiful faces (regardless of race) of today's standards, but also in pre-Modern paintings, Greek statues, and old-time movie stars. So, contrary to popular belief, the standard of facial beauty remains the same over time and across cultures. "Beautiful" body types come in and out of vogue, but the beautiful face always remains the same.

On the more daring side of quantifying beauty is the work of Juhani Risku, a Finish architect and product-creation strategist who worked for Nokia. Risku has an uncanny talent of translating complex and abstract ideas into thought-provoking graphic maps. So we ought to seriously listen to what he says. Risku's personal blog, abstractionshift, presents the following conceptual formula for beauty (fig. 11). It may look a bit strange at first but it does have its own beauty.

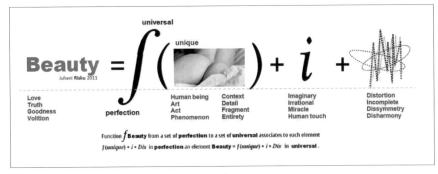

11. JUHANI RISKU FORMULA FOR BEAUTY, 2012

PART 2

Concepts of Product Form

A conjectural framework

What are the goals?

> A lot of people in our industry haven't had very diverse experiences. So they don't have enough dots to connect, and they end up with very linear solutions without a broad perspective on the problem. The broader one's understanding of the human experience, the better design we will have.
>
> Steve Jobs, co-founder and CEO of Apple, 1955–2011

In Part 1 of this book I summed up the scientific knowledge and design research knowledge pertinent to our discussion. As design research is often based on interpretation of information, I will include in Part 2 my personal observations and assumptions concerning the form evolution of contemporary product families, as they manifest themselves in Part 3 of this book, and I will add here insights as to their evolutionary behavior.

I am cautious not to call my suppositions here in Part 2 a theory. Therefore, I prefer the label them "conjecture," an opinion or conclusion formed on the basis of incomplete information. I enjoy what the dictionary has to say about conjecture: it literally means "to throw together," that is, to produce a theory by putting together a number of facts; and at one time it also carried the meaning "the interpretation of omens or signs" or "divination." So this book is not about a full-fledged theory but rather a theory outline, or at the least, a

viewpoint. Admittedly, a viewpoint means that it is subjective to my personal ideas and beliefs.

I hope that at the end of the road these observations should eventually lead to several concrete outcomes:

- find order in things (a theory)
- develop an analytical tool (a method)
- assist in predicting forthcoming product form (an application)

The purpose of this chapter is to suggest a frame that may explain an apparent order I will demonstrate later in the evolution of man-made, mass-produced products, and to discuss several issues stemming from that order. The next chapter, *Temporal aspects of form evolution*, will discuss rules or tenets that product evolution abides by. All of the rules deal with how form changes over time. After all, change is inherent to the nature of evolution. The following chapter, *Spatial aspects of form evolution*, will discuss form changes that come from the influences of parallel product families or the behavior of products being close to or far away from the user (proximity may be a better word). It seems that product form behaves differently and evolves differently when very close to our body—fashion is a well-suited word here. In the chapter about the spatial aspects of form evolution I try to define such relationships. The third chapter, *External catalysts of form evolution*, deals with the context within which form evolves, be it technology, economics, or social and cultural change. The last chapter in Part 2, *In context 2-technology*

leaders, will discuss the cultural impact of leading technologies such as skyscrapers and airplanes on our lives and thus on the shape of everyday objects we use.

Meta approaches in design

> Advancing technology, allied to extremely complex operational software and capability, are blurring the boundaries of what we understand by 'product'. Sometimes, the hardware we hold in our hand, or with which we interact, is just a small part of 'the product'. The activity of product design will continue to make inroads into the non-physical aspects of the product and even the 'virtual product' or meta product.
>
> The Design Council, UK

The design profession has a characteristic tendency to think bottom-up rather than top-down. Designers deal with specific users, feasible solutions, brand-related form, and details, not to forget production and economics constraints. As product design's body of knowledge materializes and expands, I believe that future designers will set the balance between top-down and bottom-up design at a new equilibrium. Design education was for a long time about *how*, design investigation deals more and more with *why*, eventually leading design education to a higher level of design. Call it the design of design; the gestalt of design itself. The accepted term for such a state is Meta-design.

Meta is a prefix, commonly followed by a dash or added to another word (meta-physics, meta-ethics, metamathematics, metalinguistics, etc.). Meta means beyond; transcending; more comprehensive. Meta also means "at a higher state of development." That is what design should grow into, meta-design.

What does meta-design mean? The designer Jess McMullin, in a paper titled *A Rough Design Maturity Continuum*, (Design + Business, 2005), defines several phases of design attitude, each defining a higher level of design than the previous one (fig. 1). These are the levels, as stated by McMullin:

- **No conscious design:** *Design value isn't recognized.* This attitude fosters design by default: however things come out is fine, because there are more important issues to deal with.

- **Style:** *Design is the gateway to be hip and cool.* Design is stylish, but too often is perceived and practiced as a cosmetic afterthought. Style-guides inform product development.

- **Function & form:** *Design makes things work better.* This is the classic practice of design but it is still commonly limited to incremental improvements through iteration over existing solutions. Patterns inform product development.

- **Problem solving:** *Design finds new opportunities by solving existing problems.* Design process generates alternatives within a problem space. Design also narrows down those options to a specific solution. Problems drive product development.

- **Framing:** *Design redefines the challenges facing the organization.* Framing sets the agenda, outlines the boundaries and axes of interest, and moves design from executing strategy to shaping strategy. Disruptive innovation lives here. Ideas drive product development.

Austin Govella elaborated on McMullin's ideas. In a 2006 article *Correlations Between Design Maturity, Leadership*

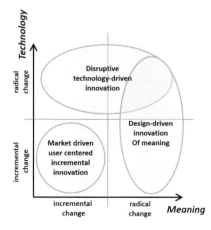

1. MCMULLIN'S LEVELS OF DESIGN

2. DISRUPTIVE TECHNOLOGY AND INNOVATIVE MEANING ARE META-APPROACH DESIGN (AFTER ROBERTO VERGANTI)

Maturity, and Innovation. Govella's ideas, widely circulated by now, outline a parallel list of management personalities, from lowest to highest on McMullin's chart: The *opportunist* or the *diplomat* (parallels no conscious design), the *expert* (style), the *achiever* (function & form), the *individualist* (problem solving), and finally

the *strategist* and even the *alchemist* (as the framer). The *strategist*, according to Govella, generates organizational and personal transformation and exercises the power of mutual inquiry and vigilance and is thus effective as a transformation leader. The *alchmist* is good at leading society. He generates social transformation and integrates material, spiritual, and social transformation.

The medieval alchemist dreamt of magical means to turn lead into gold; the alchemist designer will immerse himself in groundbreaking disruptive innovation.

Roberto Verganti, in *Design-Driven Innovation*, spots a framing attitude by design-driven industry leaders such as Apple, which compete through products and services that have a radical new meaning: those that convey a completely new reason for customers to buy them (fig. 2).

What insights can we take from science?

Before I proceed with this discussion, let me sum up the main form-related evidences mentioned in the chapters of Part 1 of this book.

Mental processing of images

- Visual cognition: our innate capacity for visual cognitive modeling.

- Perception: grasping the essential structural features of a shape to produce a "whole" or *gestalt*.

- Geons: the more simply recognized signs our brain reduces from complex images. Objects are reduced to geon elements, also making recognition less dependent on viewing angle distortion.

- Image vs. word: ongoing research on vision-word interface in the brain. We can verbalize thinking. We can also visualize it.

- Mental organization: the tendency for object memory to be grouped and located in the cortex corresponding to the nature of the images.

- Brain dictionary: the apparent visual associations essential to form recognition by comparison of images to prior knowledge, memories, and words. Semantic attributes are applied by the brain to visual representations, providing meaning, and thereby recognition.

Innate human form preferences

- Preference: We prefer forms to be simple, symmetric, geometric. They are easier to grasp and signal evolutionary fitness.

- Complexity: We enjoy complexity up to a certain level. Experience affects our fondness for complexity as experts can handle more originality than others.

- Acceptance: People tend to like culturally accepted aesthetic norms. Repetitive exposure increases attractiveness.

Language and man-made artifacts

- Language defines visual concepts: The Whorf Hypothesis states that language and culture are so closely connected that one defines the other.

- Lingual recognition: A novel product is not wholly understood and accepted until it is given a proper name and that name becomes familiar.

- Metaphors: A metaphor is something that explains the unknown in well-known terms—fundamental in design.

- Spoken languages: They change continually. The cultural needs of speakers drive language change. New technologies, industries, products, and experiences form new words.

- Visual language of man-made objects: The visual language may evolve at an even faster rate than the spoken language as it reflects not only culture but also the ever-increasing rate of technological innovation.

Technological and natural evolution

- Purpose: Technological evolution does not follow the route of random mutations in natural evolution since processes of technological evolution are *a priori* goal oriented.

- Teleology: Inanimate and animate entities evolve as if they are "intelligent," because they appear to come up with similar answers to a problem.

Culture of man-made artifacts

- Meme: a unit of cultural transmission. Memes may evolve by cultural selection in a manner analogous to that of biological evolution. Memes that replicate most effectively enjoy more success.

- Images comprehension: Society is becoming increasingly reliant on visual images in order to communicate and explain complex information.

Form-focused design thinking

- There has been a recent rise in research into the nature and meaning of form in man-made artifacts.

- Form does not arise by itself from a clean functional solution to a problem.

- Product semantics show that, often, meaning matters more than function.

- Designers must be familiar with ecology of artifacts as people attach meaning to artifacts in relation to other artifacts. This relationship has to do with cooperation, competition, dependency, reproduction, and retirement (death) of artifacts.

Archetypes

The dictionary defines archetype as an ideal example or an original model or type after which other similar things are patterned. In Jungian psychology an archetype is an inherited pattern of thought or symbolic imagery derived from the past collective experience and present in the individual unconscious. Just consider how children in western cultures insist on a specific recognized image for a house even if they live in metropolitan high-rise buildings and have not seen a real red roofed house (fig. 3).

3. A CHILD'S MODEL HOUSE SYMBOL

In useful applied terms, Helmut Leder (*Thinking By Design: The Science of Everyday Beauty Reveals What People Really Like—And Why*) suggests that an archetype is the statistical average of all examples of that product or item. Because an archetype resembles many different examples of a type, it seems familiar even if it is in fact quite new. Designers will understand the concept of statistical averaging if they compare it to a program that morphs many specimens

4. FORM ARCHETYPES USE RATHER THAN RECOGNIZE BRAND DETAILS

5. NOT ALL TWO-WHEELED BIKES CAN BE REPRESENTED BY ONE ARCHETYPE

of a product into one inclusive average form. Graphic designers will recognize averaging as intentional simplification of an image until it becomes an icon. For industrial designers, averaging means stripping the products of any design detail that relates it to a specific brand or to a specific designer. Stripping a product of its distinctive details is contrary to industrial designer's habit of adding a remarkable contribution to a product's form. In the series of case studies in Part 3, I will try as much as possible to use stripped-down archetypes (fig. 4). This will help in realizing the current evolutionary trends since designers will be prevented from being engrossed with explicit forms and details.

The archetype approach is not entirely new. Several decades earlier, Corning designed a teacup by averaging the cross section of many teacups on the market in order to come up with an ideal teacup. The idea of archetype has practical uses too. There will be some exclusions in the use of archetypes in the case studies in Part 3. On one hand, the iPhone, the iPad, and the Segway are easily identified as archetypes because they purposefully

incorporate unique archetypal qualities into their designed forms. On the other hand, if we try to describe cars only by their archetypal forms (as seen in toy cars) we will not be able to describe car evolution in time since car evolution is mostly about evolution of details and less about general contours. The same problem in form archetype arises when trying to plot two-wheel transportation devices. Bicycles and motorcycles are all about specific details and less about form averages (fig. 5), as is most furniture.

Order and classification

This book's subtitle is about deciphering the language of mass-produced objects, about how we tend to group them and interpret them. It is also about charting the evolution of man-made objects in an attempt to explain dynamic visual changes that occur in both evolutionary and linguistic terms. In a nutshell, I am trying to explain the underlying order of things.

Classification

There is an innate human tendency to see order and patterns in the world around us, even when such an order is only in our mind. The gestalt theory explains that perception is not a passive recording of all that is in front of the eyes, but is a continuous judgment of contents, shapes, and scale and color relationships. Our tendency to organize things also stems from the way our mind is organized. Object memory tends to be grouped and located in the cortex corresponding to the nature of the images, whether they be faces, animals, man-made objects, etc. Classification is the process of grouping things based on their shared traits. Classification occurs in many fields of knowledge: in the life sciences (species); in chemistry (periodic table); in medicine (ailments, medications); in libraries (Dewey and Library of Congress classifications); in the social sciences (classes, demography); and so on.

There are several linguistic terms for classification that are of interest to us. Taxonomy is the term used in life sciences to classify organisms in an ordered

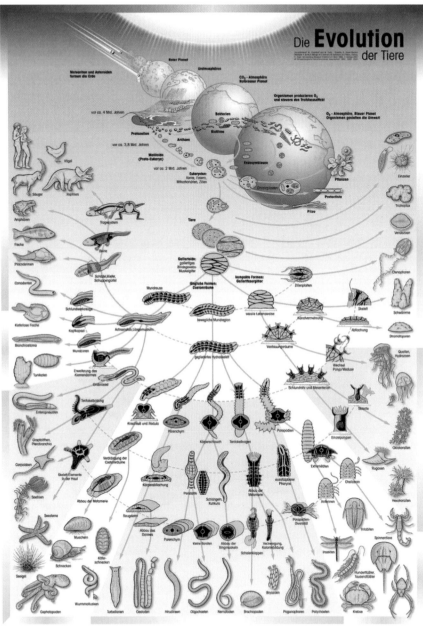

6. EVOLUTIONARY CLASSIFICATION OF SPECIES. FORM HAS A DEFINITE ROLE HERE

system that indicates natural relationships. Subsequently taxonomy generally means division into ordered groups or categories.

Typology is the classification of things according to their characteristics. Architects often use the term typology in that context.

As over a million species of organisms are currently defined, life sciences' taxonomic organization of species is quite elaborate and deeply hierarchical (fig. 6): Each species belongs to a genus, each genus belongs to a family, and so on through order, class, phylum, and kingdom. Associations within the hierarchy reflect evolutionary relationships, which are deduced typically from morphological and physiological similarities between species. So, for example, species in the same genus are more closely related and more alike than species that are in different genera within the same family.

In the study of product evolution there is no need for such complex hierarchy and classification. We can follow a simpler classification that is used in the drop-down menus of internet shopping sites such as Amazon: electronics/computers/laptops/14 inches…. There are many similar groupings of products that we use in everyday life with without really delving into the *whys* and *hows* of such classifications.

There is a deficiency of proper and agreed-upon definitions within the design community. On one hand, I am pleased that the term "design" itself is not so clear-cut, and is often vague, and instead aims to be broad and far-reaching. I hope that it will continue that way. On the other hand, I am displeased with the term "product." which I use in this book. Product is a commonly used term in our profession but, as the word "product" is used in mathematics, it is the result of something else that produced it. "Object" or even "man-made object" may be considered as too general or vague of terms. Cultural scientists prefer another word altogether: "artifact," any object made by human beings. So sheet music is an artifact. I suspect that the lack of a proper term led Prasad Boradkar to name his book *Designing Things: A Critical Introduction to the Culture of Objects*, and Donald Norman to name his book *The Design of Everyday Things*. We are not used to calling mass-produced products "things." Not surprisingly, you will find throughout this book that I tend to meander between these inadequate terms.

As you will find out when reading the case studies in Part 3, I commonly use the term "family" to denote a class of products (e.g. home entertainment objects, television screens, power hand-tools) but here and there I also use the word "class." The family is divided into branches, but sometimes I refer to sub-families. So the small food preparation appliance family will be divides into branches or sub-families named food mixers, blenders, juicers, food processors, electric kettles, and toasters. But is it really a product family? I kept finding confusing definitions of families. For example, should the word "automobile" include busses and trucks? (In this case I decided no, they are "vehicles.") What is the most defining name for the family containing portable telephones of today? (I opt to use "personal media communicators.") Do faxes, printers, and copiers belong together as a family with multiple branches? (Yes.) In proper evolutionary terms there is often a conflict with industry and marketing classifications: we are not set on definitive product family classifications.

A new design language

From the perspective of industrial design, there are two summarized main points:

1. Product design is now defined as a system to communicate product information based mainly on product use circumstances.

2. The message that a product carries has become the most important factor throughout the design process.

Chung-Hung Lin, Department of Creative Product Design, Lingtung University, Taiwan, in *Research in the Use of Product Semantics to Communicate Product Design Information*, (HCD'11 Proceedings of the 2nd International Conference on Human Centered Design)

As you may have noticed, the cerebral, psychological, and cultural relationships between the verbal language and the visual language form the backbone of my interest in product form (it seems that the Sapir-Whorf Hypothesis about language affecting perception is even more robust when it relates to artifacts). Unfortunately this is a much-intertwined area of research and I am not yet prepared to suggest a related Meta-design theory even if I point to supporting evidences in the case studies. It seems that rather than verbal and visual languages acting in parallel though separate tracks—as suggested by the left brain-right brain division premise that we designers embraced for many years, and which has recently been refuted by recent fMRI data that show many parts of the brain, left and right, acting in unison—we may eventually accept the fact that language and vision actually work in tandem.

It is a wonder why certain monosyllabic names such as *chair* or *hat* allow for such a wide latitude of form variations and yet are still easily recognized for what they are, while other words, *chisel* for example, are so specific and form-limiting. Why the word *mirror* stands for material behavior but does not define a specific shape, while the word *bucket* defines an explicit container form.

W. J. T. Mitchell, a professor of English and Art History at the University of Chicago, relates to the problem of "word and image," long debated in art history. He politely states, "The domains of word and image are like two countries that speak different languages but that have a long history of mutual migration, cultural exchange, and other forms of intercourse." Is the icon of a tree interpreted similarly as the word tree? The very phrase "word and image," in fact, is a way of demonstrating this dichotomy, but on the positive side as it opens a wide expanse for intellectual argument and historical research.

Stepping-stones leading to a theory?

I chose to reference several research works, some theoretical, some practical, some proposed by designers, some by engineers and scientists. The former prefer to use qualitative methods, the latter quantitative. What they have in common is the aim to join together language and images, semantics, emotion, and user preferences into working hypotheses and middle-range theories (fig. 7). These works use databases and accumulated information that indicate appropriate form(s) for a given product at a given situation. There is an anticipation that these works and others may eventually lead to one or more grand theories of product form evolution (fig. 7).

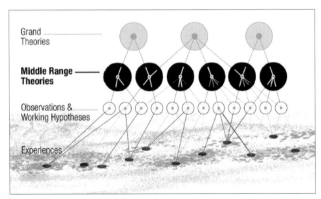

7. FROM EXPERIENCE TO WORKING HYPOTHESES TO THEORIES (STORKERSON, *DESIGN THEORY IN COMMUNICATION*, TERMINOLOGY BASED ON R.K. MERTON'S THEORY)

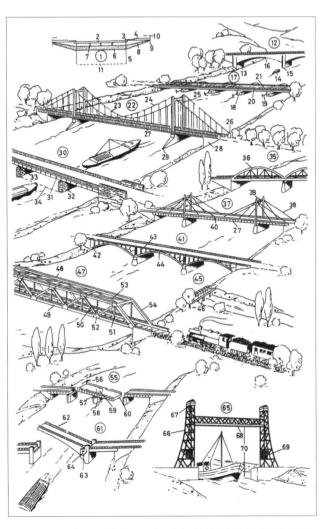

9. THE WORD "BRIDGE" IS TRANSLATED INTO SEVERAL PICTORIAL DEFINITIONS. IT IS A DICTIONARY FORM RATHER THAN A THESAURUS (SOURCE: THE ENGLISH DUDEN. A PICTORIAL DICTIONARY, 1960)

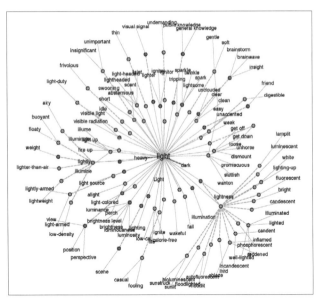

8. THE EXISTING VISUAL THESAURUS WILL EVENTUALLY INCLUDE IMAGES AND ASSOCIATIONS

Image database for product designers

Relegating the lexical organization of words into an organization of images is relatively simple if we stick to a simple word-to-image dictionary. This is the way children's pictorial dictionaries were made in the last two centuries. The German publisher Duden published in 1935 a pictorial dictionary where images covered information in which dictionary definitions did not suffice, such as the differences between musical brass instruments like the French horn, trombone, and tuba. Pictorial images are particularly helpful in science and technology (fig. 9). Now, we often use Google images in search of visual information, but Google's database, based on words, is not ready yet to suggest related images. Google is, however, experimenting with query-by-images.

Chun Ting Wu and Malcolm Johnston from the University of the Arts in London, offer a practical resolution of the "word and image" dichotomy. In a paper they published in 2005, they researched the use of images and descriptive words by product designers. They observed that different words can be used to express the same things. For example, "circle" and "wheel" could represent the same things. The importance of terms and product names in design led them to propose the development of a product design thesaurus, an interactive database of images and design related words based on the interactive Visual Thesaurus (fig. 8) that is already on the web. (A thesaurus is a dictionary of words organized by meaning rather than by their alphabetic sequence.) The use of such a thesaurus in product design processes will help to develop relevant visualizations. The sought-after word appears in the center of the computer screen and is surrounded by connecting lines to words and meanings that are related to it. Clicking on any word can transfer it to the center and consequently the designer will see relationships, defined by the word's visual form, function, and meaning. In addition, the words can be presented with images or links to relevant image databases.

Product teleosemantics

John Takamura of Arizona State University tackles another visual language dichotomy. In a paper named *Product Teleosemantics: The Next Stage in the Evolution of Product Semantics* (2007), He observes that product semantics can never offer a truly one-to-one direct translation from the designer's intended meanings to the meanings interpreted by users. Therefore he proposes a meta-design approach—that the process of designing should be teleosemantic (a self-fulfilling "prophecy" paralleling teleosemantic theories in DNA information systems). The designer embeds semantic meanings into product attributes, and it is those attributes that end up fulfilling the original intentions through their interpretation and use by consumers. This transfer of information utilizes the teleological feedback systems to understand and change cultural values that ultimately may lead to socio-economic change. Takamera suggests that teleosemantic approach in product design will aid designers with a more dynamic way to impact on our material culture.

10. A PROPOSAL FOR A NEW COFFEE MAKER FOLLOWING KANSEI ENGINEERING MORPHOLOGICAL ANALYSIS OF THE CLASSIC BRAUN COFFEE MAKER. (SHIH-WEN HSIAO ET AL, 2010)

Quantifying semantics

Pedro Company, a Spanish project management research group, uses mathematics as a common denominator in assessing products. In a paper, *Contributions to Product Semantics Taxonomy* (2004), they used quantitative measurements of the product's visual and functional qualities (the latter is of lesser importance to our topic here). Their proposal is based on Barthes, who said that an object can be considered a sign of what it does, and what it does grants it a signification. Consequently they used three separate dimensions to define an object: The first dimension is syntax, which sets out the formal relations between parts, their shape, their order, and their makeup. Numeric values are given to the product's geometry, its spatial organization, and the description of its elements and prevalence of technology. The second dimension is semantics, which associates the sign with its significance, provides us with the meaning of objects, and underlines the emotional qualities of the product. The third dimension is quality, the product's logic, usage, function, purpose, and degree of success. Quantifying the three dimensions allows for a more objective comparison between products. The acceptance of form semantics in engineering and management is to me a breath of fresh air. The authors admit that the "beautifulness" of products was

not formally considered in the past and it only recently became a subject of study in user-centered design or emotional design.

Kansei Engineering

Kansei is a Japanese term used to express one's impression towards artifact, situation and surrounding. Deeply rooted in the Japanese culture, direct translation of Kansei to other language is rather difficult. Having various interpretations by different literature, Kansei is generally referred to as sensitivity, sensibility, feeling, and emotion. Kansei Engineering is a technology proposed in Japan by Nagamachi in the 1990s. It unites Kansei into engineering realms in order to realize products that match consumer's needs and desires. A.M. Lokman, in a 2010 paper, *Design and Emotion: The Kansei Engineering Methodolog*, provides a good description of the Kansei engineering process. It is a scientific discipline in which the development of product that pleases and satisfies consumers is carried out technologically. This is done by analyzing consumer's Kansei and translates how the product design elicits this Kansei. It collects the consumer's Kansei experience and establishes mathematical prediction models of how the Kansei is connected to the product's physical characteristics. Kansei Engineering aims to improve human well-being by looking into physiological and psychological aspects that contribute to satisfaction. Shih-Wen Hsiao et al. in a paper published in 2010, provide a good example of the method, especially the morphological analysis (fig. 10). Pierre Lévy's 2014 paper, *Beyond Kansei Engineering: The Emancipation of Kansei Design*, suggests a wider context, away from the engineering world and more adapted to the design world.

Product family evolution

The methodology I propose classifies products by families and family branches regardless of firms, designers and surface styles. It allows us to investigate the formal evolution of each family and branch over time and find out the form relationship of one branch to the other or even the relationship with extraneous product families. I suggested in Part 1 that technological change, though continual, is merely a catalyst of formal change but form does not blindly follow function.

As in any cultural evolution, certain product branches decline and even become obsolete over time: the electric fan was almost replaced by the more efficient air conditioner; the home radio replaced by television. Other product families keep branching out, like the mythological Medusa hair, into different subcategories: typically portable product varieties tend to branch off from the main branch. Other product families borrow shamelessly from external families: our portable telephone doubles up now as a camera. These quite elaborate and often fast changes, branching out, intermixing, and borrowing require charting each product family's evolution over time in order to identify characteristics and form expressions exclusive to that particular family. I cannot find a better portrayal of my methodology than Paul Gauguin's famous Tahiti painting title, *Where Do We Come From? What Are We? Where Are We Going?*

The notion of persistent continuity in product design is based on the stipulation that an "out of the blue" form of a product cannot be understood for what it is and what it does. In any language a new word (and there are new words all the time) is meaningless if not commonly understood, the same goes for the visual language of products. If so, continuity means

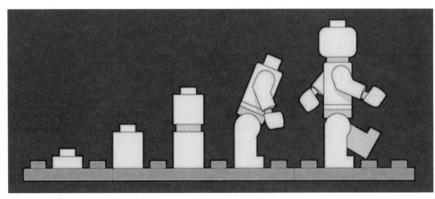

11. PRODUCT FAMILY EVOLUTION (SOURCE: GLENNZ T-SHIRTS)

that there is a gradual change in form (analogous to image morphing) as well as change in the meaning of products. Gradual is a relative term. Change may be relaxed or very swift. Industrial designers are often attentive to the "Something Old, Something New" requisite—what the design pioneer Raymond Loewy termed as "most advanced yet acceptable." The introduction of a new technology requires both a descriptive name and an acknowledged image. A new locomotion device in the early 1900s was appropriately described as a horseless carriage and it looked as such. Even the later new name automobile (autonomous mobility) was still mostly descriptive. The next chapter, *Temporal aspects of form evolution* will elaborate on the various time-related types of evolution.

Cultural and technological evolution, and consequently product evolution, not only evolve, branch out, or decline (as in natural evolution), they can also merge (non-existent in natural evolution) either within the family or with an unrelated family, or appear seemingly out of nowhere, in a short span of time, but still reflecting in its novel form the "Something Old" tenet.

wMerging of product lines is actually quite common. We were accustomed to the common all-in-one, and the more recent hybrid. Ever-increasing technological

flexibility on one hand, and production miniaturization on the other, allow for the embedding of technology taken from one product line into another product line. And not only in technology. We observe embedding visual traits from functionally successful relative branches or even from any other product line presently in vogue. A typical example of such metamorphosis is the current smartphone. It is a telephone that can browse the internet, get mail and messages, show where we are, take pictures, play music and video, and more. Who needs a map, a wristwatch, a separate music player, a portable computer, or a separate camera? This causes the name smartphone to be a misnomer that will be quickly outdated, as its root name refers to its single-function ancestor, the telephone, when the modern device is indeed so much more. The name iPhone is a proprietary one. That is why I prefer in the case study to name the family "portable media communicator" as a more suitable description of the family. But designating a name does not guarantee future public acceptance of it (remember continuity!). As branching out and merging are two related aspects of product evolution, I call them divergence and convergence. See the next chapter on spatial aspects of form evolution.

Another evolutionary feature exclusive to the evolution of science, technology, and product families is paradigm change, also described in the next chapter. Paradigm change does not happen in natural evolution. Moreover, design thinking in the corporate world is currently geared toward disruptive innovation. Unlike scientific paradigm change, which usually occurs only once in a century, disruptive change is frequent and pervasive. Bruce Mau's 2004 book, *Massive Change*, talks about this emerging phenomenon and demands a dramatic redefinition for the practice of design. The book's back cover reads, "Massive Change is not about the world of design; it's about the design of the world." Therefore design in contemporary society must function as a large, interdisciplinary methodology for solving problems.

What about creative genius?

Will a theory giving insights into the logic involved in the evolution of product form limit the freedom of product designers' creative genius? The answer is, what else, a yes-and-no answer. Industrial designers are not artists. They never had the liberty of an unlimited creative freedom. Designers always managed form successfully in spite of production limitations and cost constraints. Dealing with client and user acceptance has always been part of the design process. Design responsibility also applies to decisions on the form of the product. In recent years, the user became a major stakeholder in the design process. And the designer's solution is never alone. It has to undergo several iterations facing user groups. A hundred years after Raymond Loewy coined the statement, "most advanced yet acceptable," it still holds. Corporate industrial design will, by and large, try to cautiously move ahead with form changes, keeping them within range of the accepted archetype design of the day. IN contrast, and perhaps even conflict with this corporate caution, are design students and young designers who

will always try to push the limits of form design to the edge of "acceptable," and even beyond (what we label today experimental design). Some of these designs will not be comprehended and accepted and therefore will stay as proposals only, some will appeal to a narrow group of early adopters and eventually gain a high-end, but limited, public acceptance. Bang & Olufsen (B&O), the Danish entertainment electronics company, is a good example. Once in a while, a highly original design will even manage break away from the accepted form evolution sequence and be generally accepted as a form paradigm change. Is Dyson a good example?

On the affirmation of the creative genius side of the argument, the future probably holds more design freedom than did any time in the past. Today's advanced production solutions allow realization of almost any shape the design wishes to offer. But such excessive design freedom lays on product designers the burden of decision on what should be the *right* form (if the word *right* applies at all). Furthermore, the on-going democratization of design, the access the public has to formerly professional design CAD programs, leads to a recognition that everybody may design according to his or hers own taste and requirements. This has progressed to the physical realm through the use of inexpensive assemble-your-own 3D printers. The do-it-yourself (DIY) movement is already widely acknowledged as a legitimate public pathway, even by professional designers; thereby object form is being relegated to the public domain. No doubt we will see more and more mass-contributed product designs and crowd-established forms. The day is close when popular culture may indicate what should be the proper form for an object—the democratization of form. This development is analogous to how language keeps changing over time.

Temporal aspects of form evolution

The Cyclical Evolution in Art tenet

History does not repeat itself, but it does rhyme.

Mark Twain

People usually associate technological progress and, in general, human progress with exponential growth, or at least to accelerated change behavior, eventually reaching a plateau: the S-curve (fig. 1). Several thinkers even talk about exponential growth reaching a point of *singularity*. The renowned writer on singularity, Ray Kurzweil, defines the singularity concept in terms of the technological creation of superintelligence, and argues that it is difficult or impossible for present-day humans to predict what a post-singularity world would be like, due to the difficulty of imagining the intentions and capabilities of superintelligent entities.

Unlike most theories of social evolutionism, which view the evolution of society and human history as progressing in unique ways, Sociological Cycle Theory argues that events and stages of society and history are generally repeating themselves in cycles. Such a theory

does not necessarily imply that there cannot be any social progress. Similar cyclical theories are found in economics: Kondratiev waves, also called supercycles, are described as sinusoidal-like cycles between fast and slow growth in the modern capitalist world economy, averaging about fifty years from peak to peak.

Closer to our topic, fashion is ultimately cyclical, based on the annual seasonal cycle of summer, winter, and *demi-saison*. However, next year's fashion will certainly not be a strict copy of this year's.

Is there also a cyclical component in the design of man-made objects? I wish to distinguish between the technological

aspects, which usually grow exponentially (as in Moore's Law) and the visual contents aspects, which comprise our interest here. To answer this question we may draw an inference from arts. What does art have to do with anything here? Britannica Online defines art as "the use of skill and imagination in the creation of aesthetic objects, environments, or experiences that can be shared with others." This definition clearly embraces man-made objects of design as being art.

It seems that man-made objects of design are continually alternating between two poles. One is austere, clean, logical, functional, and geometric by nature (represented by classicism, neoclassicism, and modernism); the other is free, emotional, sculptural, decorative, and complex in nature (represented by gothic, baroque, and even in some ways post-modernism). After an era in which one paradigm dominates, there follows a paradigm shift towards the other (fig. 2).

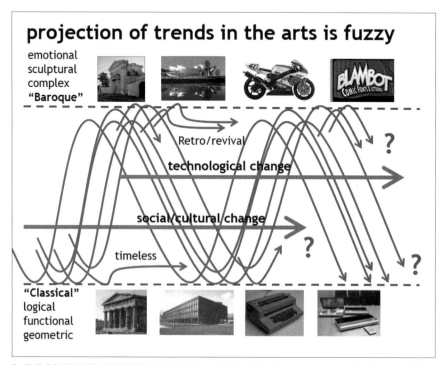

2. THE COMPLEXITY OF DEFINING CYCLICAL EVOLUTION OF MAN-MADE CREATIVE OBJECTS

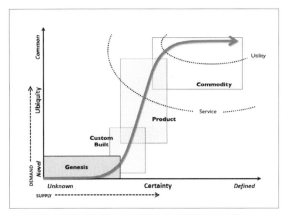

1. A TYPICAL S-CURVE SHOWING TECHNOLOGICAL PROGRESS OF OF NEW PRODUCT INTRODUCTION (BASED ON SIMON WARDLEY, 2014)

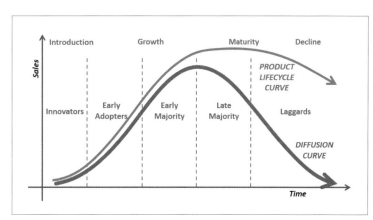

3. ROGERS' PRODUCT LIFECYCLE (BLUE) AND DIFFUSION (RED) CURVES

Bearing in mind Mark Twain's quote above, the cycle between these paradigms is never repetitious. Society changes, technology advances, styles and art movements come and go. We are speaking here about a similar principle of things, not often in actually similar things (neoclassical architecture is an exception, as the name implies). The many parallel red tracks in figure 2 represent the complexity of the cyclical process in art and design.

The terms "timeless" (referring to design classics) and "retro" appear in the diagram. I will discuss them in sections 3 and 4 of this chapter.

The Product's Lifespan tenet

Often termed "product life cycle" (personally I prefer the term "product lifespan" because it denotes a distinct beginning and an eventual end), this tenet deals with the growth and evolution over time of a specific product made by a certain company, from the moment of its introduction to the market until the product becomes obsolete and is taken off the market. That is the way marketing people understand this term. Engineers and

designers will include in the lifespan a preceding time to market—stages in which the product is conceptualized, designed, tested, and approved for mass production.

Everett Rogers introduced in 1962 the theory "diffusion of innovations," which seeks to explain how, why, and at what rate new ideas and technology spread through cultures. He explained diffusion as the process by which an innovation is communicated through certain channels over time among the members of a social system. Rogers identified 5 stages of diffusion: knowledge, persuasion, decision, implementation, and confirmation.

A lifespan of a product is measured by public acceptance (as reflected by sales) over time. It may take a form of an S-curve in certain products (a new toothpaste for example) with a slow beginning, then a noticeable growth and eventually leveling off when sales reach market saturation. Other products follow a bell curve where sales decline rather than level off due to eventual loss of public interest, introduction of competing products or innovative technology, or due to social change. In marketing terms the stages of the bell curve are referred to as the market introduction stage, the growth

stage, the maturity stage, and the saturation or decline stage (fig. 3).

As we are dealing with form development, the definition of a product's lifespan will be elastic to some degree, taking into account three related factors: (A) what we mean by product, (B) the stages by which the public accepts a product, and (C) the introduction of form modifications in the course of the product's lifespan.

(A) The term "product" may refer here to either a specific product model (e.g. Microsoft's Zune portable media device), or to all products belonging to a certain group or family (e.g. portable telephones or 35mm cameras), or even to a popular trend (e.g. military looking products, retro products). I agree that the term "trend" is quite ephemeral. I may add that in most cases a trend remains in vogue for a relatively short time; thus, trend-based products usually have a limited lifespan with no extension. Toy fads are good examples of trends.

(B) Everett Rogers also introduced the concept of product acceptance by the public. He divided the public into five groups placed along the time axis of a new product adoption, listed below (see also fig. 3, in red).

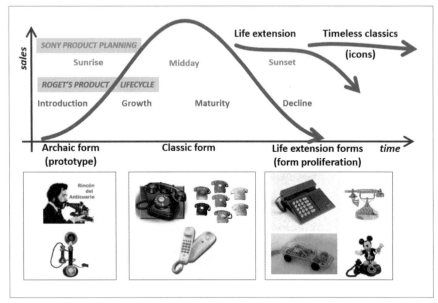

4. TYPICAL PRODUCT LIFESPAN WITH SUPERIMPOSITION OF ROGERS' AND SONY'S PRODUCT LIFECYCLE CURVES

- **Innovators:** the first individuals to adopt an innovation. Unmistakably they comprise just a small percentage of the public. Innovators are young, belong to highest social class, and are willing to take risks.

- **Early Adopters:** the second fastest category of individuals who adopt an innovation. These individuals have the highest degree of opinion leadership.

- **Early Majority:** those who adopt an innovation after some time. They are the largest group of adopters.

- **Late Majority:** those who will adopt an innovation after the average members of the society. These individuals tend to approach an innovation with a high degree of skepticism.

- **Laggards:** the last to adopt an innovation. They show little to no opinion leadership. These individuals typically have an aversion to change-agents and tend to be advanced in age, and conservative.

(C) Form shift in design usually occurs in three different stages along the bell curve of a typical product lifespan. The following diagram (fig. 4) provides examples from a long-lived, well known product family: the telephone, today known as the line telephone.

Archaic form: when an innovative product appears in public for the first time it does not yet have an established and recognized image identifier, let alone an archetypal form. Such a product often takes a crude form concept: a prototype, sometimes borrowing recognized visual elements from related products. The early telephones took the form of the Alexander Graham Bell experimental prototype. It spoke in the language of physics lab instruments. Even later models continued the same combination of brass wire connectors and turned wood body elements, keeping the already recognized mouthpiece and earpiece forms. As archaic forms are still experimental and undefined, they may assume concurrent form variations during a short time span. Today we seldom see an actual prototype

in its archaic stage, as almost all products are intentionally well designed even at the introduction stage, and the prototype form may eventually settle on a different, better recognized form. When I see today's robotic vacuum cleaners I am not sure that the basic disc geometry that all now possess will persist into the future when its market expands.

Mainstream form: When a product reaches maturity and is already accepted by the early majority group, its designed form at this stage become generally recognized. At this stage the form is the object. This form becomes the archetypal form—the iconic form—and from here on clearly associated with the product. When we utter the word telephone to someone, he may intuitively imagine in his mind's eye that archetypal form. The form becomes so deeply entrenched in our visual language that it tends to persist without change for a long time, even if it eventually becomes a boring plain vanilla form. The mainstream telephone presently etched in our mind has the ever-present black cradle, the dial ring, the 1930s sculpted form, the handset form, and of course the ever-present long spiral cord. Only after an extended time was the telephone design updated and softened, without losing any of its iconic cues. This is reflected by its continued use, still today, as the graphic symbol of the telephone. Eventually, the telephone changed color from black to white, while keeping the same form. Later, the princess telephone, designed by Henry Dreyfuss in 1959, was the first significant form deviation, yet the spiral cord was still there to signify the product.

Product decline: This stage occurs due to market saturation or due to competition from newer and better products. Therefore, a marketing attempt to visually resuscitate the product in order to make it desirable again usually follows. At the decline stage, as in fashion, you may often

6. CHARLES EAMES' 1956 LOUNGE CHAIR AND OTTOMAN ARE STILL SOLD BY HERMAN MILLER

7. THE VOLKSWAGEN BEETLE WAS NOT ONLY A DESIGN CLASSIC BUT AN ESTABLISHED CULTURAL LIFESTYLE SIGNIFIER

8. THE COKE BOTTLE IS A LONG LASTING TRADEMARK OF THE COCA COLA COMPANY

find a plethora of forms, sometimes to excess in shape, color, and detail. In the case of the line telephone, everything was allowed, from retro Victorian glitz, to transparent body, to Mickey Mouse designs.

The Sony Corporation strategy was well aware of the form-shift lifespan. Their design department used the term "sunrise-midday-sunset" in pre-planning an elaborate variety of future versions and models of their product line, to cater to any possible taste and whim (see fig. 5).

Sometimes the Mainstream form is so well entrenched in our culture to be considered a timeless design classic, thus avoiding the dreaded product decline stage. I will discuss design classics in the next section.

A radical marketing strategy is to shorten, rather than extend, the decline stage. In the mid-20th century, products' life spans were often intentionally accelerated into oblivion. This was the ill-reputed planned obsolescence strategy of Detroit's car manufacturers. Car designs superficially changed every model year significantly enough to force the public to replace older models. No one wanted to be seen in the neighborhood in a three-year-old car because it would look even older than that.

The Design Classic tenet

> A 'design classic' is an industrially manufactured object with timeless aesthetic value. It serves as a standard of its kind and, despite the year in which it was designed, is still up to date.
>
> Phaidon Press (ed.), Phaidon Design Classics, Phaidon Press, 2006

Sometimes an industrially manufactured product becomes so entrenched in the public mind so that its cultural acceptance does not decrease or fade in time. The product becomes a design classic. Recently, we also use the term "iconic," but the cultural term classic is broader. It denotes a perfect example of a style, something of lasting worth or with a timeless quality, as in classics of English literature to classic landmarks to classic cars.

There is no serious way to predict which object will eventually become a design classic. Only time will tell. I assume that a perfect archetypal image prerequisite may

5. SONY'S PRODUCT LIFESPAN. (ADAPTED FROM PAUL KUNKEL, DIGITAL DREAMS: THE WORK OF THE SONY DESIGN CENTER, UNIVERSE 1999)

Sony Walkman 1978-1999

9. RETRO 1970S INTERIOR INCLUDING PLASTIC FURNITURE OF THE PERIOD

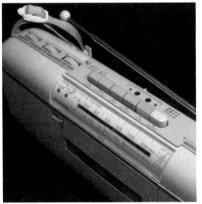

10. RETRO NOSTALGIA: POP AND MILKSHAKE. THE SHARP RETRO RADIO RECALLS THE 1970S TAPED MUSIC (LEFT) AND THE WARING PROFESSIONAL BLENDER REMINDS US OF THE ICE-CREAM PARLOR (RIGHT)

play a significant role in creating a design classic, but what makes an object become a classic design is quite ephemeral. If we claim that a product becomes a classic because it was a good design to begin with, I will argue the contradictory statement: that because the product becomes classic we assume or accept it to be a good design. Darren Bedfellow, a writer at Brand Republic, suggests four factors that occur together in a design classic: (a) simplicity and clarity, (b) consistency, (c) recognition, the icon factor, and (d) the ability to hold all the above—often contradictory factors—in one form.

It should be noted that many classic objects are design-oriented objects. By that I mean that the main attributes of the object are its form and shape or the creative ingenuity of the designer, much more than any technological or functional innovation inherent in the product, though there are many exceptions. Not surprisingly, furniture (the Eames Lounge chair, fig. 6), lamps, and cars (the original VW Beetle, fig. 7) take the lead in this category. For a good source on design classics, see *Phaidon Design Classics* (Phaidon Press, 2006). It is a mammoth, three-volume compendium of 1000 product design classics.

The term "classic" is not solely limited to product form but also applies to packaging, branding, and trademarks. Famous examples are of classic packaging are the Coca Cola bottle (its hourglass form received trademark recognition in 1960; fig. 8s) and the Heinz tomato ketchup bottle. Branding and trademarks definitely capitalize on the idea of everlasting brand recognition.

Retro products

Retro is the term used to denote a stylistic revival. Misinterpreting the first tenet in this chapter—cyclical evolution in art—we may take for granted that the revival of former styles is common. Not so! True, the evolutionary cycle moves back and forth between two opposing conceptual paradigms, but it does not return to prior form and detail. Product evolution does not embrace a previous style since cultural and technological changes during that time call for a new context, far removed from the past. Again, history does not repeat itself.

Retro revival often takes place in fashion. This is not so surprising since the yearly fashion cycle is so repetitive and exhaustive that fashion designers may seek easy answers in former styles, just for one season or so. Retro is also popular in domestic interiors as clients may find personal preference and comfort in a style of the past and this taste will reflect

11. THE 2014 FIAT 500 (FOREGROUND) IS NOT AN EXACT DUPLICATE OF THE 1957 FORM (BACKGROUND)

on furniture and accessories they buy (fig. 9). There is a revivalists market for Victorian, Art Nouveau, Early Modern, and Pop styles. Retro is also common in graphic design, often to reflect marketing aims. Retro is often associated with sentimentality and, as Elizabeth Guffey suggests, even represent a resistance to modernism.

The practice of retro in mass-produced products is by far less common as form change is costly, and is therefore less dependent on vague impulses that may fail (look up the Ford Edsel failure). There must be a good enough reason to undertake such a stylistic endeavor. Product retro mainly takes place in two areas: in electric kitchen appliances and, surprisingly, the automobile. IN the kitchen, consider that the Kitchen Aid retro style influenced the entire professional appliance segment; the notion that professional chefs prefer conservative industrial kitchen appliances took hold there (fig. 10, right). And second, considering the automotive industry, recall the reborn Volkswagen beetle, the Mini Cooper (now by BMW), and the recent revival of Fiat 500 (fig. 11). They all cater to a specific young urbanized market. If you look at form details you may notice that the nostalgic retro form feeling is there but the details are rather up to date. They say *retro*, but with a contemporary interpretation of the past (see fig. 10, left and fig. 11). Sometimes we are not even aware that a retro design initiative is taking place in a product line. A good example is the present-day digital SLR camera. It is technically thoroughly digital, but the aluminum and black exterior almost copy the form of previous 35mm pentaprism film cameras. As in cooking, we consider the older, well-established look as epitomizing professional qualities.

The Continuation but Differentiation rule

This rule corresponds to evolution in nature, where chance mutations in genes will lead to minor differences in future generations. Change is gradual and barely perceived. Most inherent human accomplishments such as language, social behavior, and culture follow the same pattern: continual but insignificant change, but a change that accumulates over time. If you read a Victorian novella, you will be familiar with the language, though some terms may sound archaic. If you read a Shakespeare play the language and spelling will be quite different but still mostly understood. Try to read the Canterbury Tales by Chaucer from the fourteenth century and you will have significant problems in deciphering the language.

Often prompted by technological, cultural, and social change, man-made objects follow the same continual but gradual change manner. The rate of change of man-made objects has accelerated significantly in the last century so that the word "gradual" may mean a much shorter time scale. The measure of gradual change cannot be subjected to a mathematical quotient. It always relates to what it changed from and why it changed.

Once society accepts a common visual image (archetype) of a certain product class, each time we utter the name of that product class (e.g. motorcycle, lawn mower, coffee maker, traffic light) people will habitually visualize that specific archetypal image in their mind. Any future change in utility, technology, material, or use environment will keep bringing up the association with the earlier version. Our cognitive faculties have to identify the archetype image of the class in order to understand it and assist in linguistically classifying it. Designers do the same. If we come with a new camera technology we still want the public to recognize it as a (new) camera, but not as a portable radio.

12. THE CLASSIC ACOUSTIC CELLO FORM AND ELECTRIC CELLOS RETAIN SYMBOLIC ACOUSTIC CHAMBER OUTLINES

We may look for signs that it belongs to the camera class (by size, lens, shutter release button, and strap), and even more, that it is a stills camera (camera orientation significantly differ from that of a movie camera). So how can we tell when a new camera appears on the market, that it is an early digital camera and not the previously commonplace film camera? The answer is found in assessing one feature: "different." The large film cassette door is replaced by a small electronic media slot. The viewfinder is intentionally not behind the lens axis, suggesting that the optic input is converted inside to electronic output. We recognize the long-established camera class but we comprehend where it differs. The differentiation is often a translation into a visual manifestation of the new technology incorporated in the now-changed product.

For a long time the cue for wireless radio was its antenna—the longer the antenna the better. The rod antenna was associated with radio, even on our car hood. Progressively the antenna became shorter, first by telescopic means. Then it disappeared altogether from most radios, but still persisted on two-way devices such as walkie-talkies and portable telephones, retaining the visual cue for the presence of high transmission power. When everyone became familiar with the pebble shape, the numerical keyboard, and the display screen, and knew that it was a mobile phone and not

14. FROM ANTIQUITY TO MODERN: A WHEEL IS A WHEEL IS A WHEEL

a portable calculator, there was no need to continue with the ever-smaller antenna symbol. It disappeared completely. This is the meaning of continuation but differentiation.

Another nice example is the electric cello (fig. 12 center and right). It does not depend anymore on the acoustic resonance box of the classic cello (fig. 12 left) so only the outline of the familiar sensuous form is left and even whimsically played with as it does not have any real functional use. The cello in the middle almost adheres to the classic contours; the one on the right is more experimental, relaying on the "S" form present in the original cello. On the other hand, the strings, being still acoustic, remain the same and their tuning head even retain the everlasting the 17th century spiraling organic form, the iconic identifier of all string instruments. This is again the power of continuation but differentiation.

By the term differentiation I signify a perceptible and enduring change in the archetypal form of the product. I do not

refer to the more superficial level of differentiation in form, superficial decoration and labeling that stems from brand identification of maker and product model. These superficial changes are usually ephemeral and seldom contribute to an enduring and significant change in the archetypal form of the product.

As an exception, when it comes to well-known design oriented firms such as Braun, Sony, Apple, Dyson, and the like, brand related changes are not ephemeral at all. Their outstanding form statements are the front-runners of the whole class of visual language of design. Thus their particular design styles eventually influence the whole product class evolution.

The tenet of The More Things Change, The More They Stay the Same

Several product classes have a remarkable diversity in form variations within the same family. Chairs, cars, and teacups come to mind. Also, but for a different reason, as explained in Section 2, certain product classes attain significant diversity of form designs as a last marketing rejuvenation before they fade into oblivion. Line telephones and portable tape music players are such examples. In both cases most of the discrete variations are not a result of innovation but due to a so-called liberty in form variation, which we cannot see anymore, as in the forest of smartphones (fig. 13). When we try to

13. IN SPITE OF FREQUENT ADVANCEMENTS, ALL SMARTPHONES STICK TO THE SAME FORM

understand why the visual vocabulary is really flexible in some cases, in chairs for example, we find out that it occurs just up to a definite visual boundary—a kind of liberty analogous to what parents may say to their children: "You can play freely in the playground as long as they don't leave the playground boundary." Cars are a good example: there are so many sculptural forms, styles, and details to cater to the individual taste of the buyer, but all fall well within the visual term of automobile or car. When we drive on the road filled with cars, unless we spot a Ferrari or a vintage finned Cadillac we will not pay attention to the lot. Like trees in a forest, they are quite the same. They are all within a certain size range, have four wheels, front grill, and headlights, etc. This is what I mean by a visual boundary. In a somewhat related analogy, I can state that a wheel is a wheel is a wheel, as long as it circular and not, let's say, rectangular in form (fig. 14).

It seems that there is also an acceptance limit on the consumer side. Out-of-line designs are not well accepted and usually fail. In another crowd analogy, they are the black sheep of the flock. It seems that "the more things change the more they stay the same" tenet is a self-balancing concept.

The Paradigm Shift rule

"Paradigm shift" is a scientific term signifying that a long-standing theory is replaced by a new theory that proves the well-entrenched older one to be wrong. Paradigm shift is an earth-moving event and it does not occur often.

A comparable event happens with product classes. Sometimes the product's change is not in the commonly accepted gradual route of evolution. The innovation is so profound that it radically breaks away from most previous notions. When change is so groundbreaking, differentiation will take precedence to rules of continuity. The paradigm change will manifest itself in clear visual terms, even if the linguistic term (product class name) still remains as it was before or becomes somewhat vague. I stress that I am not referring here to a "blue sky" product that appears without any previous precedence, thus establishing a totally new class, but rather to cases where product class A is being completely replaced by product class B. Unlike the sciences, where A deceases right away, in design it often lingers on for a while before it disappears.

An excellent example of paradigm shift is the first automobile, replacing the horse-

16. SONY'S WALKMAN, A TRAILBLAZER OF MOBILE QUALITY LISTENING

17. THE SEGWAY DEFINES A NEW RIDING EXPERIENCE

15. WITHOUT HORSES—A HORSELESS CARRIAGE LOOKS VERY DIFFERENT FROM A HORSE DRAWN CARRIAGE

drawn wagon (fig. 15). Suddenly half of the previously accepted transportation configuration is written off; the horse is replaced by a motor in the back of the carriage. No wonder that the first term to describe the new creature was horseless carriage. Only later the term was changed to automobile (literally a self-drawn moving device). Old things don't die without a fight: the measurement of the power of the new device is still rated in horsepower. In the case of the automobile, the shape of the horse-drawn carriage persisted for a while, though it obviously belonged to the previous transportation means; maybe it actually dramatized the absence of the horse.

Sony's Walkman was the first to allow private stereo listening while walking in public (fig. 16). It was not just an anticipated miniaturization of electronics. It was by far a cultural change: a concert hall within a small box, with small headphones instead of large speakers emitting a surprisingly clear hi-fi sound. In this particular case it announced the almost immediate demise of the previous portable stereo radio (only the hip-hop boom-box survived, but for different cultural reasons).

Another clear example of paradigm shift was the introduction of the Segway (fig. 17). It may not have changed the way we travel, but here too, differentiation surpassed continuation. Yes, it is a two-wheel transportation device, like the bicycle. But no, it is very different as turning and balancing was controlled by body movements activating gyroscope-driven motors. In order to loudly express this paradigm shift, the traditional two-wheel configuration was changed in a highly unconventional way, from one wheel behind the other to two wheels side by side—balancing is a completely new trick.

This tenet is certainly not a God-given rule. You may find that, for whatever marketing strategies companies have, they may stick to a proven design form, in spite of the introduction of a paradigm shift. The iPhone, previous iPad, and the hybrid electric-gasoline car demonstrate contemporary examples of a played down form.

Spatial aspects of form evolution

The Proximity rule

Be it in posh streets of Paris or in the jungles of New Guinea, you will discover the same human display of adornment: head costumes, necklaces, and arm and leg bracelets. Some will even agonizingly mutilate their body for the sake of beauty with body scars, tattoos, ear and lip piercing, neck lengthening (in certain Southeast Asia tribes), or feet disfiguring to make them tiny (in imperial China). The practice of human body adornment is universal (fig. 1). Unlike most birds and several animal species, where the male shows off with natural visual exaggerations in order to promote his genes, human males and females alike zealously participate in visually enhancing their bodies in ways customary to their culture. In that vein, we are fortunate that the tilt of the earth relative to its solar orbit causes different seasons so that clothing may be changed several times a year.

1. HUMAN ADORNMENT TAKES MANY FORMS

The proximity rule is simple: The closer the object is in contact with a human body, the more it varies. As you shall see shortly, I am not talking just about jewelry and clothing (what we commonly accept as fashion) but about any object habitually in close proximity to us. This concept also works the other way around: the farther away from contact with the human body, the less the decorative variety (see section 4). Obviously this rule is not measured mathematically. It is to dependant on culture, social and religious norms, functional requirements, and so on. On one hand, educated women in strictly Muslim communities will wear high fashion and apply elaborate makeup under their ever-present, body-covering robes. On the other hand, a hearing aid may be concealed as much as possible behind the earlobe.

Figure 2 exhibits the proximity rule in terms of objects and space. I suggest four imaginary rings around the human body. The nearest one incorporates changes induced to the body itself in order to culturally beautify the human body, from hairdo to plastic surgery. Since we confine our discussion to objects and products, I will leave this ring out of the discussion.

The second ring's objects are in intimate touch with the body—customarily clothes and jewelry, but expanded to include wristwatches and fountain pens—that act as visual personal statements more than being strict practical tools. Many of these items have been replaced recently by other useful products such as prescription glasses, sunglasses, backpacks, mobile telephones, and stereo headphones. If smartphones exist in only one design form, limiting consumer choice in expression, then the consumers will extend their options with a range of third party covers, or "skins" (seemingly culturally necessary in Southeast Asia).

As you may notice, several product classes in the diagram appear in larger fonts to indicate a wider design proliferation of these products. Take shoes for example—they're frequently a strong fashion statement. Seized by proximity law, the sport shoes that were supposed to be practical and efficient have become a vast visual design playground.

The third ring includes things with which we come in close bodily contact around the house. We sit on chairs in close bodily contact, and consequently the variety is almost endless, in any possible shape, combination of materials, and price range. Sofas, couches, and tables are close behind, not to forget cutlery and doorknobs (in Europe). Lately, lightweight laptops are carried around by hand, causing their design quality to be of increasing importance. There are two noticeable exclusions here: beds and office chairs. Beds are in real intimate contact with the body, but in formal terms they always take the mundane shape of the mattress. I am not convinced that it is just a functional constraint. There is also a social statement. The bedroom is not a public place to be displayed, but if you insist, you can decorate your bed with sheets and covers. As for office chairs, much is invested in ergonomics and comfort, but the visual statement is not personal. After all the office is a part of the corporate culture.

Here we discover an anomaly in the ring sequence: cars and homes, by their sheer size in comparison to the human body, may be excluded out of the intimate rings. Nevertheless, and I will not say something that you don't already know: they are as personal as those products in the second proximity ring. I call products in this group "cocoon," since we live within them. I am a little hesitant about the home as a cocoon, since rarely we buy our real dream house. As for the car, it is often envisioned as a direct extension of our

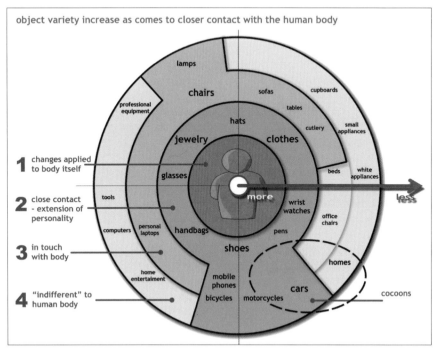

2. PROXIMITY RULE DIAGRAM

The Divergence and Convergence tenets

Divergence and convergence are two contradictory aspects of product evolution, but I prefer to discuss them together. Divergence means, of course, a splitting of a product class into two or more visually (and in our mind's eye, conceptually) distinctly separate classes. Convergence, on the other hand, is the union of separate product classes into one.

An example of divergence is the eventual split of the early vacuum cleaner (the type you still find used by hotel cleaning staff) into two distinct product classes, named the upright vacuum cleaner and the canister one (fig. 3). They basically do the same thing: suck in items and substances. But the separation of the suction tool from the canister body (enabling it to follow you instead of being pushed in front, as in the upright case) creates a visually and functionally distinct product. Later the canister vacuum cleaner branched into an additional product class: the industrial wet and dry vacuum cleaner. Consider the splitting of the digital camera into the professional SLR camera and the point and shoot camera; they contain the same basic electronics but present two very different form solutions.

3. DIVERGENCE OF FORM

You will notice that in some of the case studies later in this book that I often use the term sub-branching to denote divergence. This is because divergence behaves in a way similar to Darwinian natural evolution where one class gradually evolves into branches and even

personality. Motorcycles are quite similar, even though they may not fall under the term cocoon. If you see the rider on an expensive sports motorcycle hugging the body of his bike, becoming essentially one, you will understand the meaning of proximity.

The fourth proximity ring includes an assortment of products, some in the home and some outside. Their common denominator is our indifference. We do not relate to them personally. They include major home appliances, cupboards and storage furniture, destined to hide what is behind or inside them. Even home entertainment equipment is impersonal; we control it by remote means. Most tools, and home and hobby equipment are impersonal, though I have some doubt where cameras belong. It seems that cameras and the like, though carried on our body, are considered to be professional equipment, thus the professional aspect brands them as emotionally cold.

There are several exceptions to the product population of the fourth ring. They do not comply with the suggestion that the closer the object is in contact with your body the more it can vary. There is a vast design selection of free-standing lighting fixtures that we do not touch (or is the light touching us?). There is quite a selection to choose from in small kitchen appliances, not necessarily in close everyday contact with us (perhaps because food is the intimate intermediary).

Lately, we hear more and more the phrase, "objects of desire." This term crystallizes the process by which things we desire become more personal even though they are not necessarily in physical touch with our body. Most home decorative objects and some early adoption gadgets may apply here.

4. CONVERGENCE OF FORM

sub-branches of the evolution tree. As in natural evolution, some product branches may bloom and others will eventually decline.

Convergence is the reverse process, where two distinctly different product lines merge into one. As far as I know we do not find any parallel in natural evolution (unless you consider the sterile mule to be a successful convergence of horse and donkey). In terms of product evolution convergence turns out to be quite widespread. Consider the smartphone: it is not used anymore as merely a telephone. It also replaces a calculator (think of the old form of the calculator we used at school), a wristwatch, a digital diary, a games shelf, and even a camera (fig. 4). If you argue that this is the consequence of flexibility inherent in digital equipment and in programming facilitates convergence, you are absolutely right.

Product convergence is a recent phenomenon associated in particular with electronic equipment. The broom and the rake were quite similar in form and in the way we hold them for so many years, but no one considered merging them into one. They have dissimilar purposes. This is why we insist on giving them differing names.

As convergence is a recent phenomenon we are not certain yet about its future manifestation. Will we see in the future evidence of less and less products doing more and more tasks? I believe that the current embrace of all-in-one products,

which usually compromise on some functions in order to accommodate others, will eventually give in to separate specialized products, often living in concurrence with the converged product. A recent suggestion to support this thinking is the digital camera. Since a movie camera can take stills and a still camera can take movies, one may predict eventual convergence. On the contrary, both camera branches keep moving away from each other into separate functionally and visually defined directions.

Dr. Johnnie Chung Lee is a Human-Computer Interaction researcher and a so-called Rapid Evaluator at Google, and previously a core contributor to the Microsoft's Xbox Kinect. In a 2011 presentation, *The Mouse and Keyboard Are Not Going Away, and There's No Such Thing as Convergence*, he puts a convincing case that there is no single user interface that will perform all things well, that we are in an era of specialization; he predicts that divergence will rule.

One last point about divergence and convergence: is it a temporal tenet or a spatial tenet? It depends on how you look at it, but it is probably mutually temporal and spatial.

The Component Geometry tenet

Component geometry is about the way parts of a product relate to each other. We may not care about the arrangement of components inside a computer case (they are hidden from our sight) but we do take mental note of their arrangement when they are visually exposed. A broom-

5. THE VESTA MECHANICAL SEWING MACHINE, GERMANY, EARLY 1900S; AND THE SINGER COMPUTERIZED SEWING MACHINE, 2010S

stick will always connect to a broom in a T-type junction. The archetypal chair has a seat plate located on top of four legs, a back plate at a nearly right angle to the seat and often two armrests, one in each side (you will find many geometry variations but you will not find a seat located under the legs). In most cases components geometry is defined by the way the product operates internally (e.g. motor-transmission-chuck-drill bit in a hand drill), externally (a saw blade spreading out from the handle). In many cases component geometry is a direct derivative of ergonomic considerations. As people do not change in physique, many highly ergonomic products tent to keep the same component geometry over a prolonged period. A good example is the sewing machine geometry. Despite becoming electronic, and despite a huge change in style, the old and the new have basically the same component geometry (fig. 5), determined by the way we sew.

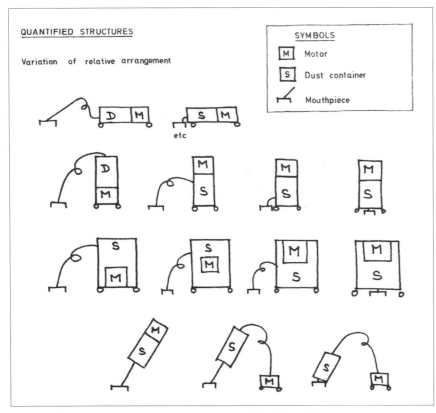

6. TJALVE'S STUDY OF FEASIBLE VACUUM CLEANER CONFIGURATIONS

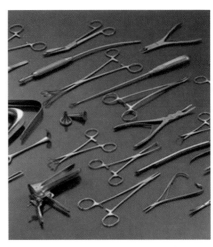

7. EACH SURGICAL INSTRUMENT HAS A SPECIFIC SIGNIFYING NAME

Component geometry is an important cue in mental recognition of form. No wonder that there are artists who enjoy creating impossible product arrangements, they always make us laugh at how irrational they are.

A new but feasible change in component geometry is a key design method in creative innovation. Erskin Tjalve's 1979 classic book, *A Short Course in Industrial Design*, encourages systematic investigation of all possible configurations before choosing the optimal one. Below is a diagram from his book where vacuum cleaner families are grouped on the basis of different component geometry. In his book he uses the term "quantified structures" (fig. 6. See also Case Study 8).

And a last thing to remember, many product paradigm shifts purposely employ novel component geometry in order to visually emphasize that paradigm shift.

The Professional Tools Classification tenet

From countless television hospital dramas, we are all familiar with the operating room scene. Next to the surgeons we spot a nurse in charge of a large tray covered with a vast number of operation tools (fig. 7). The surgeon calls for various tools by name without lifting his eyes from what he does. No one has to shuffle tools, searching for the appropriate one. To a casual observer, most tolls look exactly the same. Not so for the surgical procedure team.

In the realm of most professional tools there is a tendency to meticulously categorize them, catalogue them, and give them specific names. It is not just in the hospital, where you may justify such specificity by the requirement to avoid life-threatening mistakes. You will find the same tendency to rigorously classify in the machine shop, the car repair shop, the military, and the scientific laboratory. Closer to home you will find this inclination to classify gardening tools, tools for home repairs (fig. 8), and hobbyist tools. If you are serious about photography, yachting, mountain climbing, or golf you will find the same tendency for the carefully discreet naming of tools.

It is not only in the nature of tools. It happens with almost any professional equipment. There are so many different variants to be used for specific purposes, but not always perceptibly different to the layman. There is a need to clearly distinguish them by name more than by image. Personal objects may be quite amorphous. But not so with professional ones that we rarely identify visually. We require the assistance of language. A specific tool has an explicit name. Try to help a mechanic with a 13mm wrench instead of a 15mm one and you will hear from him, ——.

The phenomenon that tools have specific names points to the semantic manifestations of the proximity law: familiarity breeds visual recognition. This is why we almost always use less specific nouns to describe the extensive variety of formal variations of familiar objects. "Chair" is such an all-inclusive term. So are ring, broach, bracelet, and handbag. It is surprising how so few terms describe a very extensive range of clothing (hat comes to mind) or home furniture. Our lingual terminology is relatively small but visually it is quite easy to identify most proximity objects for what they are. It happens in other linguistic areas. The term for a live man-made "product," the dog, applies to so many visually, functionally, and personality distinct breeds. We may claim that the deep-rooted inclusive name evolved over thousands of years. But what is really surprising is that we apply the same mental pattern to product families existing for fewer than ten years. That demonstrates our mind's expertise in visual classification.

I assume that professional tool classification is not just for utilitarian reasons. I expect there is a social intention behind it. Each profession tends to cultivate its own language, its own jargon, and its own identifying image. Extensive tool naming

8. DEFINITIVE VISUAL AND VERBAL TAXONOMY

9. A LITERAL BLACK BOX

may be a part of that linguistic tendency for distinction.

Returning to the field of medicine for an example: physicians are very aware of personal image. Some tools of the trade have an almost ritual importance; doctors will carry on their person their ubiquitous stethoscope in order to distinguish themselves from a nurse or orderly. Years ago, when I was involved in designing computerized medical equipment, I was informed that the equipment should look "medical," not for functional reasons but for marketing appeal.

The Out of Sight, Out of Mind tenet

There are product families that are of no real interest to us or of whose existence we may not even aware. These unfamiliar products are often hidden behind doors or inside non-descript enclosures. We may contact them, if at all, by remote controls, often not knowing which box does what. To us they are "black boxes." Home water heaters, air conditioners, and alarm boxes belong to that out-of-sight class. Of course, there are many more products on the market that we rarely see, whose workings we do not understand, and thus for which we have no mental image.

In the case when the black box is visible, but we do not know how it operates, we

try rationalizing its form, or we fantasize what it is and how it works. Amusingly, ill-defined, thin-proportioned boxes of electronic equipment in the high-tech industry are habitually nicknamed pizza boxes. After all, high-tech people are notoriously familiar with delivered pizzas.

External catalysts of form evolution

Numerous parameters

In the two previous chapters we discussed two essential parameters of the evolution timeline of man-made products: temporal (when), and spatial (where, relationship, proximity). Clearly, one parameter is missing here, the context of a product form. Context is an all-encompassing parameter as it involves numerous factors, major or minor, direct or vague. Consider just a few factors that may affect the form of a product: technology (function, materials, assembly, design for service); economics (direct cost, tooling costs, indirect costs, profits, production quantities, intended market segment, local and global markets, competition, lifespan of product, etc.); social (lifestyles, popular trends, affluence, social constraints, political agendas, etc.); cultural (localism vs. globalization, national heritage, generation differences, popular culture, buzz trends, etc.); design (corporate image and corporate style, competitor's design style, the CEO's or designer's personal form preference, packaging).

Each of these factors is a world in itself, with its own professionals, knowhow and textbooks. I am going to highlight here just a few that have a known direct influence on the form of a product archetype. Purposely, the discussion here will be brief with just a few elaborations.

Hard technology

Man-made tools were considered throughout the ages to be hard technology, meaning that they had a definite physical manifestation. The concept of hardware, as distinguished from software, is a late outcome of the digital age. The mechanical nuts and bolts and gears had a great influence on the size and form of a product (please take this statement with a grain of salt. Remember David Pye's comments on that specific assumption in the previous chapter, *Reviewing the designed form*). Only with the invention of electricity, and subsequently, of electronics did there begin to be a distinct disassociation between internal working components and the outer shell of a product. Disassociation is necessarily the rule. Recall the clear effect of music media on the form of music players, from vinyl records to reel-to-reel tapes to cassette tapes to compact discs; only recently does a downloaded song have no actual physical trace. For marketing reasons, a revised internal circuit board may often accompany a new external shell in order to demonstrate an updated product.

All that said, hard technology is still the primary driver of form change in most product lines. The evolution of form will usually follow the continuation-but-differentiation rule, explained above. But major conceptual changes may instead follow the paradigm-shift rule, also defined above. The rule that the evolution of form ultimately follows in any particular case may not be so well defined. For example, if a drill bit is being replaced by a laser-boring device, will the gun form of the drill evolve completely as suggested by the paradigm-shift rule? After all, the tool-grabbing human hand has not changed. It still is a major factor in the tool's form.

Soft technology

Soft technology (also called "software") is by now ubiquitous, not just in a computer's operating system but also in the way data is collected, analyzed, and redirected at users. The internet, apps, GPS, surveillance, and cyber wars are soft technologies. The world we face in the near future will be filled with an "internet of things" network, in which our cars, appliances, and what-not will have an internal chip that will communicate over the air with other chips or servers, tell the car manufacturer about our driving habits, check how the engine is doing (and issue a warning message if needed), and turn on our home porch lights, the air conditioner, and the oven when the car

1. PERSONAL IPHONE SKINS

GPS signals our coming back home from work. I expect the internet of things to be the next big step in the evolution of technology facilitating our lives. As far as this book is concerned, the common denominator to all of these soft technologies is that they have no form.

There exists an intermediary between the physical form hardware and no-form software, called firmware, which handles soft technology. Through firmware, users just update the operating system regularly and give the product a new life boost. Ideally, all this happens without any change in the hardware. This concept may lead to form design stagnation. An ageless, purist design form that will look up-to-date for several years is better than a trendy external form, which may become visually obsolete soon. Continual revival of soft technology will promote the overuse of the tenet, the more things change the more they stay the same. This is exactly what happens to the "behind the glass" design strategy of smartphones, tablets, and laptop companies. On one hand, it is the manufacturer's dream: it can update a product and keep it from the declining phase of the product's lifecycle. On the other hand, the age-old marketing concept of planned obsolescence ('discard the old, buy the new') may lower sales profits. So manufactures may opt for non-replaceable sealed batteries that will die in time, no-service innards and, even better, limited update options after only 18 month.

The tendency of soft technology-based products to retain form for relatively long periods of time in spite of fast technological change (or at the most only in rather minor form details) does not escape the public's attention. People will find ways to combat bland form by reverting to third party external "skins." (The term skin comes from software where you can change the looks of a favorite program to fit your personal taste.) It is amazing how Apple invests so much in design language including refined details of

its milled aluminum iPhone back when almost every iPhone becomes quickly covered with a skin over which Apple has no design control (fig. 1). It looks as if third party form manipulating add-ons will only proliferate. People need a personal design statement close to their body, not just a choice of four smartphone colors such as black, white, pink and blue.

Systems economics

As both time to market and product lifespan are continually decreasing, the economic considerations involved in product innovation are becoming more crucial. Engineers use the term product architecture for design strategies that allow for a variety of products based on the same engineering design, or allow for swift transformation to future versions of the product. According to Ulrich and Eppinger, product architecture uses strategies such as modular design, the use of easily obtainable standardized components, and the design for future upgrade (of physical components), which allows room for add-ons, the adaptation to different markets (e.g. 110 or 220 volts), the easy replacement of worn parts and consumables, and the reuse of components in future models.

A good product architecture allowed HP to offer a variety of ink jet printers using the same components, but which differ in printing resolution and incorporate different options, such as scanning and faxing. The various printer models look different because they present opportunities for setting up different form designs on the same engineering chassis. A radical use of systems economics is embodied in the concept of Swatch, the Swiss wristwatch manufacturer, which in 1983 completely changed the traditional manufacturing methods of the Swiss watch industry. Low-cost automatic assembly and the use of standardized timepiece

2. SWATCH DESIGNS BECAME COLLECTORS' ITEMS

components offered together with an amazing variety of faces and straps made Swatch a design trend leader (fig. 2). Swatch even was daring enough to offer mass-produced "limited editions."

The automotive industry has faced a series of crises, the notorious one being the bankruptcy of GM, which led to the demise of such famous brands as Oldsmobile and Pontiac. Such crises led to mergers of several international car manufactures so that today many different models are built on the same chassis and with many of the same components. The French Renault and the Japanese Nissan; Ford and Mazda; Chrysler and Fiat: these are just a few joint designs. And let's not forget the Volkswagen group, which sells passenger cars under the labels Audi, Bentley, Bugatti, Lamborghini, Porsche, SEAT, Škoda, and of course Volkswagen. Also based in Europe is IVECO, a conglomerate of Italian, French, and German truck manufactures, which assemble on four continents and sells trucks all over the world.

System Economics is good at offering several models of the same product based on price segmentation. Because the market is largely teetering in the balance between features and price, you can buy a car or a personal computer or a clothing washer with features and add-ons depending on how much you can afford to pay. The approach of systems economics does not inhibit variety in form nor the proliferation of models. However, as very large ships need time and space to turn around at sea, this approach requires long-term planning. Additionally, the prohibitive cost of major production shifts will not lend itself to experimental, groundbreaking designs. Thus, form evolves according to the rule of continuation-but-differentiation, which is almost the accepted standard of evolution. The Swatch example shows that in some cases systems economics may even establish a successful design-based company.

Social status

I am not going to propose theories of class, class conflict, or classless society. I only want to call attention to the effect social stratification has on design for specific marketing segments and thus on product form. The common three-stratum model defines three classes: upper class, middle class, and lower class. The upper class, also known as the aristocracy or the elite—being of aristocratic background (in Europe) or rich or both—has strong political influence and economic power.

Aristocracy and old money tend to be conservative in taste. The newly rich try to emulate the aristocracy or reveal how affluent they are. The middle class, or Bourgeoisie, includes professionals, small businessmen, civil servants, etc. The European Bourgeoisie usually follows a certain lifestyle and cultural capital while the American middle class is less homogeneous and includes white-collar workers. The lower class, also called the working class or blue-collar workers, covers people who are employed but lacking financial security as well as the unemployed.

The upper class, due to their strong buying power, generates a whole supply market segment that caters specifically to them with one-of-a-kind, custom-made haute couture, luxury items. Apart from private airplanes and yachts (a significant industry in itself, see fig. 3), Rolls Royce and Bentley are associated with old money. The new affluent may opt for high-end Mercedes or expensive Italian sports cars. Design for the upper class market segment is based on observable conservatism, high quality, custom or hand-made, and especially at prohibitive prices. There also exists a rich sector that deliberately enjoys ostentatious taste; for example, rap singers wearing expensive Hip-Hop 'ice' as part of their social image.

Apart from the European bourgeoisie tradition, the middle class, especially in the United States and emerging developed countries such as China, capitalizes on personal social mobility. Therefore, besides investing in the family, education, and quality neighborhoods, they will tend to appreciate change and be early adopter of gadgets and objects of desire. The upper middle class will, at least in terms of affluence, try to move closer to the upper class.

Cultural globalization

Globalization is looked upon as a capitalistic economic subject but its impact is also cultural. Jet travel and the internet tend to flatten the world. When distance between nations and cultures become close, they tend to borrow from each other. Overseas business and vacation travel, internet English, satellite channels, McDonald's, Starbucks, Ikea, H&M, and Nike contribute to cultural homogeneity. Shopping centers in various places may look different architecturally but often the shop assortment is quite similar. In real life, the local partner will not totally adopt western culture and there may be a balanced compromise between global and local cultures. Both live side by side and complement each other. Borrowing and the influence of globalization usually move in one direction, aided by economic power. Still, in spite of the tendency toward blending in the European Union, modern Scandinavian design will thrive in Denmark or Sweden because it better reflects the local culture. Similarly, local culture will foster Italian design or Japanese design in its home country. Is Muji a good example of the Japanese international (fig. 4)?

In term of product design, multinational corporations may rule. No matter where one may live, one drives a Toyota,

3. UPPER CLASS LUXURY ITEMS

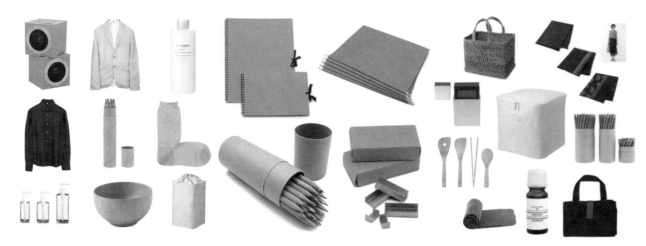

4. THE MUJI STYLE MAY BE DESCRIBED AS JAPANESE INTERNATIONAL

owns Philips kitchen appliances, holds an iPhone or Samsung smartphone, and wears Adidas or Nike sports gear. Even design school student projects tend to speak the same form language. Globalization is the great form leveler.

Cultural aspects

I keep saying that form is the cultural constituent of design. If I am right, then various cultural factors should have key roles in dictating the evolution of form evolution over time. Unfortunately, cultural factors are commonly soft factors, challenging to follow or to prove having had an explicit role in determining form (unlike technological and economic parameters, which are easier to define and quantify).

Let me remind you of but a few cultural factors. First is the modern concept of a generation. Social scientists group generations as having common but unique characteristics and holding specific social behaviors and tastes. Examples include the Baby Boomers of the post-World War II era, the Generation X counterculture, then Generation Y (or the Millennial Generation), and the recent Generation Z (or the Cyber Generation). These definitions reflect the American social scene.

You will find similar or different generation characteristics in other parts of the world, for example the Lost Generation in Europe—those whose lives were destroyed in the First World War. There are also generation sub-communities, some related to musical trends (Hip-Hop, MTV) or to fashion (Teddy Boys, Punk).

Lifestyle has to do with individual rather than group attitude and preference, such as health, sports, or environmental practices. Lifestyles are heavily associated with consumerism, as taking a lifestyle requires you to buy specific paraphernalia. Just watch what early morning runners wear.

And lastly, of course, design-associated styles such as Art Nouveau, Art deco, Streamline Modern, Modernism, Post modernism, etc. are the major cultural contributions of architects and designers.

Political agenda: the environmental movement

A political agenda is a set of issues and policies laid out by ideological and political groups, often initiated by small grass-root movements. A political agenda usually embraces a well-defined manifesto. When

a political force comes into power, its agenda may even completely change the way people live (Fascism, Marxism, other 'isms') and as a result affect the products people own, the clothes they wear, and other agenda symbols they display. I would like to deal here with just one such political movement that has a particularly strong influence on design thinking, design ethics, and the designed form: the environmental movement. It is a political and social movement that seeks to prevent impending climate, resource, and famine catastrophes, and professes a mission to protect natural resources including animal and plant species, and their habitats. Organizations such as the World Wildlife Fund concentrate on saving and preserving endangered species. Greenpeace has a broader agenda; it believes that the fragile earth deserves a voice. Therefore, Greenpeace acts to change attitudes and behaviors, to protect and conserve the environment, and even to promote world peace. Such nongovernmental organizations (NGOs), famous politicians (Al Gore), celebrities, and notorious disasters, such as Chernobyl and Fukushima, raise public awareness of ecology and pollution.

5. GREEN DESIGN OFTEN TENDS TO BE LITERAL

In terms of the influence of the agenda of environmentalists on design, several corresponding words come into design jargon: eco-design, sustainability, and recycling. The more all-encompassing term "green design" is quite fashionable now. It is even used as the name for an environmentally conscious cultural style. I am surprised as to how often green designs are literally green in color and tree-like in form (fig. 5). That is the power of verbal semantics. Lance Hosey's book, the *Shape of Green: Aesthetics, Ecology, and Design*, associates form and ecology in a rather more methodical discussion.

The environmental agenda reveals an inherent conflict in industrial design. On one hand, designers regularly lend a hand to blatant, even hedonistic, consumerism, as they design objects of desire or a hundred takes on a certain chair design. On the other hand, design thinking and ethics now involve eco-conscious attitudes that deal seriously with problems of material conservation, extending product lifespan, planning for eventual recycling, and investing in designing product second-life.

The Follow the Technology Leader tenet

Since this specific cultural factor is also a definite design evolution tenet, let me presently give it some background. A more broad and thorough discussion of the technological leader tenet will follow in the chapter "In depth 2—Technology leaders."

There comes a moment during the design process of a new product where the question, "what form shall this product take?" may arise. This question is especially important when the new product is an innovative one, with no visual precedence. There are very few cases in which the form design of a new product will appear magically with no reference, totally controlled by the personal whims and wishes of its designer. As suggested in an earlier chapter, the language of form has to be commonly understood in order to identify (and allow rational comments) on the new product. In most cases of a new design, designers will follow the Zeitgeist—the spirit of the time.

Apart from functional and technological constraints inherent to the product, the designer has a fairly wide latitude of form options. In most cases the designer will try to associate form with what seems to be the innovative trend of the time. It is better to be associated with a well-known form family, either as an unabashed marketing ploy to copying a popular image, or as something more subconscious, when the design form for the product just happens the right thing for the times. Marketing people will often advocate following successful leading companies in their particular field. This association brings us to the concept of the technology leader. A technology leader is the popular product that, in the public's eyes, symbolizes advancement in that time. Sometimes the leader is a specific product (the Zeppelin, the iPad) and sometimes it is a less specific range of advanced technology products (aviation, space exploration, etc.). The follow-the-technology-leader tenet is strongly dependent on chronological period, be it an era of a particular technological innovation (e.g. the introduction of electricity, electronic miniaturization) or to an era of a particular style trend (e.g. Art Deco, streamlining).

Individual design preferences

So far we have discussed sources of external influence on product form. What about internal influence, how the individual designer, the design team, or the design-aware corporation may affect the intended product form? Surely they must play a subjective role in how the product looks. To answer this, please go back to the end of Chapter 2.1 *A conjectural framework* to the section, *What about creative genius?*

IN CONTEXT 2
Technology Leaders

What is a technology leader?

In the last chapter, I suggested that in most cases of a new design, designers would follow the Zeitgeist—the spirit of the time. The notion of a Zeitgeist raises the question as to what is the right look of the period. Most often we will relate proper form to the ruling style of the time. Since my interest lies in defining product language archetypes I will focus my discussion on leading products and less on stylistic expressions, though sometimes it is quite difficult to actually separate them.

Here I introduce the concept of Technological Leader. What is the product archetype we desire to be associated with? A technological leader is the one that, in the eyes of the public, is the one to look up to that symbolizes the era (see fig. 1). Sometimes the archetype is a specific product (the Zeppelin, the iPad) and sometimes it is a less specific area of advanced technology (aviation, space exploration).

Since a technological leader is associated with a specific era, my discussion will be somewhat historical. I will focus more about technological leadership concepts and less about specific products and dates. By its nature it will be a somewhat superficial discussion, and of course you may contest some of my conclusions.

The age of physical machines

I will not go all the way back to the beginning of the industrial revolution, but instead I will begin somewhere in the early 1900s. Even this date is somewhat early since the notion of objects being designed in formal terms started with the rise of the industrial artist, much later the industrial designer. From the 19th century on, there was a lasting fascination with the various manifestation of physical mechanism: scientific instruments, optical instruments, electrical instruments, machine parts, assembly lines (fig. 2), and so on. It was important then to expose the nature of the mechanical device, be it an exposed engine or freestanding headlights in a car, or the cooling coils of the early refrigerator placed on top of the icebox, or emphasizing outsized wire connectors on the base of early telephones. These were considered to be the exposed symbols of modernity.

On a much larger scale were structures: bridges, transportation hubs (train stations), and skyscrapers (fig. 3). It is interesting that the pronounced verticality and the stepping façade of the skyscraper were copied into various home furnishings. Was it because architecture was then the recognized front-runner of the modern style or was it due to the vision of the futuristic movement that looked at high-rise buildings as the supreme manifestation of the future urban landscape (fig. 4)?

The Art Deco style was a synthesis of machine and structure into a purely visual representation of the age of the machine. Geometric shapes and forms, car wheels, fluted sprocket shapes, and clusters of zigzagging lightning bursts illustrated electricity and the human laborer as the spirit of industry. All were incorporated one way or another into almost any piece of furniture, product, or surface decoration.

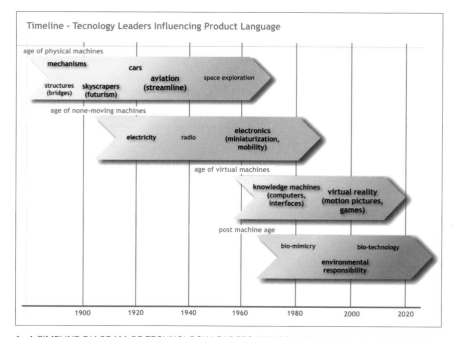

1. A TIMELINE DIAGRAM OF TECHNOLOGY LEADERS. MAJOR INFLUENCES ARE MARKED BY BOLD LETTERING

2. FASCINATION WITH MACHINES: 1900S ASSEMBLY LINE AT VICKER SONS AND MAXIM GUN FACTORY

3. THE CITY OF THE FUTURE, FROM THE FILM "METROPOLIS" DIRECTED BY FRITZ LANG, 1926

4. AN IMAGE OF THE FUTURE BY ARCHITECTURAL DRAUGHTSMAN HUGH FERRISS (1889–1962)—A BRILLIANT EXPONENT OF THE AMERICAN SKYSCRAPER

The strong influence of architecture on product design culminated with Modernism. The Modernism influence was strong and lasting because it was not merely a style but an ideology. Modernism, originated in Europe and idealized total design, from building to furnishings, products, graphics, and art (in the Bauhaus tradition, fig. 5). The Bauhaus followed the tenet that form follows function; what you see is what you get.

Generations of product designers were trained to believe in classical simplicity, to get rid of any superficiality, to adhere to functional coherence, and to use modern materials. Just to remind you of a few of the followers: Henry Dreyfuss, Scandinavian design; the German firm Braun; and recently Apple Computer. This is a case in which the technological leader was not a specific technology or product family, but the design ideology. As far as product design is concerned, Modernism did not disappear, it continued while other technology leaders came and left. I think Modernism lasted because it did not rely on following a specific technology vulnerable to eventual obsolescence.

In the 1920s and 1930s transportation became the definite leader of technology. Actually, there were two separate transportation leaders: first the car and then aviation. The car's influence on modern life (fig. 6) cannot be overestimated—front grill-like textures, front lights, door handles, and the powerful hood ornaments all appeared on many unrelated products.

Then aviation came about. Flying, in parallel with car racing, became our next technological leader. Speed was the word, streamlining was the form. Led by the pioneers of industrial design, Raymond Loewy and Norman Bel Geddes, everything got a smooth, bullet-like aerodynamic shape (figs. 7 and 8). And not only train locomotives, but even toasters and pencil sharpener were designed as if they were to fly through the air. And if at the beginning of that era you could see bird's wings appliqués (which you still see on pilots' insignia), they gradually evolved into airplane wings. It is interesting to note that this fascination with symbols of speed started with early car wheel mudguards, which were fashioned

5. POSTER FOR BAUHAUS EXHIBITION IN WEIMAR IN 1923 BY JOOST SCHMIDT

6. THE CADILLAC V-16, 1930, DESIGNED BY HARLEY EARL

7. GREAT STREAMLINE MACHINE AGE INSPIRATION. AN ART DECO CLOCK, 1930S OR 1940S, ATTRIBUTED TO RAYMOND LOEWY

8. MOTOR CAR NO. 9 WITHOUT TAIL FIN, BY NORMAN BEL GEDDES, 1933

9. TAILFINS AND REAR BURNERS ON THE ICONIC 1959 CADILLAC

to look like the bow wave of fast navy ships, continuing with drop forms of early racing cars, and culminating with Harley Earl's styling for General motors, with the notable 1959 Cadillac (fig. 9), which had tail fins, air inlets, gun sight, and rear lights that imitated rear burners of early jet fighter planes of the post-World War II era.

It was only logical that the next Technological Leader and source of imagery would be the space age, with its rockets, spacecrafts, satellites, moon landers, and space stations so visually familiar in every home, thanks to television. But it did not happen. Space may be the final frontier but not what product designers were trying to emulate. Why?

The age of non-moving technologies

The above may not be the best of section titles, but the second era of technology leadership and inspiration turned out to be less physical. It is the age of electricity and electronics. Movements of electric current, radio waves propagation, electrons and photons are not detectable by our eyes (fig. 10). Not all familiar electrical machines were totally stationary. In some we see a part moving, and in some we just hear the motor running. I have my doubts as to how to categorize early electric equipment, were they then considered to be rather electrical or mechanical? For example, the classical telephone was an electrical machine but its rotary dial still gave it quite a mechanical feeling. Even the *Frankenstein* movie of 1931 showed the brute force of huge electric controls, sparks, and sounds of storm—very physical.

10. RADIO TUBES; NO MOVING PARTS, JUST THE RADIO TUBES' GLOW

11. DETAIL FROM WALTER DORWIN TEAGUE'S "NOCTURNE" RADIO, 1936, WHEN RADIO WAS KING

12. THE FORM OF A FEW PRODUCTS GRADUALLY BECOMES ALMOST NON-EXISTENT

The underlying theme in this age of non-moving technology is that the earlier brute, raw technology—so admired in the past—is now hidden under cover, invisible. We are not interested anymore in how the office copier really works. The real non-moving technologies were the electronic equipment. During the radio tube period, electronic consumer products were emulating furniture. Radio and television receivers, in spite of their huge cultural impact, looked quite conservative, actually imitating wooden sideboards. So radio was then more of a cultural leader than a technology form giver (fig. 11).

With the advent of the transistor and the printed circuit board, you could set the new technology in almost any packaging. Products did not have a really distinctive visual form anymore. No wonder then, the age of non-moving technologies did not create a real visual technology leader. There were some minor influences: the use of modern materials, plastics in particular; reduced power requirements offered an opportunity for high mobility, eventually leading to feats of miniaturization. How small could a radio be then (credit card size), or how thin could a laptop or an LCD screen be now? In formal language, this trend is self-defeating. As a form factor it becomes almost non-existent (fig. 12).

The age of the virtual machine

If technology lost its previous glory and is no longer the panacea for all the world's ills and problems, then it is no wonder that the image of technology cannot be the leader that others emulate in their products. We are living in the age of knowledge. Our computers are insignificant boxes and only its screen seems to interact with the world. Form gives way to content. In a way, it is like sitting in a movie theater: once the lights dim we are engulfed with the virtual reality on the screen. It is the story that counts (fig. 13).

At present we have lost interest in technology leaders. We prefer popular culture leaders. The stronger the visual contents of a movie genre are, the more likely it will have followers, including in the form of everyday products. A product's form has to relate to the user, tell him a story, and be serious or whimsical. As we move more and more from the literary (books) to the visual (movies), the ultimate cultural leader is no doubt the science fiction or fantasy film. Since it tries to convince us that this is the future, shouldn't we be influenced by its imagery?

Product designers were employed more and more as set designers, drawing and building very convincing future products and environments. When the 1968 science fiction movie *2001: A Space Odyssey* translated Arthur C. Clarke's words into imagined reality, the producers approached famous technology companies in order to have them assist in designing products for the film. The idea was for them to extrapolate the products of the period into convincing

13. FILM CREATES AN ALTERNATIVE WORLD—*MINORITY REPORT*, DIRECTED BY STEVEN SPIELBERG

14. *STAR WARS* IMAGERY PROLIFERATES IN PROMOTING EVERYDAY THINGS

15. 3D ANIMATION BECOMES CONVINCING REALITY—*AVATAR*, DIRECTED BY JAMES CAMERON, 2009

forms for the end of the century. Syd Mead was hired out from Detroit's car design studios in order to create the bleak environment of 21st-century Los Angeles in Ridley Scott's *Blade Runner*. And Industrial Light & Magic was formed as a design studio in order to materialize the look and feel of George Lucas' *Star Wars* trilogy. This was also the beginning of large scale marketing campaigns that introduced toys and gadgets based on Star Wars imagery, thus influencing the form language of other completely unrelated products (fig. 14).

The introduction of computer games, computer environments and personalities (*Second Life* comes into mind), and the total immersion of virtual reality further blurred the boundary of what was real and what was not. After Pixar's photo realistic animated films, 3D computer-generated imagery (CGI) came of age, culminating in another type of total immersion experience. *Avatar* (fig. 15) introduced a new level of convincing 3D computer graphics enhanced with 3D effects representation. Should we refer to the tenet of these times as "what you dream is what you get"?

Key candidates for future visual inspiration

Are we, the toolmakers, approaching an age when physical forms are not important to us? Recall *2001: A Space Odyssey*, when the voice of the sentient computer HAL 9000 is everywhere, but at the same time non-existent. You cannot see it and cannot turn it off. I doubt if the non-existence of form will ever happen. I always wonder why most science fiction directors fall in love with empty undecorated white rooms and with boring uniform like clothing, *a la* Star Trek. If we look around at our modern society, we see individual taste; we see fashion lovers,

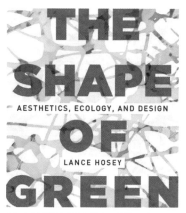

16. LANCE HOSEY'S LATEST BOOK, *THE SHAPE OF GREEN* (2012)

gadget lovers, and object collectors, not a dull society.

The promise of the Machine Age of the early twentieth century that technology would herald a better place for humanity has lost its luster after two world wars. The machine could lead either way, as beneficial or as detrimental to humans, depending how it will be used. There have been theories that we are gradually moving towards a Post-Industrial Age (Daniel Bell popularized the term through his 1973 work *The Coming of Post-Industrial Society*). If not technology and its physical manifestations than what will we look up to as a future non-technology form leader, if there is to be one at all? Some say that we have entered the age of information (how will it define the language of visual form?) while others talk about the age if creativity, where personal fulfillment does not need any leadership. There are on-going discussions of societal and environmental responsibility. So it seems that any prediction as to what will drive our visual language. At the moment, care for the environment has manifested itself in ecologically conscious design, but quite often it is a guilt removing response of designers who cater to mass consumption. Lance Hosey's Latest Book, *The Shape of Green* (2012) tries to deal with the form of ecologically respon-

sible products and environments (fig. 16). Another emerging vogue tends to follow biotechnology, often seen as a new panacea for our ills. Bio is the buzzword: organic and bio-degradable materials, bio-mimicry (fig. 17), even organic forms, as if they were naturally made (fig. 18).

The ephemeral visual form leader of the future, be it a technology leader, a culture leader, or something completely different, cannot emerge from a linear extrapolation of the past. Therefore, it may elude serious forecasting (fig. 19). After all, dreaming about the future is a wonderful advantage of the human race.

17. BIO-MIMICRY: SIMULATING THE TOES OF THE GECKO IN ORDER TO ADHERE TO ANY SURFACE

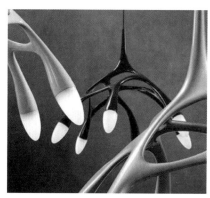

18. ORGANIC INFLUENCED IMAGERY: NLC PENDANT LAMP BY NEXT

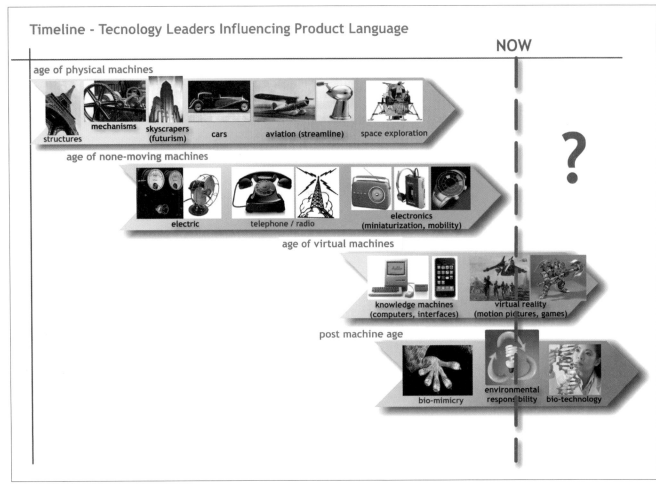

Timeline - Tecnology Leaders Influencing Product Language

NOW

age of physical machines

structures | mechanisms | skyscrapers (futurism) | cars | aviation (streamline) | space exploration

age of none-moving machines

electric | telephone / radio | electronics (miniaturization, mobility)

age of virtual machines

knowledge machines (computers, interfaces) | virtual reality (motion pictures, games)

post machine age

bio-mimicry | environmental responsibility | bio-technology

?

19. WHAT, OR WHO, WILL BE THE NEXT VISUAL FORM LEADER?

Product Form in Practice

Introduction to the case studies

A note about the selection of the case studies

The case studies in Part 3 were selected because they represent the typical varieties of evolution of recent man-made products, as outlined in Part 2. The product lines purposefully represent different evolutionary routes. Some families illustrate resistance to archetypal form change. Others are willingly and continually changing. There are families that accept convergence of several branches into one. Others resist assimilation and even grow their own way (you may have noticed that I use living metaphors here). There are also families full of confusion that are resistant to establishing definite archetypes. Electronic equipment has accelerated development within a short span of time, with less commitment to old semantic bonds; they best represent the dynamic ways in which products come into being, change, diverge, converge, and decline; therefore, I present quite a few case studies of electronic products. Other case studies deal with more traditional products such as chairs, cars, bikes, and major appliances.

The case studies represented here do not cover the whole gamut of product lines around us. There is still much research to be carried out in the future.

Visual legend

Each case study has a highlight box on the first page that points out the main themes to be discussed in the case study, followed by a detailed evolution chart of the product family. The sample chart on this page is a legend that will clarify reading the evolution charts. I suggest that you keep flipping back and forth between the text and this chart:

Sample chart

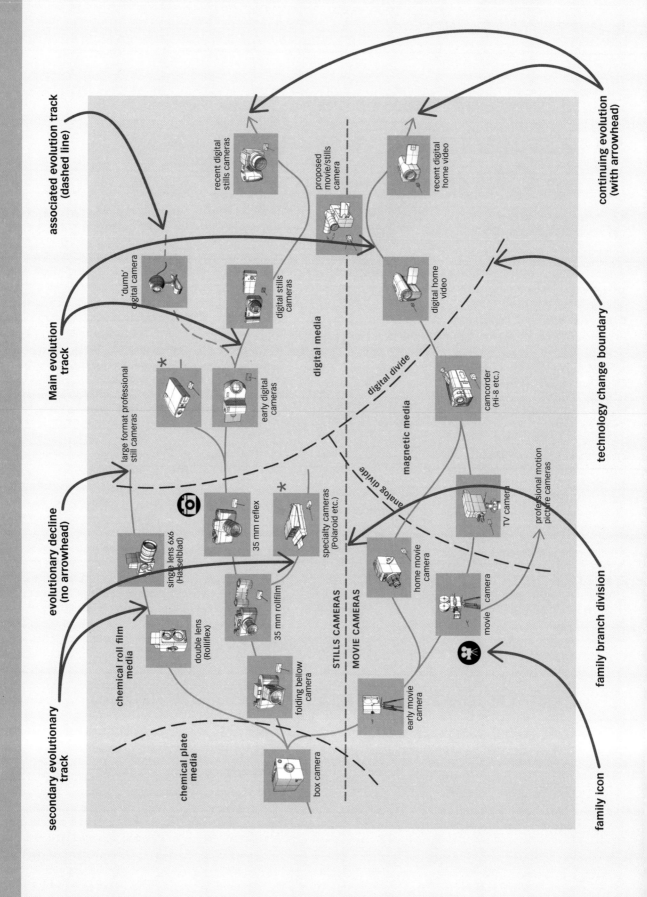

secondary evolutionary track

evolutionary decline (no arrowhead)

Main evolution track

associated evolution track (dashed line)

continuing evolution (with arrowhead)

chemical plate media

chemical roll film media

double lens (Rolliflex)

single lens 6x6 (Hasselblad)

large format professional still cameras

'dumb' digital camera

recent digital stills cameras

box camera

folding bellow camera

35 mm rollfilm

35 mm reflex

specialty cameras (Polaroid etc.)

early digital cameras

digital stills cameras

proposed movie/stills camera

digital media

STILLS CAMERAS

MOVIE CAMERAS

early movie camera

home movie camera

movie camera

TV camera

professional motion picture cameras

digital divide

analog divide

magnetic media

camcorder (Hi-8 etc.)

digital home video

recent digital home video

technology change boundary

family branch division

family icon

CASE STUDY 1
The Camera Family

I chose as the first case study a case where a very clear-cut evolutionary development takes place. An evolution into two distinct family branches presents a good example of separation according to the component geometry tenet, and the evolutionary route itself demonstrates divergence and then convergence of form. The changes in form along the way follow closely the rule of continuation but differentiation.

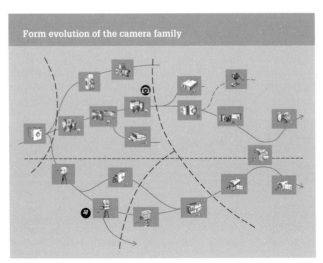

Form evolution of the camera family

SEE ENLARGED DIAGRAM ON PAGE 97

Highlights

This section tackles a typical evolutionary pattern of two family lines branching out from a common ancestor: the early camera cube form.

The stills camera branch and the movie camera branch are defined by a different optical axis relative to the camera's body: perpendicular to the largest face in stills cameras and perpendicular to the smallest, narrowest face in movie cameras.

The third possible optical axis, perpendicular to the intermediary narrow face, was seldom used in cameras. If used, it was usually to define a new or totally different camera technology. Most third optical axis cameras failed to be accepted by the public.

The evolution of cameras changed profoundly when image-capturing technology shifted from chemical media to analog-electronic media, and then again to digital media. In spite of becoming essentially computerized gadgets, cameras adhere to the optical devices' visual traits.

In each step in the evolution of the camera family the newer device tried to differentiate itself from the previous one, indicating visually where the difference lies, while continuing with the family's archetype identity.

In spite of the fact that both contemporary digital stills cameras and digital movie cameras use the same technology and can incorporate the other's feature to a degree; they did not merge into an integrated family line. Each separate branch continues to visually identify itself as different from the other line.

As media communicators (smartphones and tablets) become more popular means of shooting pictures and video on the go, the camera family loses ground in small cameras and concentrates on professional cameras, embracing the familiar visual traits of past professional cameras: complex, large lenses and the ever-present black color.

The stills camera

1. THE CAMERA OBSCURA

The first cameras of the late 19th century were basically cubical boxes with a capped lens, with no main visual axis or face. As the name of the product suggests—*camera* means "room" in Italian—it is a scaled down version of the Renaissance camera obscura, which was an actual room with a small hole on one wall that projected an inverted image onto the opposite wall (fig. 1). Not surprisingly, early cameras were analogous to scaled-down rooms, in both shape and proportion. That type of camera was commonly named "box camera," which in taxonomic terms relates the camera form to rooms and boxes. The Kodak box camera of 1887 (fig. 2) was the first really portable popular camera that imprinted the black boxy camera image in the public eye and mind.

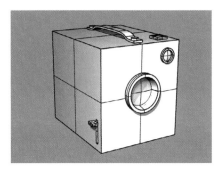

2. THE POPULAR BOX CAMERA OF THE EARLY 20TH CENTURY

Optical innovations eventually improved the camera's portability and focus: bellows (fig.3) and the viewfinder lens of the Rolleiflex camera of the late 1930s (fig. 4). The folding bellows camera set the visual rule on how an ideal portable camera should look—a flattened, non-equal cuboid with its main plain perpendicular to the optical (narrow) axis.

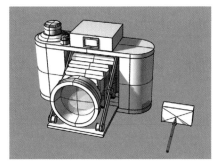

3. THE FOLDING BELLOWS REDUCED THE SIZE OF THE LENS, LEADING TO A FLATTENED FORM

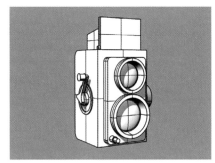

4. THE ROLLEIFLEX HAD A SOPHISTICATED VIEWFINDER AND ASSUMED A VERTICAL BOX FORM

In contrast to the common flat camera form, the elongated square cross-section form of the Rolleiflex camera was retained in the later large format (6X6) professional cameras, such as the classical Hasselblad, introduced in 1948 (fig. 5). The Hasselblad—an icon in itself, immortalized as the camera taken by astronauts to the Moon—held to the same proportions of the Rolleiflex, but with the lens placed on the small square face, and with a protruding viewing hood on top.

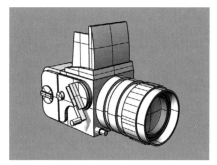

5. THE HASSELBLAD HORIZONTAL FORM PUT EMPHASIS ON THE LENS

The first modern-looking camera, the German-made *Leica*, with its superb optics that legitimized, once and for all, the smaller 35mm film format, appeared in 1930 and established the visual form of 35mm cameras to come. In this classical camera shape the lens was located in the middle of the major flat face (i.e. the face parallel to the film plane) of the camera, and the two film advance knobs echoed the location of the roll film inside (fig. 6). From here on, the 35mm camera adhered to a symmetrical form, as seen in the immortalized camera icon (fig. 7).

6. THE 35MM CAMERA FORM ECHOED THE SHAPE OF THE ROLL FILM INSIDE. THE SMALL ARROW AND BOX INDICATE OPTICAL AXIS ORIENTATION

7. THE IMMORTALIZED CAMERA ICON

Even the introduction of the through-the-lens viewing pentaprism (fig. 8) did not change the archetypal shape and orientation of the camera, except for the addition of a faceted hump on top to indicate existence of the viewing prism.

8. THE FACETED PRISM HUMP INDICATED THROUGH-THE-LENS VIEWING

It is interesting to note that the classical form of the professional 35mm camera was so firmly etched in public recognition that several deliberate trials by camera makers to get away from it failed miserably. In the 1980s, Minolta, realizing a concept that won a "camera of the future" competition in a camera magazine, came out with a radically new visual concept that changed completely the form principles of the camera and the way it was held (fig. 9). This model failed in gaining public approval and was eventually taken off the market. The new orientation was almost certainly not acceptable as a suitable camera form—sort of a failed mutation. On another model, Minolta tried to break away from the traditional "professional black" finish of the camera. It came up with a "limited edition" white camera body, which didn't gain a great deal of acceptance either, though eventually metallic finishes or even bold colors were applied to (the less professional) fully automatic film cameras. These modifications were accepted, as long as the classical orientation principle was strictly adhered to.

9. THE UNCOMMON FORMAT OF MINOLTA'S 110 ZOOM DID NOT GAIN ACCEPTANCE

The American scientist Edwin Land invented an instant processing chemical film that produced a print in minutes after exposure. His famous Polaroid instant camera was a profound advancement in photography and as such there was a justification for a paradigm-shift form to single out instant processing. After several different form experiments, the folding *Polaroid SX-70*, introduced in 1972, took the same uncommon form orientation: a lens on the long, narrow face (fig. 10). This time there was a clear justification for such a radical visual alteration. The public even accepted the unusual square format of the Polaroid prints.

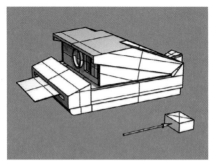

10. THE UNUSUAL FORM OF THE POLAROID SX-70 DEFINED THE FORM OF INSTANT PHOTOGRAPHY

The movie camera

Let us break away at this point from the evolution of the still camera and go back in time to the origin of the motion picture camera. The early studio camera (fig. 11) had to radically break away from the box shape of still photography cameras because it belonged to a different cultural realm altogether, though I admit that there were also functional reasons, especially the large-size film reels hidden inside. The visual differentiation was enhanced by shifting the lens location to the smallest plane of the camera cuboid, which later became the distinguishing cue of the movie camera. The mechanical turning handle was a symbol of "motion." The tripod, always linked to a movie camera (representing stability), has often been used in still camera photography, albeit not as an indispensable part of the movie icon.

11. THE FLAT PIZZA-BOX FORM OF THE EARLY MANUALLY ROLLED MOTION PICTURE CAMERA

Eventually the film reels forced their way to the exterior (usually, on the top) of the movie camera and the rotating lens exchange disc was added in front, not to forget the conspicuous lens shade (fig. 12). Thus the shape of the movie camera crystallized into a classical symbol, still used today as an icon identifying the motion picture industry (fig. 13), even if the professional film movie camera form moved significantly away from the icon and in time progressed to become a rather complex machine. One thing, though, did not change at all: the distinctive end plane orientation of the movie camera lens. It is interesting to note that movie projectors of the time (the one the general public was more exposed to) were almost matching form twins of the movie camera.

12. THE MATURE FORM OF THE CELLULOID FILM MOTION PICTURE CAMERA

13. THE CLASSICAL ICON OF THE MOVIES

The home amateur 16mm movie cameras were in vogue from the mid 1920s to the end of the twentieth century, first shooting silent black and white films and then color films with a soundtrack. It is quite surprising that, being rather small and simple in comparison to their film industry cousins, they took the same box form geometry, albeit with the small film spools hidden from view inside the box (fig. 14). The lens exchange disc and the spring winding butterfly key, reminiscent of the early motion picture camera's turning handle, were sufficient visual ques. There were models with a slightly narrow waist, to suggest the presence of the two film spools inside.

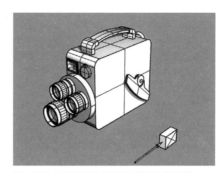

14. THE AMATEUR 16MM HOME MOVIE CAMERA KEEPS THE SAME FORM GEOMETRY

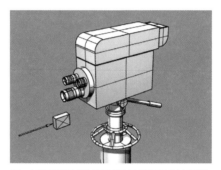

15. AN EARLY STUDIO TELEVISION CAMERA

At the beginning of the television era, the vidicon tube video camera, introduced in the 1950s, continued the film movie camera orientation, but in order to identify that this was a new technology, the telltale twin reels disappeared and a small hooded video display was added (fig. 15). The video recording magnetic tapes or the direct connection to a TV transmitter no longer constituted visual parts of the studio video camera.

The introduction of portable scale magnetic tapes and the miniaturization of the video image capturing device created a real opportunity to bring motion picture cameras—in the existence of the camcorder—into the consumers' realm. Previously, 16mm consumer movie cameras required a separate movie projector and a lengthy film developing process, not to forget cut-and-join editing. These were too complicated and expensive to make personal movie cameras

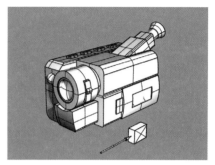

16. THE CAMCORDER BORROWS THE TV STUDIO CAMERA FORM WITH THE ADDITION OF A CASSETTE VIEW WINDOW

universally popular. The visual element of the home video tape cassette (VHS, Hi-8) was already well accepted in visual terms, deriving their form from earlier audio recording and playback equipment. So the earlier film camera's double reel visual icon returned, this time in a cassette form, to define the look of home video cameras (fig. 16). The small cassette size allowed incorporation into the camera's body, but remained intentionally visible, to indicate that no exposure-sensitive film lives here. One dominant form factor did cross over: the essential lens-body orientation that continues to set the movie camera family branch apart from the still camera family branch. It should be noted that the ergonomic components of portable movie shooting—the hand strap and the shoulder pad of the larger camcorder—were never visually incorporated, in both form and materials, into the camcorder's perceived form. On the other hand, the front microphone took visual hold, performing like a second lens.

Crossing the digital divide

The abrupt transition to digital cameras should have created, in Darwinian terms, almost a totally new species, but it did not. I would argue that the digital divide was not really a breakaway product divide, as it linked previously autonomous optical products to computers and software. However, that linkage itself did not materialized into a radically new physical form. In video photography, the evolution from a consumer video camera into a digital video camera made hardly any visual differentiation. A contributing fact was that in the intermediary stage of TV studio cameras and then magnetic media camcorders, these analog video cameras were already manufactured by consumer electronics firms rather than optics-based firms. Thus crossing the digital divide took only minor changes; for example, the tape cassette door was out, replaced internally by smaller storage media, and externally by an LCD viewer (fig. 17).

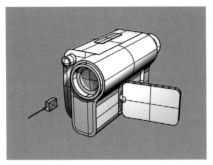

17. THE DIGITAL CAMCORDER FORM IS BASICALLY SIMILAR TO THAT OF THE ANALOG CAMERA

As for the digital stills camera, the change was, by far, more apparent than in motion picture cameras, but still considered evolutionary (though it was quite radical in industrial terms as it completely wiped out chemical film companies such as Kodak, Fuji, and Polaroid).

Actually, the first digital camera was built in 1994 by a computer firm: Apple Computer and its QuickTake 100 (fig. 18). As with computers, Apple was not committed to any previous film camera tradition. As an indication of a paradigm shift, Apple's camera had to look different, but in context it should still be recognized as a "camera." In Darwinian terms, a major evolutionary opportunity should often be purposefully visually exaggerated. So you no longer place the optics on the large face of the box, and you cannot place it at the end or it will be read as a movie camera. So why not turn to the third axis, the side plane, the one tried before unsuccessfully by Minolta (see fig. 9). To show that there is no place for a film roll, place the lens close to the body's end. The other side of the box is reserved for an electronic storage device (a diskette drive). The form of the Apple digital camera was quite rounded at the edges, shaped like bent rubber eraser (in order to claim that there are no mechanical parts or film plane inside). I am not sure whether Robert Brunner, the head of industrial design at Apple then, followed exactly this thinking process, but in hindsight it seems as if the general rationale described here was one he employed.

It should be noted that each time a major departure from the classical 35mm camera took place; the tendency was to try and place the lens on the third (narrow) axis. It happened with the Minnox miniature spy camera (not shown here) and with the Polaroid SX-70 instant camera. They were visually advertised as different, as specialty cameras. I mark these cases in the evolutionary chart with green asterisks.

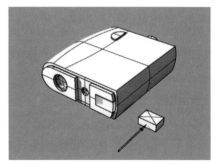

18. THE QUICKTAKE 100 BY APPLE COMPUTER INTRODUCED A RADICAL FORM CHANGE

Sony suggested a different form solution. Its Mavica digital camera retained the same large face as previous film cameras, but the lens was moved to the extreme end to indicate that there was no room for a film roll there (fig. 19). Minolta even went a little further in its digital camera; the lens was removed to an external swiveling head (not shown here).

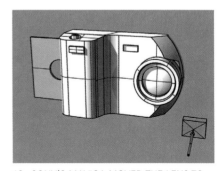

19. SONY'S MAVICA MOVED THE LENS TO THE EXTREME RIGHT. DISKETTE SLOT AT THE LEFT

After a short while, almost all optical camera companies crossed the digital divide. Unlike Apple's approach, their cameras were more conservative in form, following Sony's form approach: a zoom lens located on the large face of the box, but almost always at the right end. The viewing device, now universally an LCD screen, sometimes built like a door at the back of the camera (fig. 20). The electronic storage device, ever so small, doesn't play any role in the visual configuration.

Another class identifier is the external metallic look, often enhanced by color, as it is popular with consumer electronics (black color is generally accepted as associated with light sensitive chemical film).

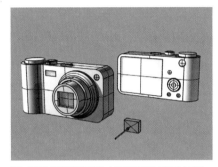

20. THE COMMONLY ACCEPTED FORM OF SMALL CONSUMER DIGITAL CAMERA

A separately evolving branch of the digital camera is the "dumb" camera, a camera that just sees, with no processing brain. Since it has no brain it takes the form of an eyeball (fig. 21). Lytro, an innovation company, came up with a rather unique product in which the recorded image data allows refocus, change of perspective, and the addition of filters to create a better photograph long after the shot is taken (maybe by a "dumb" photographer). The Lytro has an extruded rectangular form (not shown here), similar to that of exterior surveillance cameras, where information is also collected after the actual event takes place.

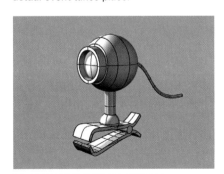

21. THE DUMB EYEBALL CAMERA

Present and future

In 2003, the sales of digital cameras in the USA surpassed for the first time the sales of film cameras. Digital resolution became good enough to attract professional photographers (who were, up to this point, using very expensive professional niche digital cameras, or applied digital camera backs). With the additional advancement of photo-editing software (Photoshop), digital photo management software and hi-quality photo printers, it was apparent that the days of film-based still-cameras were over and eventually one major film producer after another discontinued their lines of chemical films.

As with any electronic product, there exists an eye-catching range of form development possibilities: miniature, super thin cameras, folding cameras, extreme sports cameras. One rule will remain though; most cameras stay well within the accepted symbolic and taxonomic definition of a camera of the era.

Inspecting the camera family evolution chart, we may extrapolate a probable outcome: the digital still camera branch and the digital movie camera branch are getting ever closer, overlapping each other. Both have zoom lenses, LCD displays, and mass storage media. Movie cameras can shoot still frames. Still cameras can shoot short films and record sound. The obvious outcome would have been a crossover, a merger into one multi-purpose camera. The semantic question that may rise is on which of the faces the lens will be located: the main panel axis, the short panel axis, or on both, as represented in a proposal suggesting an all-purpose, omni-directional configuration (fig. 22).

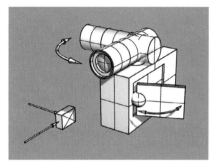

22. A MERGER OF STILLS AND VIDEO CAMERA THAT NEVER HAPPENED

This proposed merger did not occur. In fact, the two family branches are gradually moving away from each other, each branch of cameras re-defining its purpose and accordingly its looks. The moving away is by far more pronounced on the face of the digital stills camera. A professional look is the primary factor. The more the stills camera is sophisticated, the more it returns to the traditional thru-the-lens (TTL) looks (fig. 23): black body, prominent lens and hand grip, even the pentaprism hump on top, now a folding flash. One digital characteristic does survive, the next-to-the-edge location of the lens.

23. BACK TO A PROFESSIONAL DIGITAL STILLS CAMERA, AVAILABLE IN BLACK

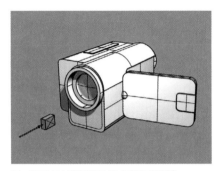

24. THE ALMOST PALM-SIZED VIDEO CAMERA

As explained earlier, the form of digital movies cameras remains basically the same with a tendency to become simpler, smaller in size, and softer in the box form to allow for easy grip (fig. 24). The larger, professional video cameras are relegated to the studios, newsrooms, and photojournalists. At this time, axis differentiation proves to be the identifier of form family, attesting to the semantic importance of hereditary family traits. Part of the explanation to this form about-face lies in the fact that most popular photography is currently being accomplished with smartphones and tablets. Stills cameras have retreated to the conservative, but well-recognized, image of the old black professional camera. We should bear in mind that most people cannot visually identify a high resolution CCD image sensor hidden inside the camera, so form has to rely on the telescopic zoom lens as the family identifier. Small amateur cameras still abound, but I doubt whether they will last for long given the overlapping and ever increasing capabilities of smartphones. After all, the ever-thinner small amateur camera has the same form factor as a smartphone. The field will be clearly divided between the professional stills and movie cameras, on one hand, and amateur smartphone and tablet photography, on the other.

One question still holds my curiosity. Why is it that past cameras rarely succeeded in surviving when the lens was placed on the narrow plane? The only semantic rationale I managed to find is that this orientation firmly belongs to and identifies another family of optical products: the binocular family (Fig. 25). I discovered, after arriving at that conclusion, that when Apple Computer came out with its first QuickTake digital camera, it was described by reporters as a "binocular shaped camera."

25. THE NARROW PLANE ORIENTATION BELONGS TO THE BINOCULAR FAMILY

Form evolution of the camera family

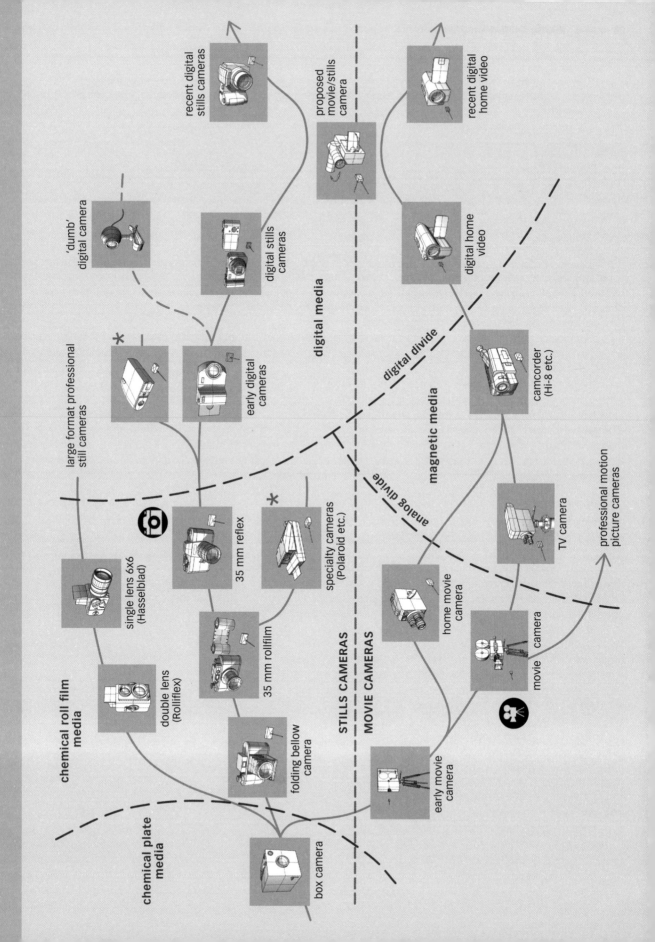

recent digital stills cameras

proposed movie/stills camera

recent digital home video

'dumb' digital camera

digital stills cameras

digital home video

digital media

large format professional still cameras

*

early digital cameras

camcorder (Hi-8 etc.)

magnetic media

digital divide

single lens 6x6 (Hasselblad)

35 mm reflex

*

specialty cameras (Polaroid etc.)

analog divide

TV camera

chemical roll film media

double lens (Rolliflex)

35 mm rollfilm

home movie camera

movie camera

professional motion picture cameras

folding bellow camera

STILLS CAMERAS

MOVIE CAMERAS

chemical plate media

early movie camera

box camera

CASE STUDY 2
Personal Media Communicators

This case study is an example of fusing previously separate classes of products into one class family. Such a merging contradicts the way that natural evolution works, where random mutations are the basis for the branching out of several distinct lines from one common ancestor. Following is a short description of how several product families of electronic equipment (media players, mobile phones, personal computers, personal data assistants like the Palm Pilot, book readers, and digital cameras) almost swiftly merge into a single "all-in-one" family, and how the visual language of that merger evolved. It should be noted that this merger takes place in a segment of the electronic industry that rapidly evolves almost day-by-day, where product lifespan is very short. Thus, visual form models are rarely preserved.

The term "personal media communicator" suggested here is not a commonly accepted term. A shorter explicit name will eventually emerge and become common in everyday language.

Highlights

This is an examination of the exceptional evolutionary convergence of previously separate product classes.

In an age of specialization and increased market struggle there is a strong argument against the inevitable convergence of previously separate product classes.

Each of the product classes that contributed to the merged offspring gradually lost most of its class's visual traits. The overall result is a decisive simplification of form. Form is delegated to the contents "behind the glass slab."

In every evolutionary step in each class, the newer product differentiated itself from previous products, visually emphasizing where the difference lies, but still observing its overall class archetypal identity.

An interesting parallel study to this case study is the conflict between the traditional vertical written paper sheet format and the horizontal movie screen format, and how to manage them both at the same time.

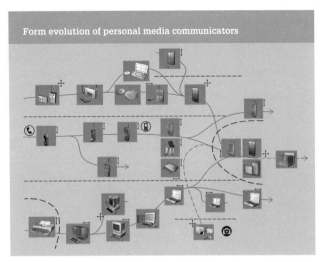

Form evolution of personal media communicators

SEE ENLARGED DIAGRAM ON PAGE 109

The mobile phone family

Leave technology aside for a moment. The mobile phone is a descendant of the familiar (in visual iconic terms) classic line telephone. The line telephone's body suggests a tabletop or wall-mounted static configuration while the handset is inherently moveable. No wonder that the ear-to-mouth element was the one destined to be carried over to the mobile phone. Interestingly, the spiral cord, which allowed the free movement of the line telephone's handset, became the absolute hallmark of the line telephone.

1. MILITARY WALKIE-TALKIE OF WORLD WAR II: A UNION OF TELEPHONE HANDSET AND RADIO TRANSCEIVER

The precursor of the mobile telephone was the military transceiver. The technology was wireless (thus mobile) but the handset was taken verbatim from the classic telephone. The first instance of merging the transceiver with the handset was the military walkie-talkie (a very apt verbal description) of the 1940s. The integration of these elements created an odd hybrid: a boxy form with two protrusions indicating where the earpiece and mouthpiece were (fig. 1)—a case of the rule of continuation but differentiation. In spite of miniaturization efforts it was rather bulky equipment, the size of a man's arm, but nonetheless handheld. The whip antenna became a distinct element, visually indi-

cating that what we saw was wireless equipment.

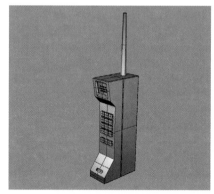

2. MOTOROLA'S DYNATAC, THE FIRST TRUE MOBILE TELEPHONE, APTLY NAMED "THE BRICK"

The extensive engineering innovation and development of wireless technology of cellular phones are of no concern to our discussion as we focus on the visual appearance. Motorola's *DynaTAC* (fig. 2) of 1983 was the first truly mobile phone. In visual terms it was a heavy bricklike version of Ma Bell's Trimline telephone, less the cradle. But having an antenna, it signified mobility. Again we see the rule of continuation but differentiation.

From here the shape of the mobile phone evolved continually through several intermediaries into the ubiquitous pebble or soap-bar, hand-fitting mobile phone

3. THE CLASSIC FORM OF A CELLULAR PHONE AND A MOBILE PHONE ICON, BOTH IDENTIFIED BY KEYBOARD AND ANTENNA STUB

(fig. 3). No wonder then that its evolution was termed in Wired Magazine, "From Brick to Slick" (February, 2009). The typical, possibly iconic, cell phone had a small LED screen and a bulging short antenna stub, rather than the previous extended antenna. The antenna was still a required visual cue, or how one could differentiate it from, let say, a portable electronic calculator. It could be argued that the calculator and the phone have reverse numeric keypad arrangements, but this is not significant enough in formal terms.

Let us sidestep for a moment. The previous walkie-talkie form did not completely vanish. It branched laterally into a line of professional military and civil (police, fire fighting, medical, and marine) handheld wireless communicators (fig. 4). In order to denote an evolving separate branch, the antenna was retained as a strong visual element (the rule of continuation but differentiation). The communicator's surface was almost always professional black. Most of the controls are on the top face (recalling family distinction through accentuating different box faces in the camera family case study).

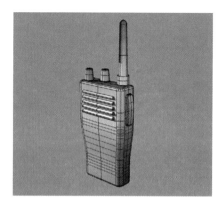

4. MILITARY AND CIVIL HANDHELD WIRELESS COMMUNICATOR IS RUGGED AND MADE TO WORK IN DARKNESS CONTROLS

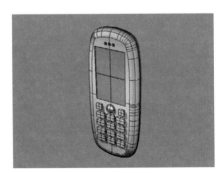

5. THE LATER PEBBLE FORM CELLULAR TELEPHONE NO LONGER REQUIRES AN IDENTIFYING EXTERNAL ANTENNA

6. SLIDER TELEPHONES TRY TO OVERCOME THE EVER SMALLER ALPHANUMERIC KEYBOARD PROBLEM

7. MOTOROLA'S STARTAC—AN HOMAGE TO STAR TREK—OFFERS A PHYSICAL OPEN-CLOSE INDICATION

Returning to the cellular phone's form development, the pebble or soap-bar form proliferated into a glut of visually non-significant variations of the basic pebble form, often playing with the way the cellular phone opened up and folded: clamshell, slider, rotational folding (see examples in figs. 5, 6, and 7). As the mobile phone became ubiquitous, it was enough for it to be recognize by the screen and keyboard. There was no need for the previously identifying antenna stub (which could also be a reminder of a radiation health hazard). Again, we see an example of the rule of continuation but differentiation. An interesting variation in that crowd was Motorola's *StarTAC* (fig. 7), which paid homage, by both name and look, to the folding communicator used in the *Star Trek* TV series of the 1970s. Therefore, it kept the antenna as an indispensable element of that historic allusion.

The ever-sophisticated operating systems and availability of applications (messages, games, images, music, etc.) obviously necessitated a much larger color LED display, leading to competition with the keyboard for room on the surface. Moreover, messaging became a much more important feature, requiring an ergo-nomically adequate alphanumeric keypad, or even a miniature alphanumeric keypad. This led to a new distinctive family, the smartphone, which will be discussed in detail later.

I do not believe that the smartphone configuration heralds the demise of the basic no-nonsense cell phone. Technology has a tendency to progress towards over-complexity. We should bear in mind that there is a huge market for a basic unsophisticated communication device, a telephone and nothing else, and not only in the Third World.

The portable media player family

Historic media players included the phonograph (record player), the reel tape recorder, the radio, and eventually the television set. These were bulky and heavy, with delicate radio tubes inside, requiring cords and power outlets. Thus, portability of these players was almost out of the question. They were ment to be static home devices.

When we say portable media players, we most often mean different types of audio players, mostly for recording and for listening to music. Admittedly, there are also video players in the market but they are not very common, unless watching a movie in a car counts as portability. We should also be aware that a new media player is always the byproduct of a new and different physical media. There were several awkward failures in introducing new media standards as replacing a global media music library is always a huge undertaking. Thus, some new media routes were experimental dead ends.

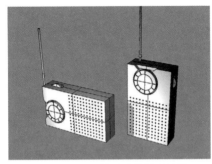

8. A MINIATURIZED TRANSISTOR RADIO MAY BE HELD OR PLACED AT ANY ORIENTATION

The invention of the transistor in the late 1940s allowed for significant miniaturization of media players for the first time. The transistor's low power requirements allowed the use of small batteries in lieu of a power cord. These factors led to the introduction of the transistor radio (fig.8). Radio reception itself was not a new, but Miniaturization and portability were. They became the really important things about radio. Thus, form considerations were of less concern: a small brick with telescopic antenna as a characteristic media signifier and a loudspeaker mesh. Radio waves flow in, sound comes out (again, the rule of continuation but differentiation). Later technological innovations, always hidden inside the transistor radio, did not much change its external form, except perhaps the insistence on a symmetrical layout, to indicate the existence of stereo loudspeakers (see *Case study 5—Home entertainment*).

As vinyl records were large and sensitive to sunrays, absolutely unsuited for outside portability, subsequent development was focused on an encased magnetic tape media—the cassette tape. The portable tape player was basically an oversized stereo transistor radio with a tape door. The real breakthrough in the development of cassette players came about with Sony's Walkman, where the heavy oversized stereo loudspeakers were replaced with a more minimal and better substitute, high fidelity stereo earphones (fig. 9). The idea was revolutionary then: an introverted music player. No one else hears what you are listening to. The shape was a throwback to the small brick-like transistor radio, without the telescopic antenna but with a transparent door to visually display the cassette media (the rule of continuation but differentiation plus form-follows-media).

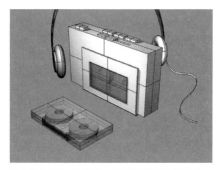

9. MOST HAND-HELD CASSETTE PLAYERS FOLLOWED SONY'S WALKMAN GROUNDBREAKING CONCEPT

Cassette tapes were not without their faults, such as occasional spilling of tape and sensitivity to inadvertent magnetizing that erased the recorded music. The next technological media solution was the compact disc (CD), a miniature reminiscence of the vinyl record, though with huge capacity and a non-physical, scratchproof reading device incorporating a laser beam reader. Here again, the form-follows-media approach dominates: a circular door suggests the disc media. Soon, the CD player acquired an overall circular, or almost circular, form (fig. 10).

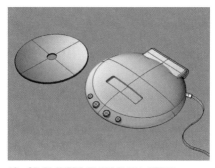

10. CD PLAYERS CLAM SHELL FORM REFLECTED THE ROUND MEDIA FORM

In the next evolutionary step, the introduction of the video compact disc (DVD) demanded a display screen, leading to a DVD player that looks like a hybrid of a Discman and a small laptop computer, but with no keyboard (fig. 11). In evolutionary terms, the DVD player was just a temporary sidetrack soon to be forgotten.

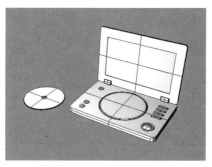

11. DVD PLAYER: A NOT-SO-RECOGNIZED FUSION OF A CD PLAYER AND A LAPTOP SCREEN

The memory chip came next, smaller than any previous media, with no moving parts prone to breakage. The memory chip is easy to format and upload and has playlist arrangement capabilities. As there was no need to access the memory chip, it was set on an internal circuit board, never to be seen externally. Naturally, the question arises: "What form should the new media player take?" The answer suggested by Apple Computer designers was almost iconic: place a circle within a rectangle (fig. 12). It was a tribute to, or reminiscence of, the earlier CD player and the record player. If you look closely, almost all previous media players had a circle within a rectangular form somewhere. Apple's early iPod had, rather than an internal memory chip, a miniature hard disc, echoed by a round external control. A small display screen was added as a practical indicator of the playlist, thus getting nearer in its form to the mobile phone and setting the stage for a future class merger.

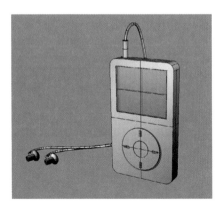

12. MUSIC PLAYERS HAD NO VISIBLE MEDIA CUES. THE IPOD CLASSIC'S AND IPOD MINI'S CIRCULAR CONTROL MAY REMIND THE USER OF PAST CDS AND VINYL RECORDS

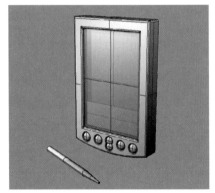

13. PALM PILOT IMPRINTED THE VISUAL IMAGE OF THE PERSONAL DIGITAL ASSISTANT

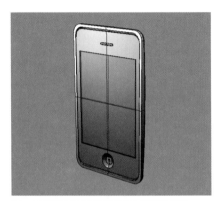

14. APPLE'S IPOD TOUCH IMPLIED THE FORM OF THE FUTURE ALL-IN-ONE MEDIA GADGET, YET WITHOUT THE PHONE PART

Let us step backwards in time to investigate a separate family of portable products, the hand-held personal digital assistant (PDA). It was almost a reflection of the scribe's clay tablet of four thousand years ago. Thus, it had a glass-topped rectangular plate with an interactive stylus—also a historic name (fig. 13). The groundbreaker here was the Apple Newton of 1987. Unfortunately, it was still immature for its time and eventually a marketing failure. Later, the idea was followed by the successful Palm Pilot line and other similar devices. Somewhat later, in the same form but different in use, was the family of e-book readers: the Kindle, Nook, and others. The PDA and e-book reader families are quite similar in form, though not necessarily in size. The readers had the size of a soft-cover pocket book, but both had in common an almost flat box shape with a large screen and minimal token buttons. Concentrating on the language of form, I bundle the two functional classes together as one.

Eventually the media player, the calendar, and the book and video screen configurations, so similar in form but still diverse in use, were united by Apple into one object, the iPod Touch (fig. 14), introduced in 2007, which incorporated, music, photos, video, games, and productivity software.

I should remind the reader that in spite of popular belief, Apple was not the first to introduce an all-in-one media player. Sony already came up with its Clié in the year 2000 (fig. 15). The Clié (an acronym at different times for creativity, lifestyle, innovation, and emotion; or communication, link, information, and entertainment) was much more than just a personal digital assistant. Unfortunately, the operating system (OS) could not yet live up to the full realization of that idea for lack of comparable operating software.

Apple gained the competitive edge by developing a magnificent media-oriented operating system and a truly revolutionary intuitive gesture control. The iPod was still missing voice telephony and internet connectivity, but it was only a question of time to integrate those, too.

15. SONY'S CLIÉ, INTRODUCED IN 2000, WAS AN EARLY SOLUTION OF AN ALL-IN-ONE MEDIA PLAYER

The personal computer family

The personal computer (PC) was heralded by a long lineage of mechanical word processors. The mechanical typewriter—the one with a keyboard mechanism, a moving carriage, and typing on inserted paper sheets—dominated the office environment for over a century (fig. 16). The typewriter existed for a long time before the digital computer. I go back

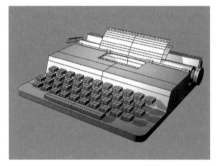

16. THE LOW PROFILE OF A 1960S TYPEWRITER CONTRIBUTED TO THE FORM OF FUTURE GENERATIONS OF PC KEYBOARDS

in time to refer to it here because the keyboard layout (QWERTY) and keys have been stubbornly carried over ever since. The standard typwriter was greatly improved by IBM, introducing the elec-tromechanical Selectric in 1961. In the Selectric, the carriage was replaced by an internal, moving typing ball, allowing for a variety of fonts. The exterior was built as one form, without an externally visible mechanical carriage. Before the personal computer appeared, there was a short-lived interim electronic word processor (not shown here). It was quite similar in look to the Selectric typewriter, but with a one-line display—a really strange concept in today's terms.

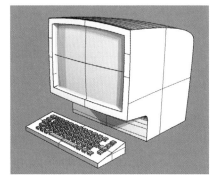

17. THE IBM 3270 FAMILY OF DISPLAY TERMINALS (CA. 1972) HAD A UNIQUELY SCULPTURED FORM

The conventional image of computer in the 1960s was the massive main-frame, occupying a large room together with its huge magnetic tape readers, printers, and control terminals, almost dwarfing the humans operating it. No one envisioned then the likelihood of a small-scale offshoot of that colossal computer. Eventually, office workflow necessitated the extension of mainframe input devices into the office proper via network cables. These input devices were called X-terminals or even dumb terminals (they did not have a brain of their own). X-terminals had the familiar keyboard and a CRT (Cathode Ray Tube) screen, which was quite similar to the familiar TV screen

at home (fig. 17). The display then had one color (generally green or orange) and was only alphanumeric, with no trace of graphic capabilities.

It always puzzled me why the CRT terminal had a horizontal orientation, since the typed page orientation was (and still is) universally vertical. It seems to me that there are several reasons for this oddity. The CRT orientation followed the pervasive TV screen at home (using the same technology). The orientation was of less importance because what was typed on the screen did not look at all as the final, typed page, which was completely trusted to a programmed printer. The keyboard had the horizontal orientation of the typewriter age and it naturally paralleled the horizontal CRT in its width. Actually, you will notice that the past mechanical typewriter and the IBM Selectric were basically horizontally oriented machines; only the typed page was vertical. So I assume that what was taken for granted then became the defini-tive visual rule later on (even the QWERTY layout is a heritage we could not replace later).

IBM was the first firm to cut the umbil-ical cord to the mainframe (or at least, loosen it) by introducing the personal computer (IBM PC). Though the indepen-dent personal computer was a revolution in terms of office work, in formal terms it did not deviate from the traditional looks of office equipment. A new CPU box was simply added to the previous X-terminal keyboard and CRT. Luckily, the CPU box provided a pedestal for the CRT display, allowing for a better viewing angle. The notion of the PC made of separate elements connected by cables became the accepted standard for a long time in order to create a visual uniformity. As a group, the components had an identical width and the same surface color and details (fig. 18).

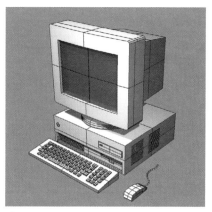

18. A TYPICAL PC CONFIGURATION

In spite of the effort to relate the PC elements to each other, peripheral devices were considered as separate entities, and not even necessarily as coming from the same manufacturer. There were really few exceptions to the ubiquitous separate components approach. The early Apple Macintosh and Lisa computers, in which the CRT was placed in the computer box, were almost singular exceptions. Speaking of exceptions, a company named Radius, almost as an oddity, tried to resolve the horizontal-vertical issue of the CRT by designing a rotatable CRT for Apple computers (fig. 19). This approach was quite logical as both Apple and Radius catered mainly to the graphic design

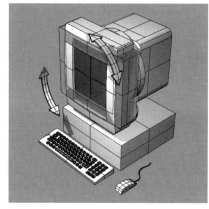

19. A HORIZONTAL-VERTICAL ROTATING CRT BY RADIUS WAS THE ONLY PORTRAIT-LANDSCAPE ORIENTATION SOLUTION TILL THE ARRIVAL OF THE IPAD

community. Graphic designers had to see their designs on the screen exactly as it will appear in print; hence the importance of WYSIWYG (what you see is what you get).

The introduction of the flat liquid crystal screen provided an opportunity to change the entrenched PC configuration. If the CRT display occupied a large area of the desk, then the thin LCD display could be placed almost anywhere and be of any size. As the keyboard and the display were slim, the computer box was obviously at odds with the thin components and had to be removed from the desk, to be hidden somewhere in the background or below the desk (fig. 20), where it became almost visually insubstantial. As in driving, what you see on the screen counts, the rest could be invisible while working. In the same vein of thought, several PC models integrated the processor board into the back of the display screen, and cluttering cables could be replaced by Bluetooth radio connection between components.

20. A TYPICAL COMPONENT BASED PC. THE COMPUTER BOX, NO LONGER A PARTNER-IN-FORM, COULD BE PLACED ANYWHERE

Portable laptop computers have been around for quite some time, mostly in the business sector. They were bulky, limited in performance, and quite expensive—only for real corporate road warriors. As performance improved and cost and weight kept going down, more and more laptops were sold, eating into the desktop PC market. PCs may eventually end up as niche products for office work and heavy-duty computation.

Mark Dean, IBM's CTO for the Middle East and Africa, reflected on the dawn of the desktop era and looked forward to its seemingly inevitable demise:

"When I helped design the PC, I didn't think I'd live long enough to witness its decline. But, while PCs will continue to be much-used devices, they're no longer at the leading edge of computing. They're going the way of the vacuum tube, typewriter, vinyl records, CRT and incandescent light bulbs."

Posted in Engadget.com, August 12, 2011

The laptop form configuration is simple and straightforward with a thin, book-like folding (fig. 21). Minimalism is the accepted rule. Razor thin, the Mac Air and ultra-laptops have become the look in vogue, justified by lighter weight but also by refined looks. The ever-thinner and lighter laptop, now commonly labeled "ultrabook," looks more like a folder than a book. A smaller version, though limited in performance was made to connect to the internet, aptly named "netbook" (fig. 22). The introduction of high performance tablets led to the netbook's short lifespan as products.

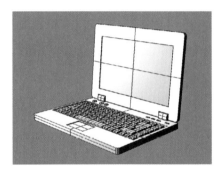

21. THE FOLDING BOOK CONFIGURATION OF THE LAPTOP MOBILE COMPUTER BY VARIOUS MAKERS WAS BASICALLY THE SAME, DIFFERING MAINLY IN PERFORMANCE, SCREEN SIZE, AND WEIGHT

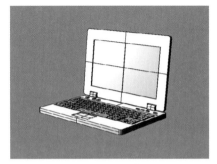

22. THE NETBOOK WAS A LOW PERFORMANCE SMALLER BROTHER OF THE LAPTOP

The multi-function device family

If we take a tally of the different product classes we dealt with in this case study, we realize that they gradually came to share the same visual traits: hand-held, flat, ever-smaller, centered around a large color screen. This is not an arbitrary evolutionary accident. Almost all share similar functions and operate in more or less similar ways, so that quite often we cannot tell the difference between devices. Technological advances allow for incorporating all the different functions mentioned previously into one device, even adding a camera function (as we dealt with in the previous case study) and often GPS, all set in one physical entity, dominated by a gesture-operated super-screen. Multi-function has come to be a catchword. Why carry on your body several independent gadgets if you can combine them into just one? The preeminent visual manifestation of the smartphone is its display screen, accompanied by minimal controls and, until recently, accompanied by a human-friendly rounding of corners and edges—a pebble or soap-bar shape (fig 23).

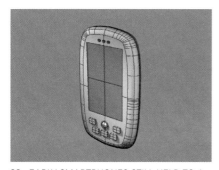

23. EARLY SMARTPHONES STILL HELD TO A PEBBLE FORM, WITH AN EVER-LARGER DISPLAY SCREEN AND ONLY A FEW BUTTONS

Very quickly, the personal media communicator turned into an omni-functional, omni-directional, Swiss Army Knife-like product. An emphasis on contents and the removal of physical controls in favor of motion gestures comes in lieu of product distinction. Soap-bar smartphones are being replaced by ubiquitous iPhone look-alikes. Even personal communicators and the larger tablets look the same; the differences between different brands are summed up in minor nondescript details.

At this time we do not have an appropriate accepted name for this "all-in-one" product. We still call it a smartphone, denoting that first and foremost it is a communications device. The first part of the name, *smart*, relegates authority to the brain of the product rather than to any physical appearance. Apple Computers markets all its variations of "all-in-one" under the "i" prefix, as a market dominance scheme. Possibly the market dominant name iPhone may become a dictionary word, the likes of Frigidaire and Xerox. Another possibility is that the word tablet, by its historical connotations, now assigned to the large sized version, will become the inescapable name for that variety, or not.

I believe that since our hands will not change in size in the foreseeable future, a small-sized product is a rational ergonomic solution. Our visual acuity prefers a larger screen size in order to perceive text and images. This size conflict may lead to two parallel product lines doing the same things, the smaller palm of your hand communicator family (fig.24) and the larger tablet family (fig. 25), with a variety of screen sizes in between. Since they are so similar in form and operation, I doubt if they are still to be considered as separate archetype classes. We do not classify fashion by size. In form archetypal classification there is no distinguishable difference, a screen is a screen is a screen.

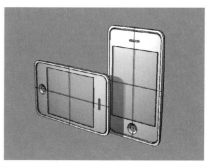

24. PRESENT DAY COMMUNICATORS FOLLOW THE IPHONE'S FLAT AND THIN RECTILINEAR CONFIGURATION

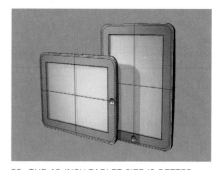

25. THE 10-INCH TABLET SIZE IS BETTER SUITED FOR WATCHING, READING, LEARNING, AND PLAYING, WHICH CONSTITUTES A TRUE MEDIA MACHINE

It should be noted here that product evolution no longer follows the rule of continuation but differentiation we have encountered so often in this case study, that newer products differentiate themselves from the previous product, visually emphasizing where differences lie, while at the same time following the overall family archetypal identity. Similarly, a major technological change, what I have termed earlier as "crossing the technological divide," might be expected to have resulted in a pronounced appearance change (according to the paradigm change rule), denoting the beginning of a new technology era. It simply does not happen in the case of personal media communicators. On the contrary, when Apple introduced the iPhone, it did not even bother to show a distinct difference from the iPod Touch except by name.

26. THE SLATE AND WOOD TABLET OF THE 19TH CENTURY SCHOOL

The two are essentially indistinguishable in form. Is it the arrogant manifestation of Apple's brand market dominance? There certainly is a grain of truth in that. The other players in the market were almost doomed to follow the market leader.

I dare to suggest here another explanation. Others have already pointed out that Jonathan Ive, the Senior Vice President of Design at Apple, was heavily influenced by the German industrial designer Dieter Rams, and that iPhone appears to have been directly influenced by Rams' 1978 Braun calculator. Therefore, in strictly formal terms there is not any new visual message here. As for the iPad, the older and almost forgotten word "tablet" brings us back to the school children's slate of over a century ago, even down to the bezel's details and radii (fig. 26), though the original wood frame and slate were replaced by aluminum, plastic, and glass. It seems that Apple's design approach, after so many unique past designs, has one clear design message, based on Bauhaus' modern minimalism: the "i" products are timeless icons. However, we should not forget that in visual language terms that these interesting references to the near and far past escape most people today.

Convergence: do all roads lead to Rome?

As suggested earlier, personal media communicators are Swiss Army Knife products. Their emphasis on content and absence of physical controls in favor of touch gestures makes a product designer's nightmare come true: a featureless product; a chameleon—"tell me what you want to do and I will change accordingly." No wonder, then, that the industry calls this approach "behind-the-glass design."

As far as I am aware, assimilation of different evolutionary classes into a single class does not occur in Darwinian natural evolution. Branching like a tree, and the extinction of unsuccessful branches, are patterns mirrored by natural evolution.

Johnny Chung Lee, a Ph.D. in human-computer Interaction and a Google researcher, previously of Microsoft Kinect fame, suggests a concrete evolutionary trend. In his well-publicized lecture *Myth of the Dying Mouse*, Lee states, "The mouse and keyboard are not going away, and there's no such thing as convergence." He argues that we are now in the

In this case here, it seems that teleology rules. Teleology is a philosophical account that holds that final causes exist in nature; in our words, the end result is unconsciously predefined at the beginning. How did the different product families know to gradually metamorphose into one plain-form product class? On a higher level of design thinking we may ask, Is it the age of convergence?

So, are most of the roads leading to the demise of diversity? I would like to say, "No." This is against the way culture works. If diversity is not provided by the electronics firm themselves, we will see the proliferation of personal covers and skins. That is already happening. If you investigate the charted development of personal media communicators at the

age of specialization; professional requirements and different personal usages necessitate a variety of tools. In terms of input and output devices, there cannot be one scheme that will cover the gamut of computer devices from the hand-held to professional computer to the even larger-size media screen (fig 27).

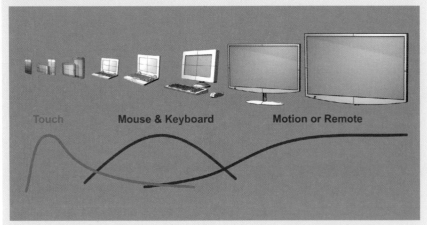

27. OPTIMAL INPUT DEVICE VS. SCREEN SIZE (FOLLOWING JOHNNY CHUNG LEE)

beginning of this case study you will find that, in spite of what now seems to be a general convergence of most personal media communicators into one branch. After the initial convergence excitement, we may encounter a certain degree of backlash into an array of portable products, dedicated to different tasks but sharing functions and operating systems across the array, creating a flexible divergence. Judging from the recent ultra-laptops, industrial design will even take a more fashionable role, not unlike handbags. The proximity rule applies here.

It is only logical that these size varieties will continue in parallel for a while. In the evolutionary chart, I divided them into three closely related evolutionary lines, akin to giants and pigmies in the human race. The smaller one, which I label "basic communicator," will still differentiate itself as a more practical telephone. The middle one is the "all-in-one" group of gesture-based communicators in a range of display screen sizes. And at the other end, I grouped all the high-power-plus-keyboard portables. For lack of a better term, I call them professional portables (the word portables will eventually disappear). Naturally there will be much form and capability exchange between these groups, and boundaries will continue to be ill defined. Evolving shared operating systems will allow such cross-pollination.

And what may lie ahead...

Going back in time just five years, we would not have guessed at all how fast and how soon the personal media communicator would develop. Who could have thought that kindergarten kids will be able to intuitively operate and play on these clever devices? Consequently, any discussion of future development of personal media communicators should be taken with more than a grain of skepticism. Seeing recently some amazing academic research on advanced human-computer integration, I am certain that the industry-leading players are investing heavily in the next big things of the future. Deducing, albeit conservatively, where the next generation of personal media communicators may evolve brings several possible general directions to mind.

The first possible direction will resolve the conflict inherent in sizing: "smaller is better for portability" conflicts with the interest in ever-larger screens essential to visual quality and content legibility. This may be done by folding or collapsing the screen, possibly using a soft screen that can be rolled. Soft folding will bring about a new form factor. We already see in the market new ways of incorporating detachable keyboards and docking stations doubling as screen covers.

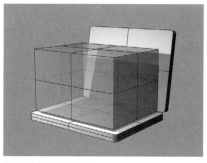

28. A SCHEMATIC PATENT DRAWING FOR A 3D MEDIA MACHINE. THE DRAWN BOX IS VIRTUAL, OF COURSE

The second possible direction is the splitting of media communicator devices into separate elements: a small one for quick access, and a larger one for intensive work. We already see pioneering approaches to the smaller devices in Google Glass and communicator watches. As glasses and other bodily adornments, they will allow a large variety of form solutions. What will happen to the larger device is less predictable. Will it be the same smartphone or tablet, part of a purse, or even a wearable computer?

The third possible direction is one that will concentrate on experience enhancement, following the same route of 3D movies in the theaters. In formal terms this will require new definitions as to how to suggest a virtually occupied three-dimensional space, be it physical or a virtual design solution (fig. 28, as taken from a recent US patent application. Patents already applied by major players in the field give us a hint of future concepts.) Figure 29 is a designer's concept of how such a 3D space may look.

The fourth possible direction is the almost total obliteration of any physical manifestation of the personal communicator by means of movement toward virtual reality or augmented reality, creating an almost total immersion experience. In such a direction, the only physical manifestation left may be a computerized eye display,

29. CONCEPT FOR MACBOOK 2020 BY TOMMASO GECCHELIN. BACK TO A (VIRTUAL) TOOLBOX?

indistinguishable from today's fashion glasses.

And further away lies the possibility of a totally different product realm. Science (no longer just fiction) already investigates the possibility of implanting electrodes directly into our brains.

Vertical versus horizontal orientation

An interesting sidetrack to this case study, still quite important in terms of physical form manifestation, is the spatial orientation of the products in this class. In order to attract attention to the question of a vertical orientation versus a horizontal one, I placed a small orientation signifier next to most products in the personal communicator evolution chart in the end of this case study.

Ergonomically, hand-held objects that are slightly longer than our palm are naturally held like a soap bar, hence in a vertical orientation. This is almost the rule with mobile telephones (following the iconic cord telephone handset that was held vertically in use but that sat horizontally in the cradle when not in use. Is it also a semantic indication that mobile phones are always on? In portable telephones, orientation was naturally resolved. But in other content-oriented devices, there is often a vertical-versus-horizontal conflict. The two common content orientations (formats) we are familiar with are the written or printed page (almost always vertical) and the movie screen (always horizontal and even widening in proportion over time, as does the HD format). The only "indifferent" media is the photographic print, which may be by choice vertical or horizontal. We can trace this duality in our computer printer's terminology that labels orientation as portrait or landscape. The Polaroid format was

a neutral square, though printed on a vertical card. Nowhere had this conflict manifested itself more than in computer screens. I have mentioned earlier that the computer's CRT screen, rather than adopt the anticipated typed-page orientation, "chose" to follow its cousin, the television screen, which itself was a re-embodiment of the horizontal movie screen.

There was no reason for a vertical-versus-horizontal conflict in the audio media players. They could be held or played in any orientation in space. The only time the orientation dilemma arose was with stereo loudspeakers, but that was resolved with miniaturization to earphones.

The more still-image and video content was ingested into portable devices, the more the screen orientation conflict became a problem, leading to a screen rotation, multi-directional solution, as manifested in orientation sensitive detectors in Apple's "i" series family. Unfortunately, this dual orientation further contributes to the already featureless nature of recent media communicators.

Form evolution of personal media communicators

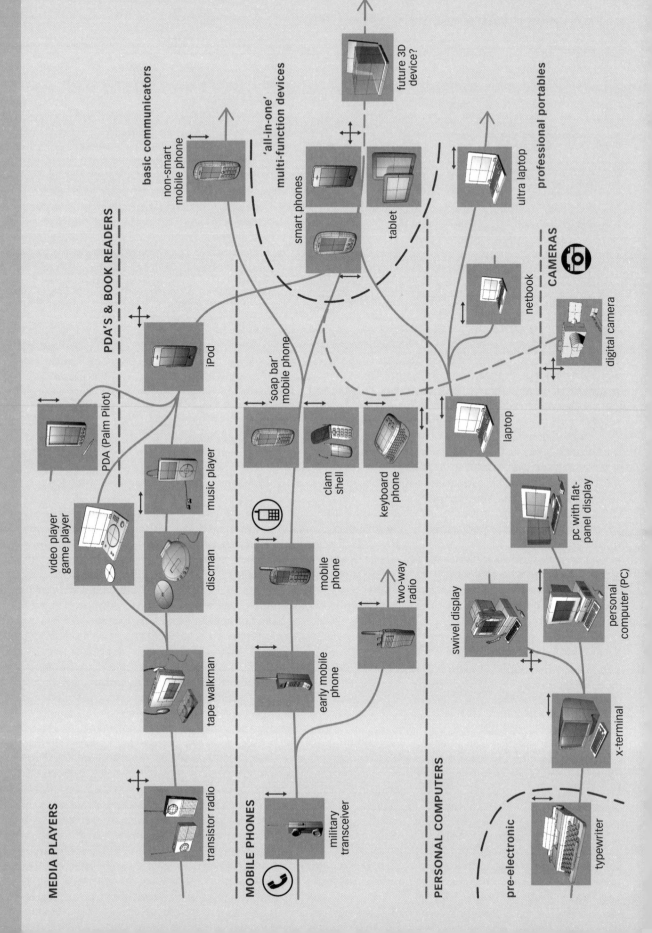

MEDIA PLAYERS

transistor radio

tape walkman

discman

music player

video player
game player

PDA (Palm Pilot)

iPod

PDA'S & BOOK READERS

MOBILE PHONES

military
transceiver

two-way
radio

early mobile
phone

mobile
phone

'soap bar'
mobile phone

clam
shell

keyboard
phone

smart phones

'all-in-one'
multi-function devices

non-smart
mobile phone

basic communicators

tablet

future 3D
device?

ultra laptop

professional portables

netbook

CAMERAS

laptop

digital camera

pc with flat-
panel display

swivel display

personal
computer (PC)

x-terminal

typewriter

pre-electronic

PERSONAL COMPUTERS

CASE STUDY 3
Faxes, Copiers, and Printers

If you investigate the diagram at the end of this chapter you will see a perplexing evolution picture: many cross tracks, continual technology-sharing between parallel lines, and frequent introductions of new technologies.

Faxes, copiers, and printers—once markedly different families— had in common the translation of an electronic page into a printed physical page, and vice-versa. This purpose did not change much over time, despite the repeated promises of the paperless office.

Today, these three families have been made digital and quite often act as input and output devices for personal computers. With a common output and universal technology share, we may infer that these product lines have so much in common that there should be a problem in visually distinguishing one line from the other. Surprisingly, this is not so. They still persistently present distinguishing visual marks that have been carried on from earlier ancestors.
In this case study, we will investigate why these device families act the same but still look different. One possible factor is that they are still very physical products, with particular electromechanical guts. Another factor may have something to do with the fact that sending a fax, copying a page from a book, and printing color 4x5 prints are quite different activities in our minds. Faxes, printers, and copiers are profoundly technology-driven. Any introduction of a newer and better technology into a preexisting product affects how it performs and how it looks. Since our theme is form development, I will often describe in a few words the kind of technology involved, but will not elaborate on it. So I apologize in case I omitted thermal printing, bubble inkjet technology, and fax protocols among the other technical topics.

Highlights

The products in question retain the recognized visual traits of their primary uses despite their shared technology, their common digital platforms, and their ability to act like each other.

Most defining archetypal traits are persisting continuations of past equipment probably because we consider sending a fax, printing a letter, or copying a document to be separate, distinctive tasks.

Innovations in these families were introduced in the corporate office. Therefore, office equipment design language strongly prevails.

Faxes, copiers, and printers are peripheral equipment. Makers come from different core businesses. Therefore, there is little incentive for visual coordination with other computer products.

The location and direction of the paper trays plays a significant role in defining whether what we see is a printer, a fax machine, or a copier.

The tendency for highly specialized equipment exists concurrently with general purpose equipment. All-in-one machines tend to be relatively inexpensive and are designed to be "one size fits all."

Fax machines are declining and are replaced by other devices. It is probably a breed soon to vanish.

3D printing is a new concept yet without an established archetypal form. As 3D printers reflect a definite paradigm shift they may look fundamentally different in that they are the only printers in which seeing what is created inside may be compulsory.

Form evolution of faxes, copiers & printers

SEE ENLARGED DIAGRAM ON PAGE 117

Early printers

Let us begin by investigating printers, since they have the longest evolutionary roots, being the offspring of the typewriter, the reigning office machine of the pre-digital 20th century.

As you may recall from Case study 2, the mechanical typewriter and its follower, the electromechanical typewriter IBM Selectric, had the same basic form factor: an inseparable keyboard and a visible roller carriage that holds a sheet of paper against printing heads, surrounded by one exterior shell with openings in it. It only seems logical that the first printing-only device, the dot matrix printer, will take the form of the recognized electromechanical typewriter with the omission of keyboard. In fact, the stand-alone printer had a much older parent, already in use in the mid-19th century, the teleprinter. Also called teletypewriter or teletype, the teleprinter is an electromechanical typewriter used to communicate typed messages through telegraph wires. The teleprinter, not commonly seen in public, replaced the Morse code telegraph in Western Union offices and in newspaper's newsrooms.

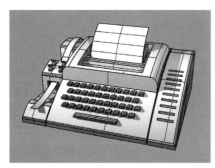

1. THE TELEPRINTER WAS A RATHER UNGAINLY, COMPLEX ELECTRIC TYPEWRITER

The teleprinter (fig. 1) looked quite like the familiar typewriter with a continuous paper feed in lieu of separate sheets and an attached punched tape input device. In archetypal terms it was a leftover from the telegraph days. The teleprinter's contributions to subsequent computer printers were the concept of printing from a remote location and the use of a continuous paper feed. Rather than the teleprinter's paper roll, the early dot matrix printers' continuous paper was a flat stack, folded back and forth on itself, with the perforated strips on both sides. A steel printer stand was often used to accommodate both the printer and the large paper stack. Since the dot matrix printing head was quite noisy, it was often covered with a soundproof enclosure. Dot matrix printing quality was quite poor.

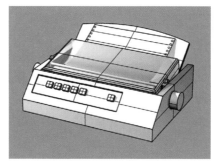

2. THE OKI DOT MATRIX PRINTER IS STILL AROUND IN SPITE OF RATHER OBSOLETE TECHNOLOGY

Dot matrix printers were to be found in the dedicated mainframe computer rooms of corporations and shared in the open space office, parallel to the office copier. A smaller version of the robust office dot matrix printer became common in small offices, and next to personal computers (fig. 2). Note the familiar carriage and the external carriage advance knob on the side. Even without a keyboard, it indicated clearly that it was a kind of a typewriter.

The main drawback of the dot matrix printer (other than the nerve-straining noise) was that it could print only prescribed alphanumeric symbols. Crude pictures could be made only with many x's. The computer screen's increasing use of quality graphics indicated that the days of the dot matrix printer were soon to be over, except in the accounting department. The time was ripe for graphic printing.

Graphic printing was previously in use in a specialized niche, as pen plotters for architectural and engineering drawings. An ink-drafting pen was moved around to mark on paper along x- and y-axes. It used what is called vector printing, the pen running along a computer prescribed route. Pens of different thicknesses and colors could be substituted. There were two versions of plotters: a flat plotter for small drawings (fig.3) and a drum plotter for large-scale drawings (not shown here). As plotters were used only in professional environments, their form was not commonplace. Interestingly, the drum component of drum pen plotters kept reappearing in later printers such as the laser printer.

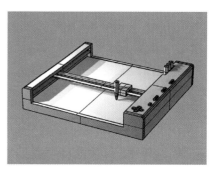

3. DESKTOP X-Y PEN PLOTTERS WERE COMMON IN ENGINEERING OFFICES

Inkjet printers

The ever-popular inkjet printer is in many ways a compact evolution of x-y pen plotter, spraying minute ink droplets rather than using a pen. The inkjet printer movement mechanism is simple, small, and quiet, but it required an increasingly sophisticated printing head and means of registering each printing run to the previous one in order to print a complete image in several back and forth runs. Very soon full color printing took hold, using separate printing ink containers. The external shell of the inkjet printer could have taken several differing forms, since the internal mechanical elements occupied a relatively small space. But the most common convention is the version with the input and output paper trays in front, the latter above the former (fig.4).

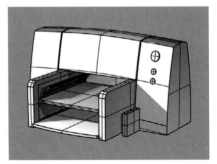

4. A TYPICAL INKJET PRINTER HAD A HOUSING TO COVER THE INK SPRAYING MECHANISM

We will see that the location and direction of the paper trays in relation to the main body will play an important role in defining whether we face a printer, a fax machine, or a copier. I will elaborate on this later. The paper advance carriage is still there but hidden inside the housing now, without any external hint.

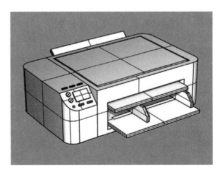

5. THE ARCHETYPAL PHOTO JET PRINTER IS RATHER BOXY AND BLACK IN COLOR, OFTEN WITH A LASER COPIER PLATE ON TOP

Inkjet printing became popular in the small office and in domestic use due to its image printing quality, small footprint, and low cost. But in due course, inject printers were separated into two different branches according to usage. One branch is dedicated to high-resolution photo printing, thanks to ever-increasing inkjet technology sophistication. The basic inkjet printer configuration remains the same, but with fewer external physical parts. The covering skin is now lower and deeper in its proportions relative to the multi-purpose inkjet printer. It is typically black in color, which is not only a move away from the previous office light grey but befitting anything that is associated with photography (fig. 5). The sophisticated electronics component is pronounced visually by integrating a small LED image preview screen. The remainder of the sophisticated elements required to print quality color images is delegated to the photo-processing software.

The second track is in the all-in-one inkjet printer, to be discussed later in detail. (I should also mention here that there are intermediary versions of inkjet printers in that many photo-quality printers also have an image copier incorporated on top of the printer.)

Laser printers

The laser printer is an entirely different breed, different from any other image-making technique. It is a desktop derivative of the office xerographic process copier, dedicated to printing only. With such a different beginning from other printers it only makes sense to assume it may also have a different form.

The laser printer, introduced by Xerox in 1971, was designed with the office environment in mind. The laser printer is a reliable high-volume printer with a fine quality output and never-fading prints, though (at the time) only in black and white. As the various stages of the xerographic process are of no interest to the user, their complexity is concealed under an undistinguished cube-like cover. Only when we have to change toner are we faced with some of the intricate innards. The box form design is copied from the ubiquitous office copier. So how can we tell what it is by its form? A printer or let's say an office telephone exchange. There are two visual signifiers that tells us what it is and what it does: the frontal paper supply drawer, borrowed from the office copier and by the output tray bed on top (fig. 6). These are the same signifying directions already established in other printers. The input and output trays of the printer are facing the front and not the left and right sides of the office copier.

6. A DESKTOP LASER PRINTER IS A PLAIN CUBE THAT HIDES WHAT IS INSIDE. ONLY THE TRAYS REVEAL WHAT IT IS

7. THE EARLY HOME LASER PRINTERS: HP'S LASERJET 5L (LEFT) AND APPLE'S APPLEWRITER (RIGHT) HAD DIFFERENT FEED AND OUTPUT SOLUTIONS

Fax machines

I do not mean to give the impression that the laser printer design has reached its accepted form configuration that easily. There were several initial printer versions that were designed quite differently. HP's Laserjet 5L (fig. 7, left) had vertical input and output paper trays, probably in order to reduce tabletop footprint. Apple Computer's version had input and output trays on either sides. In an early version, the AppleWriter II, the outside form reflected the cylindrical form of the internal xerographic process drum (fig. 7 right). Eventually the office environment cube shape described earlier stuck. These unique design solutions were outward manifestations of the continuation but differentiation rule. The laser printer

8. THE POPULAR PRINTER ICON IS ABOUT PAPER TRAYS

will almost always be taller from the low photo inkjet printer and if it takes a slightly rounder design, it will be done on a different plane than photo inkjet printers. In spite of these differences between the designs of the laser and inkjet printers, the accepted symbol (icon) for printers makes the most of the paper trays' location relative to the printer box (fig. 8).

The color advantage of the inkjet printer prompted laser printer manufacturers to come out with color laser printers. As the color laser printer is more complex, it is visibly much taller that the black and white laser printer; thus, its characteristic visual signifier is similar, but more upright (fig 9). Being expensive, and thus less common, color laser printers do not have a generally recognized image yet.

There are several recent attempts to get away from the plain boxy look of the laser printers, usually by bending its form, like a bent or twisted rubber eraser (fig. 10).

The origins of the early fax machine, then named facsimile machine (only later shortened to fax) are quite parallel to that of the teleprinter. Both used telephone lines, but the facsimile machine was designed to remotely transmit images. We often see in old crime movies FBI agents waiting for a mug shot to emerge out of a strange contraption, the early facsimile machine. Working like an earthquake seismograph, the reading sensor and the writing pen traveled along a paper-covered drum, though at a closer distance (fig. 11). The image was converted at the transmitting facsimile machine into sound signals that were transmitted and picked up at the receiving end by a telephone handset placed on the receiving facsimile machine.

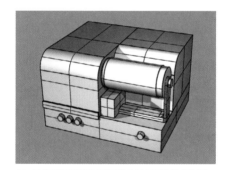

11. THE EARLY FACSIMILE MACHINE READ AND WROTE ON A DRUM, SIMILAR TO THE FIRST PHONOGRAPH OR THE SEISMOMETER

The fax machine we are more accustomed to came about in the mid-1970s. It united the facsimile modus operandi with the design of the telephone. The new fax machine looked like a common multiline office telephone, always with a sloping front and with the handset cradle on the side and the telephone key dialer on front (fig. 12). Technically it could be used as, and even be mistaken for, an office telephone, if not for the addition of two trays on top (one for feeding the outgoing documents and one for fresh paper supply to be printed by incoming faxes) and an

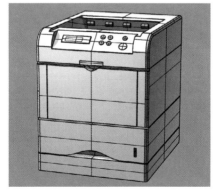

9. THE COLOR LASER PRINTER HAS THE SAME FOOTPRINT AS THE BLACK AND WHITE ONE, BUT IS MUCH TALLER

10. THE SOFTER "BENT RUBBER ERASER FORM" OF THE XEROX PHASER 856 COLOR LASER PRINTER

additional horizontal slot in front for the original documents to come out. The fax machine used a photosensitive reading bar and a disposable black wax-coated roll to transfer the electric image to the paper.

12. THE FAMILIAR INCLINED FACE AND PHONE CRADLE OF THE FAX MACHINE, TWO INPUT TRAYS AND A COMMON OUTPUT TRAY

13. THE FAX ICON RELIES ON TELEPHONE HANDSET AND DIALING KEYBOARD CUES

14. THE LASER FAX HAS A FUSED FORM OF A LASER PRINTER (BOTTOM) AND FAX MACHINE (TOP)

This form configuration became the classic archetype for fax machines (fig. 13). This archetypal form did not change much over time. Newer heavier-duty laser fax machine (fig.14) carried over the sloping front face with the same input-output trays, albeit no longer with a phone handset and instead placed on top of a well-recognized laser printer form.

The fax machine as we know it is a vanishing breed. Faxes are commonly sent, received, and stored by software programs on our personal computers, supported by a nearby copier or scanner. The all-in-one printer still has explicit fax capabilities and even carries over the familiar fax panel, but the freestanding fax machine will no longer be a recognized feature in the small or home office.

Copiers

Copying documents is as old as writing itself. For centuries copying was done by hand. The invention of printing put an end to manuscript copying but the need for copying specific letters and documents only increased. In the late 19th century, duplicating was accomplished by inserting thin carbon paper between several paper sheets placed together in the typewriter. Photography was often recruited in order to duplicate original images. Later, fast-development photochemical processes were used instead. All these methods were quite crude and time consuming.

Xerography (or electrophotography) is a dry photocopying technique invented by Chester Carlson. The first commercial copier, the Xerox 914 (fig. 15), was released by Haloid/Xerox in 1960. Xerox's domination of the patent and consequently the market made the name

15. THE XEROX 914 REVOLUTIONIZED OFFICE WORK BUT WAS HUGE IN SIZE. IT BROUGHT ABOUT THE "COPIER ROOM."

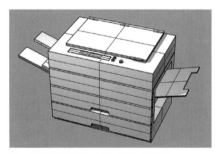

16. THE PERVASIVE OFFICE COPIER EPITOMIZED THE OFFICE EQUIPMENT LOOKS, NOT TO MENTION THE BEIGE COLOR

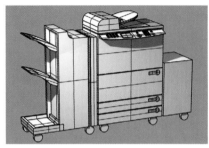

17. AUTOMATIC OFFICE COPIER/SORTER

18. THE COPIER ICONS ALWAYS SHOW THE SLANTED FEED AND OUTPUT SORTING TRAYS

Xerox almost synonym with copying.

The xerographic process is quite complex to comprehend. It encompasses several distinct steps: first reflecting the original image on an electrostatic charged metal drum by optical means; then an even spreading of fine black powder (toner) over the drum's surface. The powder adheres only to static charged areas on the drum. Then the machine transfers the powder image to a sheet of paper. And in the end, it fuses the toner into the paper by heating it. Not surprisingly then, the Xerox 914 was quite a monster with a rather incoherent experimental prototype form, as often happens to blue-sky inventions. One prominent external element was carried over to subsequent models: the glass plate and its hinged cover (seen on the left of the photo). The glass plate and the hinged cover are still universal cues of copying.

Subsequent models of the Xerox copying machine succeeded in packing the copier into one coherent and recognized form (fig. 16), with a top glass plate, a hinged cover, and a paper feed tray on one side and copied paper collector on the other side, both slanted relative to the main body. The elongated box with the two wings became the iconic image of the copier (see also fig. 18).

Eventually, the growing demand for batch copying added an automatic feeder of originals on top, large capacity paper supply drawers underneath, a large sorter, and even a stapler on the output side. The resulting design took a modular configuration, the recognized copier in the middle flanked by sorter and paper stack units (fig. 17). The technical solutions helped in establishing a definite visual product differentiation through the location of paper trays. Printers commonly use frontal trays but copiers use side trays (using the continuation but differentiation rule).

Eventually, copying became increasingly digital by networking the copier as a printer. Image sensing replaced optical projection, allowing images to be digitally enlarged, reduced, and corrected. As previously, none of these innovations manifested in the external form of the copier.

Copiers belonged, for a long time, to the realm of the big office. The advent of digital copying provided an opportunity, both in reduced price and physical size, for the shift of copiers to domestic settings, by integrated it into a home inkjet printer without actually changing the printer's appearance (see fig. 5). This development made functional sense as the printer turned into an input/output device.

19. THE CORPORATE MASS PRINTER IS NO LONGER A PART OF THE OFFICE VISUAL ENVIRONMENT

Concurrently, digital copying and printing also took a turn to large-scale solutions in the form of the corporate printer that produces millions of pseudo personal letters, monthly bills, or short runs of in-house book publishing (fig. 19). The corporate printer is already a highly specialized machine, no longer recognized as a common image.

All-in-one machines

It was realistic to predict, since there was such an exchange of technologies between copiers, printers, and fax machines, that eventually they will merge into one. That makes economic sense. Also, no one ever had enough room for these three separate products on a home desk. It was a natural form merger. In the mind's eye copiers, printers, and faxes are considered to be one family of input and output devices.

The all-in-one product (fig. 20) borrows a little from each of its contributors: the recognized copier document feeder

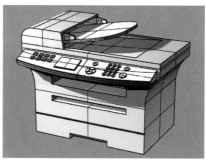

20. A TYPICAL ALL-IN-ONE MACHINE FORM REFLECTS THE FORM OF ALL THREE PREDECESSORS

stays on top; the familiar fax keyboard combined with copier controls in front; and the input/output trays of the inkjet printer image remained underneath and in front. We may learn from this retention of recognized element that it is still important for us to visually recognize each of the involved partners in the all-in-one machine. The all-in-one machine is not the ultimate solution that will end once and for all the previous separate lines of products. Usually each component has to yield in performance for the sake of the others components, similar in the synthesizing of the off-road vehicle with the fast hard-surface car. The results are a compromise.

Three-dimensional printers

21. THE MAKERBOT REPLICATOR CAGE TALKS IN THE LANGUAGE OF HOME SELF-ASSEMBLY. A PLYWOOD FRAME ADDS TO THAT IMAGE

Three-dimensional printing, professionally referred to as stereolithography, is at present an entirely separate equipment domain dedicated to industrial design and engineering prototyping. Except for the word "printer," it has had nothing in common with the office or the home environments. It is possible that the two separate domains will cross paths in the future. As we have seen before, engineering plotters were the basis for the inkjet printer mechanism (still 2-dimensional). Movies and display screens are turning into 3D, as are virtual reality games. Recently, MakerBot designed an inexpensive 3D printer called the Replicator to the DIY (do it yourself) market (fig. 21). As prices go down, desktop-size 3D printers will be common peripherals next to our PCs.

3D printers are quite similar in principle to the inkjet printer. Rather than using ink, most use a fast curing heat melted liquid plastic. Each printing head pass, controlled by x-y-z moving mechanism, gradually builds a three-dimensional object, be it a sculpture, a toy, or a functional one-of-a-kind product. The object itself is designed with modeling software on a home computer and the instructions are sent directly to the printer.

22. STRATASYS' UPRINT-3D-PRINTER MAY BE THE WAY THE FUTURE 3D PRINTER FORM WILL TAKE SHAPE

In common two-dimensional printing, you wait for the printed page to come out of the printer. Since 3D printing is a slow process and involves chemicals and fumes, the printer may eventually take the form of an external rectangular shell with an access door and a viewing window (fig 22). It is still too early to expect an accepted archetypal form of the 3D printer but it will come eventually. Since build-your-own-design is a real groundbreaking occurrence, we may expect a concurrent visual paradigm shift form to materialize.

To me, the idea that a printer's working innards are so exposed, becoming the center of attention, is something that never happened previously in the paper printer family. This is already a form paradigm shift. In terms of form we may see a close similarity to the microwave oven. We want to see what's cooking.

Several collective observations

Let me begin with the observation that we can still perceive a strong office environment influence on all three product lines discussed here. Most inventions were applied first in the corporate office and there acquired their inherent visual language: boxy, visually flavorless, and, of course, ubiquitously beige or off-white. Only photo-quality inkjet printers made an attempt towards a different design language, possibly taken from the photography world, to include, for example, an overall black overall color.

The location and direction of the paper trays in each of the three lines (though based on historical technological solutions and rarely on user interface considerations) play significant roles in defining whether we see in front of us a printer, a fax machine, or a copier. So paper movement and direction (note that is the common denominator of all three lines) play a major visual identification role in combination with characteristic design details of each product line.

In spite of shared technology, a common digital platform, and the capability of most current equipment to double as a printer/copier/fax machine, the recognized visual traits of the primary use of each line of product remain strong. You cannot mistake an office copier as anything else except for what it is, even if you can use it as a printer controlled by your PC. That insistence on archetypal form character-

istics is analogous to what happens in the camera family; you can take movies in a stills camera or snapshots in movie camera, but you know by looks what the principal use of each camera is. The all-in-one machine cannot even hide the three contributing family lines' visual characteristics. Will this differentiation last? I am not sure. On one hand, we are at an age of equipment specialization. We prefer the best equipment for its purpose. On the other hand, who needs three boxes on your desk? They take more space than our desktop-replacing laptop.

The manufacturers of copiers, printers, and faxes come from different core businesses. For example, Xerox was always in the office copier environment, Canon (printers) came from the photography area, and Panasonic (fax machines) from the telephony area. I am not sure if there is one manufacturer that specializes in making all three product lines; but two out of the three, yes.

An additional hindrance is semantic. In the home office environment all three product lines are considered to be peripherals to the computer. Therefore, unlike a home theater system, fax/printer/copier is never considered as a single visual family. People may consider and buy each peripheral separately. There seems no chance for a visual family coordination. Even companies that make both computers and printers—HP comes first to mind—they are made by different divisions and designed by different designers. Xerox copiers and Xerox laser printers are different breeds, unless you consider the office off-white color as coordinated branding. I recall only one company that consistently tried to coordinate its printers' image with the rest of its products: Apple Computer, though it does not sell printers any longer.

Will the paperless office concept ever happen and make all these paper-to-electronics equipment redundant?

Form evolution of faxes, copiers & printers

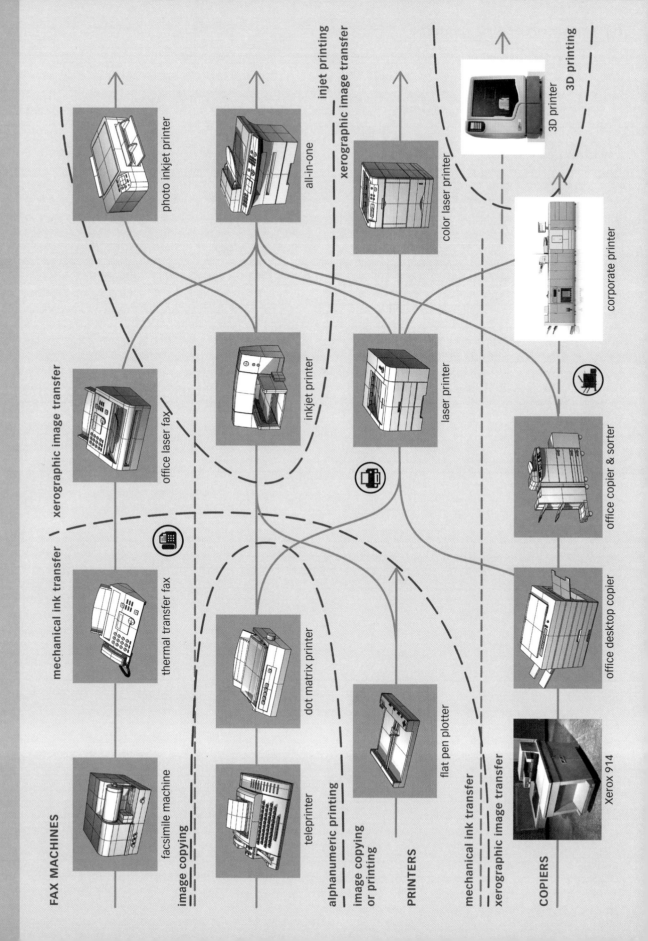

FAX MACHINES

facsimile machine

thermal transfer fax

office laser fax

photo inkjet printer

mechanical ink transfer

xerographic image transfer

teleprinter

dot matrix printer

inkjet printer

all-in-one

inkjet printing

xerographic image transfer

alphanumeric printing

flat pen plotter

laser printer

color laser printer

3D printer

3D printing

image copying or printing

PRINTERS

mechanical ink transfer

Xerox 914

office desktop copier

office copier & sorter

corporate printer

COPIERS

xerographic image transfer

image copying

CASE STUDY 4
Television Screens

The home television screen is a highly popular media entity. With many competing manufacturers, it is reasonable to expect that form designs of television screens will be quite common and highly visible. But it is not so, either because the technology is such a primary form factor or the media is the message; the screen is merely a window to contents. It seems that both factors play a role in gradual form dematerialization of the television screen. Semantically, we should be reminded that the word "screen" originated in the theater. It is the partition supposed to mentally disappear in order for us to focus on the show.

This chapter will plot the development of the television screen from a masterpiece of living room furniture to a mere picture on the wall.

From here onwards the words television and TV will denote the appliance used on the receptor side of the media.

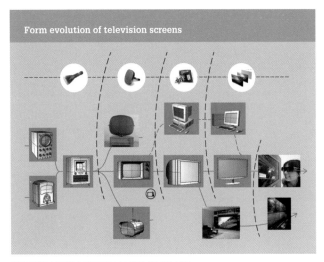

Form evolution of television screens

SEE ENLARGED DIAGRAM ON PAGE 123

Highlights

Technology—specifically, the electronic means of picture presentation, from the cathode ray tube to LED—has been central in defining how a television set looks.

The evolution of television screens followed a single route. Deviations from the main route, such as experimental forms, portable TVs, and rear projection TVs, were short lived.

There has been a clear path from a small screen within a large enclosure to an ever-larger screen within a minimal enclosure, from a boxy enclosure to the thinnest sheet possible.

There has been a continual change from a spherical display face to a flat, rectangular one; from an almost round screen to a movie-like screen.

The end result of form development is a substantial dematerialization of form, from a strong physical entity to an anonymous two-dimensional wall-hanging rectangle.

Television screens are now just the large-scale terminus of a gamut of digital media equipment sharing the same contents.

Extrapolation of form development of the television screen may lead to a non-form "picture wall." Will future glasses-free 3D imagery bring about form change?

Early television sets

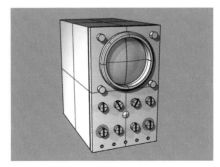

1. A TYPICAL INDUSTRIAL OSCILLOSCOPE

In the first half of the twentieth century the radio—wireless sound transmission—ruled supreme. While in the motion picture industry voice was a later addition to the picture itself, it was the other way around in the broadcasting industry, which searched for a way to send pictures over the ether to the radio. Military technologies such as RADAR and SONAR and scientific oscilloscopes (fig.1), all developed rapidly between the world wars, providing a monochromatic visual representation on a cathode ray tube (CRT). CRTs were then quite small, with a circular face (still apparent in the way we use a fake revolving beam on modern RADAR screens). Concurrently, the invention of RCA's iconoscope allowed the conversion of a photographic image to an electronic signal that could be transmitted over the ether. The first regular TV broadcast began as early as 1931.

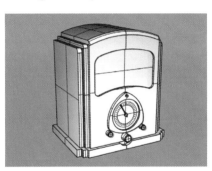

2. A RADIO RECEIVER HOUSED IN AN ART DECO WOODEN HOUSING. ONE OF MANY FURNITURE FORMS

Clearly, early television consoles were an integration of a CRT into the typical radio receiver of the time. As radios then were usually packaged in wooden boxes, the early television was packed in a much larger furniture-like console, making it a living room centerpiece, fit for the family to sit in front of it (fig.3). Legs were added to the console, to bring the screen to a height suitable for seated viewing. The round CRT face was placed behind a somewhat rectangular mask or bezel, an obvious reference to the movie screen. Some TV consoles had folding doors to cover the screen when not in use. These may have also borrowed from the theater or movie hall. In retrospect, it is quite surprising how diminutive was the size of the CRT in comparison to the wooden console—almost a peephole.

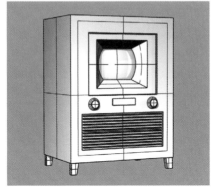

3. AN EARLY TELEVISION CONSOLE: A SMALL SCREEN IN A LARGE CABINET

The golden age of the television's physical form

The 1950s and 1960s were the decades where independent TV form explorations really took off. Technology advances improved the size and proportions of the CRT, bringing it closer in shape to the

4. AN EXPOSED CRT, THE 1950 PHILCO PREDICTA

5. SPACE AGE. THE PANASONIC TR-005 ORBITEL (KNOWN AS THE "FLYING SAUCER"), LATE 1960S

6. A CLASSIC TELEVISION SET

movie screen aspect ratio (the movie studios fought back with Cinemascope-wide proportions). As a result, the CRT screen became for the first time a dominant form factor. The previous wooden console furniture was split into two products, a TV set and a separately manufactured TV stand. Following space-age visual influences (at the height of the race to reach the moon) there were several bold explorations of form, such as taking the CRT totally out of the box, but they did not prevail for long (figs. 4 and 5).

Television sets became less and less furniture-like and were gradually acknowledged by designers to be what they really were: electronic equipment. Wood appliqué, if any, became minimal, usually imitating thin picture frames, but often completely replaced by modern plastics. Increasingly the well-recognized visual form of the TV set came about (fig. 6) with a large screen, a rectangular bezel around it, and two large channel switching knobs placed vertically to the right of the screen, all encased in a simple, unadorned rectangular box. Often a "V" type indoor antenna at the top indicated that this was a TV set (radio sets that had just one telescopic antenna). At last the television set got its recognized iconic form (fig.7).

7. A TV SET ICON

Regrettably it was a single-view form, only the front really counted. That was the beginning of what I refer to as the form dematerialization of the TV set, which may sound like a paradox since TV sets were quite deep and heavy then. When color TV technology was introduced, incorporating a sophisticated three-ray gun tube and an internal color mask, there was no external visual change whatsoever. A classic form tends to resist change (the design classic tenet).

Portable television sets

The 1970s brought about another spin-off to the home television set. Taking a television set out with you did not make much sense, with serious sun glare problems and short battery life, not to mention that small screens disagreed with the ongoing trend for larger and larger screens. But miniaturization was an engineering challenge and designers enjoyed the opportunity to deal with a TV set as an all-around sculptural form.

Clearly, early television consoles were an integration of a CRT into a typical radio receiver of the time.

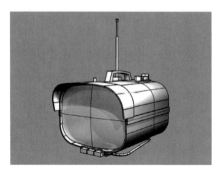

8. A TYPICAL PORTABLE TV CONFIGURATION. THE 8-INCH SCREEN-SIZE SONY ALL TRANSISTOR TV, 1960

9. THE BRIONVEGA ALGOL TV: A DESIGN CLASSIC DESIGNED BY RICHARD SAPPER AND MARCO ZANUSO IN THE 1960S

Some of the best designs milestones came out of Europe (Brionvega, fig. 9), and Japan, in an early sign of Sony's dedication to good design (fig. 8). Regrettably, the portability trend soon died out, perhaps substituted by non-portable small TVs in the bedroom. It is interesting to note that the acceptance of small screen viewing had to wait for several decades, until smart phones and tablets came about.

Flat and thin is better

In the 1990s the buzzword was a perfectly flat television screen. The CRT technology required to accomplish it was not simple. It might have been just a marketing ploy but it made sense in term of recalling the movie theater screen. Similarly, computer screens of the day, with similar flat CRT technology, emulated the printed page and the photograph.

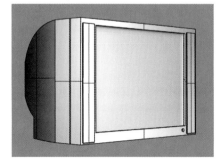

10. A FLAT SCREEN FRONT, BUT IN FACT DEEP AND HEAVY

Flat screens led to a minimal bezel or to having none at all. The introduction of stereo TV transmission brought about speakers on each side of the screen. Control knobs were hidden as controls were taken over by the remote tool. So the TV screen turned into a flat and totally symmetrical entity, with minimal details (fig 10). What was seen in front was a glass screen with barely a frame around it, analogous to framed paintings. As the actual depth was not to be mentioned, everything was done in order to hide the enormous CRT appendix in the back by minimizing the volume of the back cover and painting it in black; it is not an element to be seen. The flat-faced CRT was in fact faking flatness.

At that time the only practical way to make even larger screens was by projecting the image on a screen, the same way that movies are projected in the theater. There were two methods: front-projection and rear-projection. In front-projection, the projection device was an electro-optical projector lowered from the ceiling or placed on a table-sized small enough for home use. In rear-projection, the projection device was hidden within the same flat TV form seen in fig. 10. Both methods did not do well as picture quality and ambient lighting interference were problematic.

Current technology

Display technology advanced in great strides recently, resulting from the incorporation of innovative display physics: liquid crystal displays (LCD), plasma screens, light emitting diodes screens (LED), and organic LED screens. When cost and production issues were resolved, TV screens (and correspondingly computer screens) now indeed turned into just flat screens. Wider screens and high definition quality could match or even outdo the movie screen and bring the movie theater to the living room. There is no form left to deal with. The frame is minimal and commonly as black as the screen. It is only a question of time for the screen to be just one large sheet of glass illuminated all the way to the edge.

In fact, computer screens and TVs are the same, differing only in size. Computers play TV programs and movies (and conversely, TV screens may have their own computer). The only element, if any, left for designer to play with is the form

of the screen's pedestal, and that is solely relevant to desktop computer screens and small TVs (fig. 11). Most living room television screens are now wall mounted. The only design gimmick left to play with is the thickness of the TV screen, as if it really matters in a 50-inch screen. Reduced thickness is an engineering feat and not a form feat. It only makes practical sense in portable computers.

11. A FLAT SCREEN HD TV DISPLAY

As TV screens are evolving to be just the larger-sized end of a variety of digital screen devices (smartphones, tablets, laptop screens, TV screens, all sharing the same contents), the TV screen is losing its separate evolutionary line characteristics, even though it is one of the few products of real significance in defining the home interior environment, having the role of the family's evening campfire.

And what will come next

TV studios and rock concerts brought about super large screens made by splitting the image into a matrix of many flat TV screens. You are still able to notice the screens' edges, but that may not be possible to resolve. When an entire wall becomes a display—and it will—it will also be the end of the television screen as a physical entity. It will turn out to be moving wallpaper, the complete triumph of contents over context. Recall the ubiquitous feminine voice of the computer

12. AN 8-INCH LCD TV, BY NAOTO FUKASAWA, FOR PLUS MINUS ZERO

HAL 9000 in the movie *2001: A Space Odyssey*—it will be a visual world without a body.

Figure 12 is sort of a retro rebellion or comment against the increasing two-dimensionality of contemporary TV screens, incorporating it within a CRT-reminiscent enclosure. The designer, Naoto Fukasawa, says, "It's not about making things thin just because you can."

Is it a farewell to a product family? In terms of form, we can see that there has been a continual path from a small screen within a large physical enclosure to an ever-large screen within a minimal enclosure, from a boxy enclosure to the thinnest depth, from an almost round screen to a wide aspect ratio, movie-like screen—a "moving picture wall" (fig. 13).

Will there be a form revival stemming from the semantic context of three-dimensional televisions or will form manifest itself only in the 3D glasses worn by the spectators (fig. 14)? It is fascinating to consider a stage space allocated for 3D action, not unlike boxing ring ropes.

13. A CONTEMPORARY MULTI-SCREEN IMAGE WALL

14. ADVERTISEMENT FOR PANASONIC STEREOSCOPIC 3D IMAGES TELEVISION SCREEN

Form evolution of television screens

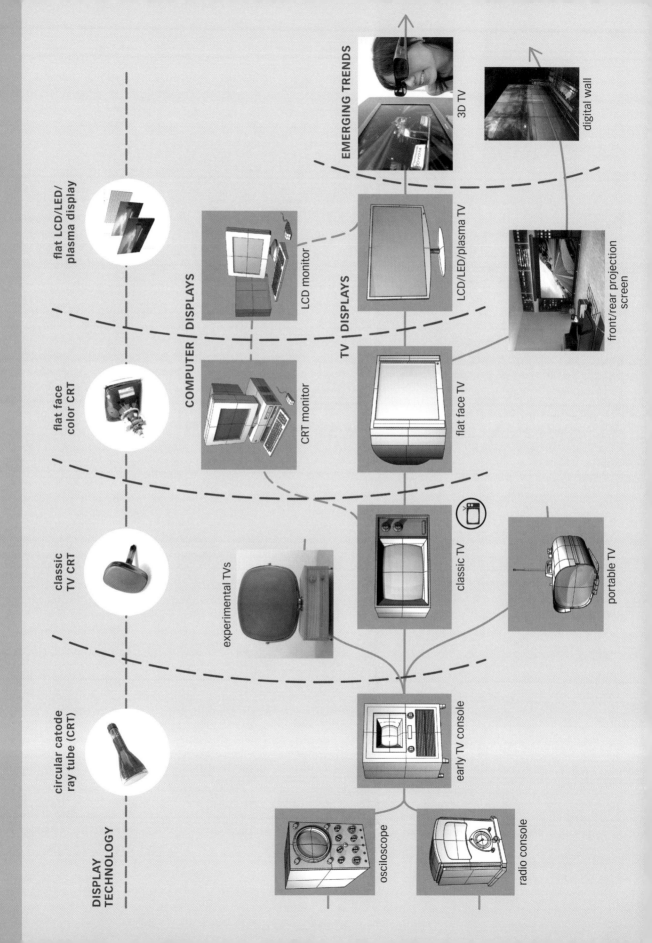

DISPLAY TECHNOLOGY

circular catode ray tube (CRT)

classic TV CRT

flat face color CRT

flat LCD/LED/ plasma display

COMPUTER | DISPLAYS

CRT monitor

LCD monitor

TV | DISPLAYS

osciloscope

radio console

early TV console

experimental TVs

classic TV

portable TV

flat face TV

LCD/LED/plasma TV

front/rear projection screen

EMERGING TRENDS

3D TV

digital wall

CASE STUDY 5
Home Entertainment

Home entertainment is the present-day term, in lieu of the previous home theater, previously stereo, before that hi-fi (high fidelity) and before that radio and phonograph. Home entertainment is a catch-all term for equipment that allows you to stream your on-demand movies, arrange your playlist, watch your photo album, browse the internet, video get-together with friends, play interactive games and ever search for new gadgets that may connect to your system and enhance your experience.

This products line is a good example of a family that, with few exceptions, did not establish a coherent form archetype (unless you assume that boxy contours are unique to this family).

Why? Is it because this particular field has changed immensely in a short time span? Is it because so many names and terms have been in use to define various elements of the family, or the words components and system permitted assembling non-form-related elements according to personal preference? Is it because engineering innovation took priority to user-friendly design (recall the then notorious programming the VCR impediment)? Or is the cause even more profound, as literally you close your eyes in order to listen? So the bottom line is "the more content is offered, the less clear is the language of form".

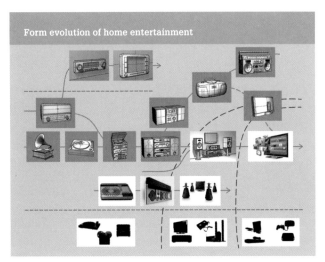

Form evolution of home entertainment

SEE ENLARGED DIAGRAM ON PAGE 131

Highlights

Home entertainment systems had continually evolved in time, new components added, sometimes replacing old ones. Sometimes clustered together, sometimes placed apart. Continual expansion and change may lead to an eclectic attitude.

Eclectic approach means that components chosen from diverse vendors prevent the establishment of a coherent visual language.

As purpose of systems and names of components tended to ever change, consequently not allowing for semantic coherence. Same attitude reflected in equipment's panels, where no user recognized layout prevailed

Easiest way to put together disparate components is to design of similarly shaped boxes, leading to unclear function identification.

At early evolution stage, input devices were visually easily recognised (record player, reel to reel tape, radio receiver). Gradually they vanished, replaced by hidden "in box" non-descript devices.

Output devices (loudspeakers, TV screen) became spatially separated but kept strong rectilinear form. In some cases loudspeakers boxes exposed a semantically recognized loudspeaker conical form.

Several design based firms invested in creating a coherent components' design language but failed to influence the on-going trend. They mostly catered to exclusive consumers.

Formal language was recognized again when components were grouped together into one definitive entity – portable stereo and car radios.

Due to increased functionality, variety and complexity, it seems that future trends will concentrate on senses, probably leading to ephemeral physical elements.

The early days of audio

Photography, which permitted our great-grandparents to record faces and events and keep them in albums and on the wall, was society's first modern recorded media. Early films, though quite popular, dictated public projection facilities and were not watched at home. The first true home entertainment systems were of black vinyl records and the phonograph, the gramophone, or the patephone—three different names, but actually the same device invented by Thomas Edison.

1. AN ACOUSTIC PHONOGRAPH

It was a purely mechanical acoustic device. In spite of the different labels given to the devices, their black round records, winding handles, and conspicuous horns immediately produced a powerful visual archetype (fig. 1), later immortalized by "his master's voice," RCA's long-standing advertisement campaign in which a dog listens to a phonograph.

The invention of the radio tube, wireless transmission, headphones, and loudspeakers brought home the prevalent radio. Photos of a family sitting around the radio listening to a popular radio drama became very common. Soon the phonograph's sound was amplified by electronic means and the phonograph was frequently connected to the radio box. Even after the technology and form abandoned the acoustical horn, the circle-within-a-rectangle shape was a very recognized image, unchanged even by later introductions of long playing records and automatic record changers (fig. 2). Home radios, almost always encased in wooden furniture, but sometimes in plastics (Bakelite), had universally common controls: two knobs on either side, one a tuning knob and the other a volume knob (fig. 3), with the tuning indicator between them.

2. A RECORD CHANGER. A LONG-STANDING ICON

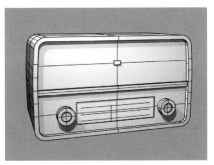

3. THE RADIOS OF THE MID 20TH CENTURY HAD MANY STYLISTIC DESIGNS BUT A RECOGNIZED LAYOUT

High Fidelity

4. HI-FI COMPONENTS WITH SIMILAR DIMENSIONS ALLOWED STACKING

The goal of faithfully recreating a concert hall's audio quality without any distortion—known as "high fidelity" (commonly abbreviated to Hi-Fi)—required costly professional equipment, similar to what was in the recording studio. Since professional studio electronic equipment was often installed in large standardized frames—the so-called nineteen-inch racks—the nearly professional home Hi-Fi equipment took the same form. Nineteen-inch wide boxes, typically black in color, but sometimes finished in brushed aluminum (fig. 4) could be stacked one atop the other: a tuner, a pre-amplifier, an equalizer, a power amplifier, and a turntable placed uppermost, sometimes with the addition of a reel-to-reel studio tape recorder (fig. 5), which facilitated home audio recording. Similar to professional photography (also in black and aluminum), there were often mysterious counter-intuitive controls, understood only by the real mavens.

5. INPUT COMPONENTS: RECORD PLAYER AND REEL-TO-REEL TAPE RECORDER

As the proliferation of knobs and switches spelled "professionalism," and since impressive specifications (which most people did not understand) were the deciding factors for the typical buyer, the common practice was to get each component separately, often from different vendors. This meant that the only common form denominators were similar width and color. This practice led to the emergence of the component concept in home entertainment, in which over-engineered sophistication overshadowed clear user interface.

Stereo audio systems

The introduction of a separate audio track for each ear in the 1960s produced amazing sensual results. You could close your eyes and feel as if you were in the middle of a concert hall. Stereo system components were physically similar to earlier Hi-Fi equipment; most of the changes were in internal circuitry. The continuation but differentiation rule required a visually significant external manifestation of the stereo concept, symmetry. The duality of loudspeakers, on the left and right, indicated a stereo sound system (fig. 6).

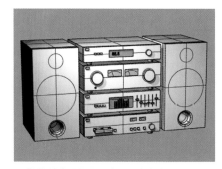

6. THE ARCHETYPAL STEREO SYSTEM WITH SYMMETRICALLY PLACED LOUDSPEAKERS

Now, the loudspeakers turned into the most prominent visual elements in the system, by their sheer size and vibrating sonic presence. The often-exposed loudspeakers' cones became familiar icons of sound itself (check your phone's speaker and mute symbols).

The old record player was eventually replaced by audiotape cassette players, and later by the compact disc (CD) player. As both newcomers were small and hidden within one of the visually standardized boxes, they did not have any real effect on the overall visual form. Gradually, most of the previously separate Hi-Fi components, except for the input devices (CD player etc.), were integrated into one unit, now given a new and rather

elusive name, "receiver." True, the stereo receiver still has a tuner/display panel and two large knobs, as in old radios, but not necessarily volume and tuning. Surprisingly, a very esoteric element borrowed from the obsolete record player, the thick four shock absorbing cylindrical feet, were established as the almost universal tell-tale indicators of sophisticated stereo devices (fig. 7).

7. ALL RECEIVERS HAVE ESSENTIALLY THE SAME FACE

When transistors replaced radio tubes, the obsession with electronic miniaturization brought about smaller and smaller versions of the full size stereo system (admittedly being of lesser audio quality): first the mini system, and then the micro system (fig. 8). The separate physical components were gradually fused into a single box, often with external decorative visual layering of the previous stereo elements (an example of continuation but differentiation). The loudspeakers, often still separate, completed the shape. It was only a matter of time for the micro system to become one portable unit.

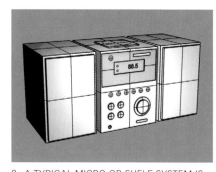

8. A TYPICAL MICRO OR SHELF SYSTEM IS MAINLY ABOUT SMALL SIZE

Portable stereos

Portable stereo systems were almost the only branch from the linear evolution of the home entertainment line of products (I consider the car entertainment systems as a separate breed altogether). It had to come about as an improved sound quality successor to the portable transistor radio. All that had to be done was to fuse the electronic unit with loudspeakers on each side, add a carrying handle, and provide for battery power.

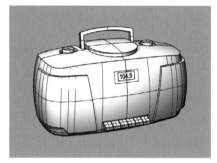

9. AN "AVERAGE" OF MANY DESIGNS OF THE PORTABLE STEREO

10. THE WIDELY HELD FORM FORMAT OF THE BOOM BOX

In terms of form design, fusing the traditionally separate components together created a first opportunity for a well-defined sculptural form. The portable stereo branch was where the styling variety of product design is most evident. The common boxy nature evident in home stereo systems evolved into highly sculptural portable products. Symmetry of form was strictly adhered to in order to signify

stereo sound. In spite of the large variety of designs, the portable stereo is well recognized visually as one product group (fig. 9). The change from tape cassettes to CDs barely influenced the overall form.

One fascinating offshoot of the portable stereo branch is the so-called boom box popularized in America by the Hip-Hop culture. Here, the bigger the better, as long as one can still carry it (fig. 10). Here, too, was a gradual evolution from a pseudo home stereo system to a more sculptural entity, though exaggeration of the loudspeakers was an expected outcome (fig. 11).

11. JVC'S VERSION OF A "SUPER" BOOM BOX

In this discussion, I keep referring to the portable stereo branch in the past tense as advances in super miniaturization (e.g. the Sony Walkman) completely took over. High quality miniature earphones did a better job than boom boxes in music fidelity, and boasted a separation from street noise. The Walkman family and its

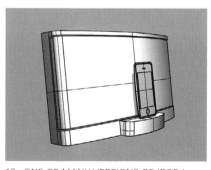

12. ONE OF MANY VERSIONS OF IPOD/ IPHONE LOUDSPEAKER ADD-ON GADGETS

later descendant the iPod are by their nature introverted gadgets. You cannot hear what the carrier is listening to. The portable stereo is definitely extrovert. Thus, I believe it will not disappear completely from sight.

Another semi-portable variant tries to extrovert the introverted: the recent proliferation of iPod type music players' add-ons that add loudspeakers to the portable device. In a way, it is a return from the portable to the home stereo, but without the hidden identity of the portable player unit (fig. 12).

Home theatres

It was only a question of time before the home television set and video player joined forces with the stereo system to become one system. Audiovisual became one word. It made good sense to combine the visual and auditory sense experiences. Social fashion advocated watching movies at home rather than in the movie theater. Engineering routed a video player's output to the stereo amplifier, provided a surround sound effect, and added a theater-rumbling subwoofer loudspeaker. Consequently, the physically separated components concept returned with the placing of at least five different speakers around a living room. The ever-larger and eventually flat TV screen became the dominant visual element (fig. 13). One can hardly escape perceiving the image of a home shrine.

The home theater receiver and associated video players, cable TV decoders, and other paraphernalia are less conspicuous then before and are often partially hidden in dedicated entertainment center furniture. The video recorder/player became an increasingly vague entity, with so many media designs making previous or competing standards obsolete at a rapid pace (Betamax, VHS, DVD, Blue-Ray). As

13.　HOME THEATER SETUP (REAR SPEAKERS ARE NOT SHOWN HERE)

14.　INTERNET TV BECOMES AN INTEGRAL PART OF HOME ENTERTAINMENT

evidence for the variety of equipment, you have only to count the number of remote controls on the coffee table. In formal terms, we see that complexity and fragmentation of visual consistency is ever increasing.

Home entertainment centers

Since the audiovisual experience also took place on personal computers, with the advantage of internet connection to Netflix, Hulu, and other movie services, it was just a matter of time to combine the best of the two worlds together. The buzzword is the all-encompassing (and quite vague) "entertainment." Now, one can add any electronic device one likes in order to create an experience. We call it configuration. One prerequisite holds. Unlike portable and personal entertainment devices, home entertainment exists in a well-defined place, usually in the living room or den, but in some cases even a dedicated room—theater seats included.

As this case study deals with tangible form I am not going to dwell much on the ephemeral or content portion of the experience. The physical side of the experience may be divided into three components groups: input devices, "mediating devices" (I take the liberty of introducing this term for my purposes in this book), and output devices.

As far as the highly visible output devices are concerned, not much has changed from the home theatre, except in sheer size—they present the same layout of screen and loudspeakers.

Input devices have expanded immensely, and not just music and video players but a growing list of interactive devices: gaming controllers such as Wii, PSP, Xbox, Kinect (that also senses your moves), video cameras, musical instruments (Guitar Hero and any MIDI instrument). Other devices are computer based: the internet, apps, and social interactive programs. I am certain that I did not exhaust the list here (fig. 14).

The mediating devices are all those boxes that talk with each other electronically: multi-channel receivers, CD and Blu-ray players, dedicated entertainment computers (Apple TV for example), recording devices (Tivo), streaming devices (Apple TV, Roku), video cameras, wireless routers and modems, a variety of dedicated remote controls, and of course laptops and tablets.

All these mediating devices speak with each other electronically, but not visually. They constitute a hodgepodge of unrelated shapes sizes and colors.

As far as contents go, this is great. As far as form is involved, it is a real menagerie. What was traditionally a not-so-form-conscious is currently a totally fragmented playground. One moves from experience to experience, though without actually moving. Even dedicated home entertainment furniture cannot visually tie elements together. As each user selects his or her own individual set of components, it is almost impossible to see a unifying solution. I dare to say that it is a very provisional situation. Very likely, most components will become visually intangible, hidden behind the walls, comparable to collecting many apps in one tablet.

Car stereos

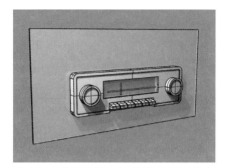

15. THE ARCHETYPAL CAR RADIO DID NOT CHANGE IN SEVERAL DECADES

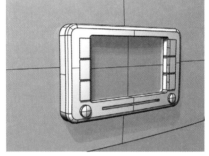

16. TODAY'S CAR RADIO. A LARGER SCREEN BUT A LIMITED NUMBER OF KNOBS AND PUSH BUTTONS

Unquestionably, the car radio does not belong to the home environment, nor to the evolution of home entertainment systems. It belongs to a specific environment, the car, where it is increasingly an integral element of cockpit design. I mention car systems here because the car radio (fig. 15) was a direct descendant of the domestic radio, borrowing only the flat front panel configuration, with no visual presence of loudspeakers. As the panel opening in the dashboard was standardized in most cars, it is no wonder that car radios—often bought and installed by car owners, with no relationship to the make of car—were almost visually identical. It is surprising that the visual identity of car audio, from old car radios to today's sophisticated stereo (fig. 16), has not changed that much; the screen grew in size, a minimalistic CD slot was added.

The reason is that car radio is still largely about listening. Also the need to simplify ergonomics to prevent driving distraction is a strong form restraining factor. In addition, as cars have coherent flowing interior lines, car radio devices are not likely to fragment into separate elements as did home systems. Loudspeakers and amplifiers were always well hidden behind panels. External add-ons, such as smartphones and GPS devices started a fragmentation process. But In due course, smartphones and GPS devices will merge into one device. I doubt that the combined visual display of GPS, telephone, and car data may change their form radically.

Design-based visual coherency

Not all entertainment systems makers gave in to the ubiquitous high engineering, low visual imagery trend. Several makers, admittedly not many, were concerned with the visual form of each and every component of the system and with the overall visual experience. This approach forbade buying separate components from different vendors. You have to buy a complete system from the same maker.

I name this concern "design based visual coherency." Such coherency requires a distinct design-oriented corporate philosophy, not unlike the route taken by Steve Jobs' Apple. This philosophy often created a form language singular to the particular maker, although it may sometimes be criticized as elitist and not widely accepted. It's no wonder that the German company, Braun (during the radio and stereo days) and more currently, the Danish Bang & Olufsen (B&O), catered mainly to small, design-conscious, exclusive buyers and often failed in the general marketplace, despite high quality and out-of-the-box innovation.

17. THE B&O EARSET 3I ADJUSTABLE EARPHONES, DESIGNED BY ANDERS HERMANSEN, 2011

18. THE B&O BEOVISION 9 HOME THEATRE, DESIGNED BY DAVID LEWIS, 2006

19. B&O BEOSOUND 9000 MUSIC SYSTEM AND CD CHANGER, DESIGNED BY DAVID LEWIS, 1996

I decided to show here several images of the unique language of Bang & Olufsen over several decades. Note the form treatment of record player, CD player, and loudspeakers (figs. 17,18, and 19).

Form evolution of home entertainment

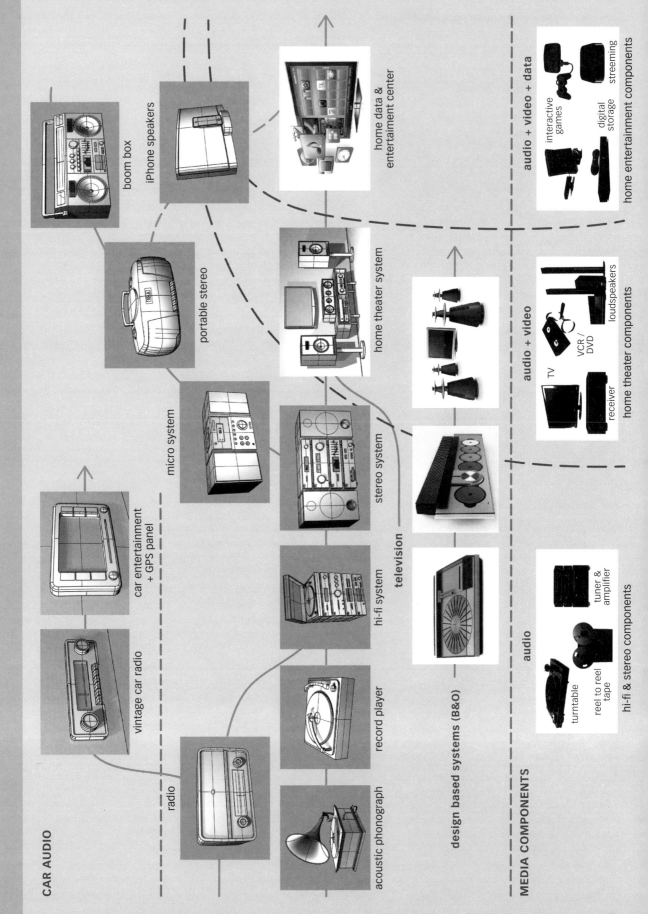

CAR AUDIO

vintage car radio

car entertainment + GPS panel

boom box

iPhone speakers

home data & entertainment center

portable stereo

micro system

home theater system

radio

hi-fi system

stereo system

television

record player

acoustic phonograph

design based systems (B&O)

MEDIA COMPONENTS

audio + video + data

interactive games

digital storage

streeming

home entertainment components

audio + video

TV

VCR / DVD

loudspeakers

receiver

home theater components

audio

turntable

reel to reel tape

tuner & amplifier

hi-fi & stereo components

CASE STUDY 6
The Automobile

The more things change,
the more they stay the same.

French novelist **Alphonse Karr** (1808-1890)

Designing the aesthetic aspect of the car is easy.
There's nothing to that. It's very easy to design a
car. What's hard is finding a story to tell. I often
make the analogy between the car industry and the
movie industry. If you don't have a story, you don't
have a movie. If you don't have a story you don't
have a car, either.

J. Mays, group vice president, Design, and chief creative
officer, Ford Motor Company, quoted by Larry Edsall, Concept
Cars, 2009

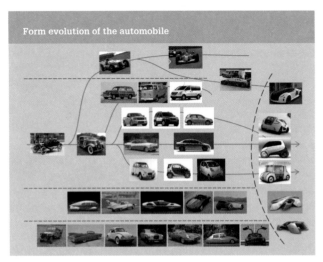

Form evolution of the automobile

SEE ENLARGED DIAGRAM ON PAGE 145

Highlights

In relationship to the human body, the automobile is
a cocoon, even an extension of the human body. The
automobile embodies the personality and aspirations
of its owner, not unlike the clothes people wear. The
human-car relationship is a love story, often more
emotional than logical.

The automobile family is divided into three form
sub-families: personal or family car, racing cars and
their derivatives, and an assortment of working cars.

In spite of the remarkable variety of car models, the
core automobile archetypal form is basically the
same, with few exceptions. That remains true even
in periods when the automobile goes through major
technological changes such as hybrid and electric
cars. The variety expresses itself solely in styling
and in superficial details. Therefore the term "car" in
the human mind has an almost universal imprinted
image, where four wheels are the dominant
identifiers.

The car has few basic form configurations, predominantly expressed in the side view. These configuration differences became gradually less discernible,
as most recent cars acquire aerodynamic free flowing
forms rather than joined boxes.

There is a common tendency by automobile makers
to adhere to or to copy the universally accepted
styling fashion of the day. Thus, in spite of many
historical landmarks, there are few automobiles that
are really different in formal concept that could be
labelled icons of form.

1. THE AUTOMOBILE AS AN OBJECT OF LOVE

There are not many man-made products that have been as immersed in form design as the automobile. Actually, the word "styling," often associated with superficial design connotations, was strongly allied with giving a car form (Styling Department was the name given by the legendary Harley Earl in 1937 to the preceding Art & Color Department at General Motors). It was often stated that cars are sculptures in motion. No other product class has so many books devoted to its design history. No other modern artifact has engaged so much emotion and gut feelings of love and hate.

The term "automobile," though somewhat outdated in North American culture, is common in Europe (shortened to *auto*). I will use this term here interchangeably with the term "car." I will limit my discussion here to four-wheel vehicles used for personal or family transportation, excluding any work vehicles such as trucks, busses, and specific duty vehicles such as fire engines, ambulances, shovels, and campers. Nor will I delve into exhaustive car styling history. There are excellent books available on this topic. I will concentrate mostly on form archetypes and concepts and less on a thorough chronology of car form development.

Unlike most of the case studies in this book, where I use simplified computer generated archetypes in order to concentrate on basic forms, the accompanying examples here will be fully photographic. Cars are all about detail and personality (fig. 2). One representative archetype simply does not work here. Still, most of the visual examples I will show were chosen to depict a zeitgeist-typical appearance and not a specific make and model. Only when referring to iconic cars will I refer to the appropriate specific models.

2. IN THIS CASE STUDY, PHOTOS ARE OFTEN USED TO REPRESENT SCULPTURAL DETAILS

The automobile as a visual archetype

3. WE RECOGNIZE RIGHT AWAY THAT THIS IS A CAR

We all recognize a car right away, cars of whichever make and model, be it a late model car or a vintage one. We immediately identify them as cars from any angle and distance (fig. 3). In spite of what may seem to be an almost endless variety, the car archetype in our mind will not be distracted by any specific configuration, make, model, color, or superficial details. A car is a car. As a form geometry archetype it is basically a large, rounded container with four wheels and with several standard silhouette varieties. We can easily identify where the car is facing.

What is the reason for such universal object recognition? There is another product line where broad form latitude falls under one name: the chair. We identify chairs of different structures, materials, forms, and story contents, whether classic or wild experiments. They are all chairs. But chairs have been around us for three thousand years and so the formal concept of a chair is quite ingrained in out visual vocabulary and language. On the contrary, the automobile has been around us for a short time, just over a hundred years.

I propose here several likelihoods to explain this form recognition phenomenon: reason A., because the automobile is such a dominant object of our society and culture that our mental terminology of

the automobile accepts perceptually wide latitude falling under one linguistic term. Or reason B., that we are so concerned with specific makes, models and production years so that the term automobile is just a generic term like furniture or medicine. Or reason C. that cars are not really as different from one another in formal terms as we are inclined to think. It seems to me that all three reasons apply here, but I will try to show here that reason C, so contrary to our belief, may be the key reason.

We all may be closely familiar with models of cars we drive now, or had in the past, and recognize them immediately. Most of us remember the shape of some outstanding car models. Other than these, most cars are basically quite similar in overall form. We can hardly tell them apart, one from the other. If you are not convinced yet, look at the images of eight common 2012 model sedans selected

5. A DETAIL IS THE INDISPENSABLE IDENTIFIER OF CAR MODELS (THE TOYOTA EMBLEM)

at random by Paul Sanderson in figure 4. You most likely will not be able to identify the make and model. When you compare only the outlines (the lower part of fig. 4) you might be surprised how identical they are. Paul Sanderson rightfully suspects that this is not due to aerodynamic requirements but rather due to marketing conservatism; makers prefer to play it safe and conform to current trends.

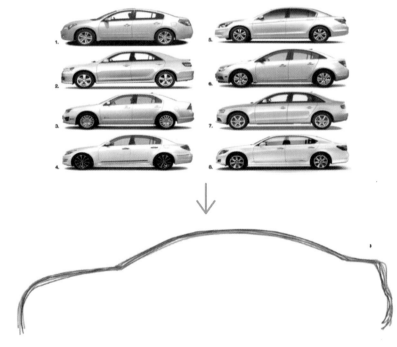

4. MOST CONTEMPORARY CARS SURPRISINGLY HAVE THE SAME OVERALL CONTOUR (FOLLOWING PAUL SANDERSON BLOG, HTTP://5THCOLOR.WORDPRESS.COM/2012/03/14/WHY-DO-ALL-NEW-CARS-LOOK-ALIKE)

6. A DETAIL IS THE INDISPENSABLE IDENTIFIER OF A CAR MODEL (THE JEEP GRILL)

It is easier to identify a car by its front view or rear view. We may recognize the grill, the front or rear light forms, or hood lines (fig. 5, 6). These are detail design, not a full form design. No wonder the Chevrolet or Toyota emblem is essential to any identification.

Why is that? My contention is that the proximity rule applies here. We treat cars as cocoons around our bodies, or even as expressive extensions of our personality. Therefore, we socially consider our car as artifacts adjacent to our bodies, as adornment. In spite of their relative sizes, cars are—please forgive me—quite similar to shoes. Let us admit: car styling may be in the domain of fashion.

As a result, cars have a remarkably limited variety in form. It is not an oxymoron, because variety exists but within a strict defining formal rule. Like shoes! This phenomenon means that we only allow for a huge variety in the decorations and minor details. We accept several varieties of cars in terms of size, for example, but not in terms of form principles. We accept several form division configurations as long as the car's defining cues, such as wheels, headlights, windshield, and doors are there, in one form variation or another. When we see a herd of sheep of the same breed grazing in the countryside, we tend to see them all as absolutely identical, even if on close inspection they differ

slightly. The same is true with herds of cars on the highway or in the parking lot. They are not individuals.

If you are not convinced yet, let me try a differentiation approach. Take any car model and turn it into a taxi. All that is needed is a color scheme (not necessarily yellow), a decal on the side, and usually a taxi sign on top. From here on we see it as a taxi. The car model has not changed but we do not pay attention to it.

Only few cars are plainly identified by a unique form and not by detail. These are usually icons of design, or retro cars: the VW Beetle and the Jaguar E-type (fig. 7) are good examples.

7. JAGUAR E-TYPE HAS A UNIQUE CAR FORM

How do we identify a tree in the forest?

Well, to quote Mies van der Rohe, "God is in the details." In the case of cars, God is not in form concepts. Very few cars were ever radically different in their form concepts (perhaps Citroen and Volkswagen in the past). Like morning cereals packages on the market shelf—same boxes but with different graphics—car branding is branding at its extreme. And remember what I have stated earlier—the automotive industry is time and again about adornment, not unlike the fashion industry. With that in mind, consider how we differentiate cars:

- By make—different models of the same maker usually have related family brand form details.

- By model lineage—features are retained over the years (Rolls Royce, Ford Mustang).

- By production year—age differences are quite pronounced. In the past it was blatantly done via planned obsolescence policies (read Vance Packard's *The Waste Makers*, 1962); now it is done by more subtle "improvements." Style aging still rules.

- By make and model—cars are differentiated by stating the model, by displaying the maker's emblem, crest, or hood statue (Jaguar, Mercedes, Bentley).

- By size—cars are divided into subcompact, compact, intermediate, full size, etc.

8. DISTINCTIVE ROLLS-ROYCE FRONT GRILL AND STATUE

9. FAMILY CAR SUB-CLASS (1950S VINTAGE)

- By social segmentation—cars are made exclusive by price range and rarity. How many own a Bentley or a Ferrari? Also, cars are differentiated by the maker's perceived status: Buick is considered classier than Chevrolet.

- By gender differentiation—models are designed with young men (muscle cars) or women (urban cars) in mind.

Archetypal automobile families

In terms of both form and function, the automobile has three archetypal sub-classes:

a. Personal or family cars

b. Racing cars

c. Working cars and trucks

The third sub-class, working cars and trucks, has form configurations strongly related to specific work requirement (e.g. the fire engine, the ambulance, the camper, and even the hearse). In formal terms, members of this sub-class have both highly recognized specific traits and overall form. Every child easily recognizes a fire truck for what it is. As I mentioned earlier, working cars and trucks are outside of the scope of this discussion.

The second sub-class, racing cars, is heavily determined by technology and sport-racing rules. Formula 1 is a typical

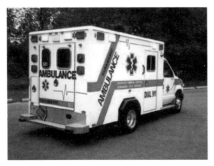

10. WORKING CAR—THE AMBULANCE

11. RACING CAR SUB-CLASS—FORMULA 1

12. CONVERGENCE—SEDAN OR HACHBACK?

modern representative. The racing car is as recognizable as the working car, except for stock car racers, which are visually (and only visually) similar to common production cars. The racing car strongly influences the form sculpture of limited production sports cars (Ferrari and the likes) and urban sports cars: usually aggressive two-seaters with powerful engines and a long low silhouette.

Hot rods and drag racers are the free-spirited, underground variety of the racing car.

A related variety is the convertible car, which is a sports car and a sedan at the same time. Increased air pollution and use of interior climate control may force the early demise of the convertible car.

The first archetypal sub-class in the list, the personal or family car, has itself several varieties or species, based mainly on side silhouette forms. I use here the terms commonly used in car design terminology but sometimes with different contemporary names:

a. **One-box configuration**—vans and minibuses. Not many exist outside of the working cars and truck class.

b. **Two-box configuration**—formerly known as station wagons, now recognized as hatchbacks, crossovers, and sport utility vehicles (SUV).

c. **Three-box configuration**—mainstream sedans, often seen as the core car-like archetype of the automobile. Come to think of it, the pickup truck has also a three-box configuration. I hesitate to place the pickup truck in the personal car class. Originally it was a pure work vehicle but often we find the pickup truck as a family car with an open trunk. In linguistic term, a truck is a different breed from a car.

In the early days of the car, when wind drag was of no importance, the box configurations were quite pronounced due to the common vertical-horizontal lines of cars then. Nowadays, the box distinction is far less pronounced. It seems that the configuration distinctions are gradually blending into one. Today's sedans and hatchbacks display a soft and continuous transition between the previously so-called boxes, resulting in one flowing sculptural silhouette. I believe that the term crossover—a combination of SUV features with the features of a passenger car, especially those of a hatchback—is an indication of the evolving sub-classes merger.

So we witness a general convergence of the automobile. Then again, a new sub-class emerged in the last decade: the city car, also so-called the subcompact. Actually, it has been around for quite a long time in Europe and Japan; the Fiat 500 of the 1950s is a well-known example, now being revived. Recently, with the rise of environmental concerns, the city car has become more and more common, especially in Europe, but also on the American freeways. Present examples are

13. SMART CAR, ORIGINALLY DESIGNED BY SWATCH

14. CHRYSLER'S GEM-PEAPOD EXPERIMENTAL ELECTRIC CAR

the Smart Car (fig. 13), Mercedes-Benz A-Class, and the Indian made Tata Nano. We may see additional models around soon since fully electric city cars will likely proliferate (fig. 14). Since city cars differ radically in their proportions from larger cars, and since they still are fresh design concepts, they tend to be quite distinctive visually. There are even experimental models that can be driven sideways into a small parking space.

Notes on historical car forms

As we are inclined to perceive car form as sort of an art form—a sculpture in motion—it suggests that the major influence on car form will be the prevailing art and design style of the time. Following design styling trends, car styling tends to oscillate in time between angular forms

15. THE HORSELESS CARRIAGE

and soft forms. Design styles may have a major influence but, of course, they are not the only ones. Even fashion has its influence (whitewall tires echoing the black and white shoes in the 1930s).

The early automobiles were popularly called horseless carriages (fig. 15); they drew their form from the earlier horse-drawn carriage, even the driver's seat was very much a coachman's bench, sometimes kept out in the open air, while the passengers sat inside the coach. The motor, be it a steam motor, an electric motor, or an internal combustion motor, was totally exposed, to suggest the means of power.

The moment the chassis, engine, transmission, and steering mechanism were hidden under the carriage and hood, designers were more free to exploit form as the main expression of the car (the sound of the engine, muffler, and horn is still a part of the experience, but it rarely has any visual manifestations, except in hot rods or muscle cars with their supercharger inlets). Cars were likely to visually express the ideas of speed and direction of movement; in the 1920s and 1930s they often emulated speedboats, with air piercing bows and bow wave-like mudguards (fig. 16). In the 1950s and 1960s the airplane played a role model, lending tail fins and air intakes (fig. 17).

Recently, though less obvious, the inspiration is sometimes the racing car: spoilers, body graphics, and a low drag coefficient.

Since we tend to perceive the car in an emotional context, the means of power are of no visual importance, be it a gasoline engine, diesel engine, hybrid engine, or fully electric propulsion. This is perhaps why hybrid cars did not require a major form shift as an indication of a new paradigm shift and it seems that the fully

16. 1930 CADILLAC PHAETON—BOW WAVE, SEARCHLIGHTS, AND WHITEWALLS

17. 1959 CADILLAC SERIES 62—FIN TAILS AND JET FLAMES

18. TOYOTA PRIUS—FIRST HYBRID CAR WITH A CONVENTIONAL FORM

electric car will only affect the form of the energy supply pump. The engine location is of no consequence to most people, be it in front, in the rear, or in the middle of the car, as it is found in some sports models.

In spite of almost strictly adhering to prevailing design styles, car forms tend to introduce, here and there, indications of technological advancements, such as windshield glass-bending technology in the past. And, later, innovative chassis construction replaced the separate chassis and body with a monocoque body. And, most recently, such obvious inclusion of technology is seen in the introduction of new skin materials, especially plastics. And let's not forget that forms also change in compliance with safety regulations: front and rear bumpers and folding rear view mirrors.

If there were noticeable changes in car form over the years, they were

mainly in two areas. One, mentioned before, is the continual shift from boxy forms to free-flowing, aerodynamic sculptural forms. The second one is the wheels-to-body relationship. In the past, wheels were external to the main car block, necessitating visually prominent mudguards. During the 1930s and 1940s the mudguards slowly became part of the car's body, and since the 1950s, the wheels moved inside the main body for good.

There were even isolated attempts to hide the wheels altogether, especially the rear wheels in luxury cars, but these attempts did not last. They just indicate that "car" is defined by four wheels. Take out the wheels, or hide them, and you tamper with the car's form recognition (fig.20).

A recent car interior design trend—the car as a gadget—has negligible influence on exterior form. True, interiors become more and more important to the user, and not only with leather seats and a radio as in the past, but with every conceivable electronic and computerized device being incorporated into the instrument panel. The electronic specifications are at times more important than the drive-train specifications. This only emphasizes that the car is our cocoon. We still keep playing the role of the pilot in the cockpit (fig 21).

More than a few car elements strongly adhere to past traditions. The front grill expressed, and still does, social status (Rolls Royce, Volvo) or brand recognition (BMW, Alfa Romeo, Jeep). The headlights, formerly separated and later incorporated into the body, give the car front that ever-present look of a face. Actually, the symmetry of the car face form is an essential car feature, not to be played with.

Any referral to tradition had usually been confined to localized car details and not to the car as a whole. Only recently car manufacturers were daring enough to introduce revived car models. Retro cars, though inspired by past models, were not exact copies of the old models, not only with a modern drive-train under the hood, but also with some stylistic changes in order to conform to current taste. It started with the return of past icons, such as the Mini Minor, now produced by BMW; the VW Beetle (fig. 23); the now out of production Chrysler's PT Cruiser (fig. 24), which is return of a form idea and not of a specific model; and more recently the Fiat 500 in Europe.

19. 2005 HOLDEN EFIJY CONCEPT CAR (AUSTRALIA)—A CONTEMPORARY PLAY ON MUDGUARDS

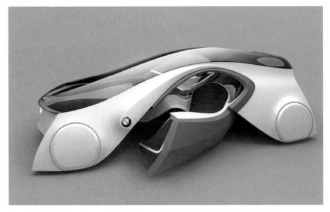

20. BMW-2015 CAR CONCEPT—ARE WHEEL INDICATIONS SUFFICIENT TO SUGGEST A CAR?

21. 2009 CITROEN HYPNOS HYBRID CONCEPT CAR—COCKPIT DESIGN REIGNS

22. THE 2008 BRETA RELIGIOUSLY ADHERES TO THE ALFA ROMEO TRIANGULAR GRILL

23. THE MODERN VW BEETLE

24. 2000 CHRYSLER PT CRUISER

The car as an object of desire

The main impact of the automobile in the first half of the 20th Century was in providing an agile and dependable means of mobility. The automobile caused remarkable social changes: people living in suburbia, building drive-in cinemas and drive-in diners, having more time for leisure (but no longer thanks to gridlock), and not to forget the old promise: a car for every worker. The automobile also contributed heavily, and generally detrimentally, to changes in our environment with highways, gridlocks, and pollution.

The following short story illustrates the car as a social dream fulfiller:

During the Second World War, millions of GIs were out in the cold, rain, and mud, wet, tired, and missing home. Above them they saw airplanes flying over the front, and then back. How envious they were of those Air Force guys, soon back to base in England, to drink in a cozy bar, meeting the lovely local girls. They wished to be pilots too. That was their dream. Back at home, after the war ended, when new car models were introduced (there were no new models during the war), some airplane elements were intentionally added to car designs, simulating airplane gun sights, fighter plane noses, air intakes, and eventually, more bluntly, tailfins and jet flames (following early jet fighters of the Korean War). GM styling, at the hands of Harley Earl, was directly catering to dreams of being in the pilot's seat.

25. 1950S CADILLAC AS A DREAM FLYING MACHINE

26. CAR ON TURNTABLE AT AN AUTO SHOW

Cars are objects with designs to inspire dreams: flying airplanes, being a racecar driver, or at least, especially for teen-age boys, to impress the girl sitting next to you. Come to think of it, even in today's auto shows, new car models are displayed on turntables with beautiful hostesses around them (fig. 26).

Car designers always were, and still are, a special breed of product designers, playing with line, form, speed, and emotion. For many years, and unlike their usually anonymous colleagues, the product designers, car designers' names were well known to the general public. Their names were often displayed on cars—Bertone, Pininfarina, Ghia, Porsche, just to name a few. Not unlike famous fashion design houses.

The car as a memorizable form

Automobile historians composed a long list of cars that became universally recognized icons and collectors' items. Several models immediately come to mind: Ford Model T, Duisenberg, Rolls Royce Silver Shadow, 1959 Cadillac De Ville, Citroen DS, and Mercedes SL. There are also quite a few sports car icons such as Jaguar XK, Ferrari Testarossa, GM Corvette, and Porsche 911. Please forgive me if I omitted some others. The list of memorable cars is quite long and sometimes contentious.

But if we try to suggest a list of icons in terms of a form that can really stand out as groundbreaking, a form that breaks away from previous conventions and instead influences subsequent car forms, the list shrinks and becomes quite small. I am not overlooking the fact that the car form was never at total liberty to branch off in myriad directions. It has had to comply with drivability and road and safety regulations. There will be a disagreement as to which should be on that list. The chart at the end of this case study suggests a few iconic cars. Let me mention several outstanding cases, especially of current and less historical interest:

Jaguar E-type Coupe (fig. 27)—I chose it as a representative of the sports car sub-class. By their highly extrovert sculptural form and upscale market, the sports cars' form is generally easy to recognize, in contrast to most production line cars (red or yellow paint only helps). The E-type, debuting in 1961, epitomizes the sports car: a very long hood in front dedicated to the large engine under it, and a small two-seater cockpit way at the back, and still all one flowing sculpture. Even the headlights are part of it. The very successful E-type is still a recognized form, at any angle and in any color, rather than in local details.

27. 1962 E-TYPE JAGUAR

28. JEEP—MILITARY ALL-TERRAIN VEHICLE OF WWII

29. 1960S VOLKSWAGEN BEETLE

Willys Jeep—the famous military car of World War II (fig. 28). Not surprisingly, it came from such a different form and vehicle use category that it influenced all subsequent civilian off-road cars, all the way to the outrageous Hummer S3. Seventy years later, Jeep is still a recognized brand and form.

Volkswagen type 1, the Beetle (fig. 29)—the immensely successful German car. 21 million units were produced between 1938 and 2003 (the later years in South America), and you still see them around. The Beetle was the longest-running and most-manufactured automobile of a single design platform

anywhere in the world. It is a small car with a rear-mounted engine, external mudguards, and a characteristic round top. The basic idea here was a simple car model that does not change with time (almost). It became also a cultural icon by being associated with the counterculture movement of the 1960s. Its worldwide success was never to happen again, even if you consider the recent Beetle.

The French **Citroen 2CV** (fig. 30)—a less-known small groundbreaker was in production from 1948 to 1990. Along with clever cost-cutting innovations (one shock absorber for two wheels, windshield wipers operated by speedometer cable), the 2CV incorporated uncompromisingly utilitarian and unconventional looks, lacking even a guise of styling. In time, that self-aware unpretentious look became a distinct style of its own.

Smart by Daimler AG (Mercedes)—the precursor of modern small urban cars (fans of the revitalized early Fiat 500 and the Austin Mini Minor please forgive me). Based on the manufacturing techniques of the Swatch watchmaker, it embodies a totally new concept, in production and in

30. CITROEN 2CV

31. SMART CAR—THE FORERUNNER OF CITY CARS

32. THE LONDON TAXI—A WELL-RECOGNIZED LONG GONE ERA STYLE

33. CITROËN DS19, 1955

34. CITROEN DS19 INTERIORS

use of limited internal volume. In a way it is an antithesis of the E-type jaguar form, with barely any hood.

I would like to add to this list the **London Black Taxi** (fig. 32)—manufactured by Austin and others. It is a piece of wonder, amazingly comfortable and practical, turning on a dime. Eccentric like the London double-decker bus, it is totally oblivious to any contemporary styling trend. Unfortunately, its form is a 1940s style. Since it is a working car, I hesitate to list it here; although the Nissan Cube of 2002 shows that there is a market for such non-designed cars.

The **Citroën DS19** (fig.33)—again, another Citroën. Stephen Bailey, the well-known cultural commentator and writer about cars, calls it "perhaps the single greatest automobile design of all time." The DS was produced from 1955 to 1975. Citroën's designers, led by Flaminio Bertoni, were thinking differently (their maxim: study the possibilities, including the impossible). The DS's unconventional engineering and form solutions did not follow the styling conventions of the time, just to mention its sloping hood, covered rear wheels, highly placed brake lights, and one-spoke steering wheel (fig. 34). Its engineering was not less innovative: a super smooth ride, a self-leveling suspension due to adjustable hydro-pneumatic shock absorbers, an air cooled engine, and an almost-digital driver's display.

The DS inspired Roland Barthes (the French philosopher who initiated the investigation of popular culture) to write, "Cars are our cathedrals." Pure individuality has its drawbacks. Citroën was losing money until Peugeot bought it and it thus lost most of its originality (quite a parallel fate to that of the German consumer electronics firm Braun).

If we define a car form icon as a car that we can recognize even when covered with a white skin so we do not identify any individual details, we will not find many of them after 1970. Perhaps the blame for the lack of major trend-setting icons lies in the now pervasive follow-the-crowd approach. The absence of different or even eccentric automobile design was often ascribed to the huge investment involved in any new car model. The cost of failure is exceptionally expensive. It is always safer to follow successful and well-accepted trends. Globalization, common solutions to widely different tastes in different markets, and common car platforms all added to the common predictability.

Concept cars, dream cars and cars of the future

Only the automobile family has that unique phenomenon of concept cars, the one-of-a-kind dream car, never to be mass-produced. Concept cars were introduced during the early automotive years, mostly as racing cars, made to test speed and maneuverability.

The concept car as we are familiar with it was devised as a marketing ploy by General Motor in the 1950s. They were called then "dream cars" ("concept cars" is a later term). Some were so futuristic that they looked more like airplanes, with no regard to highway realities (fig. 35). Dream cars were supposedly experimental feelers of public opinion, indicators of technological advancement, or initiators of dreams. Actually, concept cars were displayed in auto shows to instill in the public's mind where car styling was going. In its heyday, GM had amassed such public influence that other car makers had to follow similar trends or be liable to failure.

35. 1930S STREAMLINE CAR CONCEPT

36. 1971 PININFARINA MODULO CONCEPT FOR FERRARI

Automotive designers are adept in suggesting advanced designs and mockups (fig. 36), but now you find them mostly in car magazines. Dream cars of the 1950s and 1960s were often naïve but very futuristic in looks.

As the futuristic style went out of fashion, concept cars became more realistic but less experimental (fig. 38). Recent concept cars are by far more restrained in form, but sometimes there are sparks of fresh ideas, such as BMW's feasibility study of a soft skinned body (fig. 39).

Hollywood was always in love with the automobile, and cars have taken prominent roles in many movies, from *Bullitt* to *Batman*. With the no-restraints artistic

40. LA POLICE SPINNER 2019 BASED ON SYD MEAD'S 1980 *BLADE RUNNER* DESIGNS (ART BY FERNANDO FARIA)

37. 1958 PONTIAC FIREBIRD III CONCEPT CAR

38. DESIGN PROPOSAL OF CROSSOVER CAR

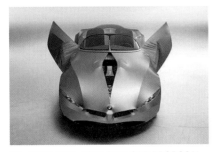

39. BMW GHIA SOFT SKIN CAR PROPOSAL

freedom of sci-fi films, it comes to reason to investigate futuristic motion pictures as sources of inspiration for the future of the car.

Futuristic fantasy genre movies such as *Star Wars* are so good at depicting fantastic space ships and flying machines, but not cars. Why we do not recall futuristic cars in these movies?

Syd Mead, the definitive futuristic designer, was a car designer in Detroit. He calls himself a "visual futurist" and concept artist. Mead is best known for his designs for science-fiction films such as *Blade Runner*, *Aliens*, and *Tron*. When you inspect his car designs for *Blade Runner* (fig. 40), advanced as they are for 1980, the year *Blade Runner* was filmed, you can tell right away that the Spinner is a car, and in fact, a police car. The protruding front wheels could flip horizontally, allowing the Spinner to levitate and then fly. Syd Mead was mindful of retaining the archetypal car form and adding a paradigm shift element to suggest a future flying car.

41. FLYING TAXI AND POLICE CAR IN THE FILM *THE FIFTH ELEMENT*

42. DELOREAN CAR USED IN THE *BACK TO THE FUTURE* FILMS

Try other fantasy designs such as those in *The Fifth Element*. In that movie, Bruce Willis drives a flying New York City yellow cab. It is a shamelessly, absolutely retro (fig. 41). And *Back to the Future*'s time machine car is just a beefed-up 1983

44. REALITY IN EUROPE—REVAI IS AN URBAN ELECTRIC MICRO-CAR SEATING TWO ADULTS AND TWO CHILDREN, SOLD IN THE UK SINCE 2003; IT IS A JOINT INDIA-USA VENTURE

43. AUDI AVATAR CONCEPT CAR

45. TOYOTA'S CONCEPT FOR AN ELECTRIC CAR POWERED BY FUEL CELL TECHNOLOGY, 2015

46. FIAT'S MIO FCC III IS A 2010 PROPOSAL FOR A FUTURE CITY CAR

DeLorean (fig. 42). Why is it so difficult to come up with a unique concept of a futuristic car? There are no real-life limitations. Designers can be visionaries as much as they like.

Well, it is the archetype image of the car with four visible wheels and a flat bottom that blocks us. Take them out and your imagination will soar. But what we see then is not a car anymore; it is a vehicle of fantasy.

But even serious car designs are still considering what will happen if the wheels are visually eliminated. Is the Audi concept (fig. 43) still recognized as a car or an underwater vehicle, considering the resemblance to sea turtle flippers? Or try picturing it as the form of fabric blown in the wind.

And a final word on the more serious side: unlike in films, the technological future of the car is quite clear. The approaching end of fossil fuel, the environmental costs, and growing congestion will direct manufacturing toward smaller efficient cars, driven by electrical motors (fig. 44). The energy source will be a charged battery, eventually a fuel cell. Computer-controlled driving, eventually fully automated driving with no driver's seat are on the horizon.

Since green cars are so important nowadays, why they still look like other cars. Is current fashion acceptance more important than a new transportation paradigm? When Toyota introduced the hybrid Prius, it looked the same as conventional cars (unless you consider the spoiler in mid rear window a herald of a new age). And GM's Volt is new by name, not by looks. Even Toyota's future fuel cell car, the acknowledged electric technology of the future (fig. 45), is just another run-of-the-mill car design. Why not come with a paradigm shifting visual concept? Is the car in fig. 46 realizing it any better?

To me, it only validates time and again the fact that the automobile is first and foremost expressing its driver and not the technology aboard.

Form evolution of the automobile

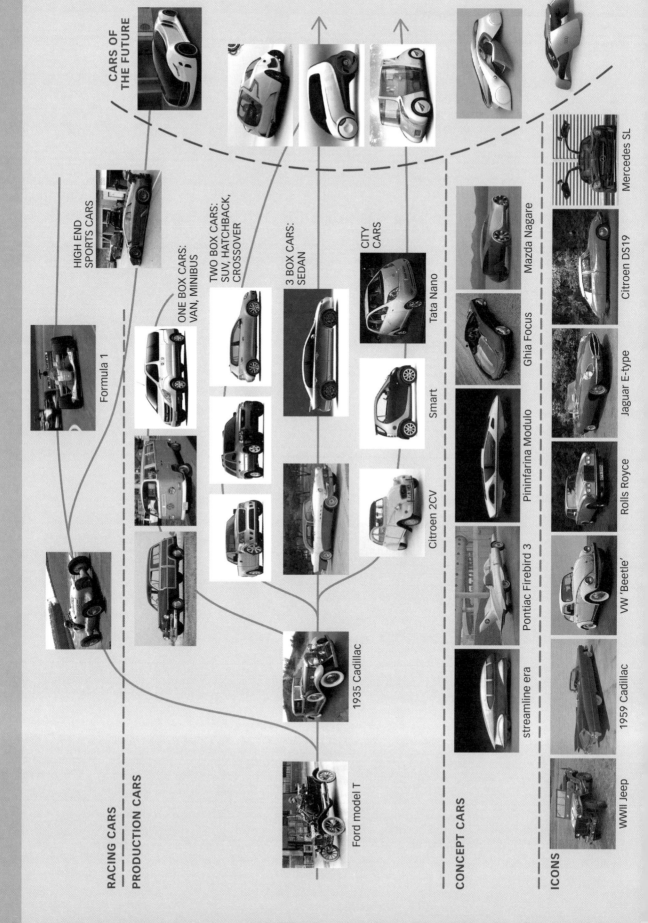

RACING CARS

PRODUCTION CARS

Formula 1

HIGH END SPORTS CARS

ONE BOX CARS: VAN, MINIBUS

TWO BOX CARS: SUV, HATCHBACK, CROSSOVER

3 BOX CARS: SEDAN

CITY CARS

CARS OF THE FUTURE

Ford model T

1935 Cadillac

Citroen 2CV

Smart

Tata Nano

CONCEPT CARS

streamline era

Pontiac Firebird 3

Pininfarina Modulo

Ghia Focus

Mazda Nagare

ICONS

WWII Jeep

1959 Cadillac

VW 'Beetle'

Rolls Royce

Jaguar E-type

Citroen DS19

Mercedes SL

CASE STUDY 7
Two-Wheel Transportation

The popular two-wheeled vehicles are the bicycle, motorcycle, and scooter (both the human-powered scooter and the motor-powered). This case study exhibits a product line that is so iconic that it does not change much over the years. Such conservatism happens more with mechanical devices that are around us for quite some time rather than with electronic devices, which are of a more fleeting nature. Does the longevity of such optimal mechanical solutions go hand in hand with ingrained classical forms, which tend to defy swift change?

As in the automobile case study, when an outer shell covers the familiar frame structure, primarily in motorcycles, it may lead to proliferation of surface forms. Therefore, I have to depend on photo examples rather than simplified computer archetypes.

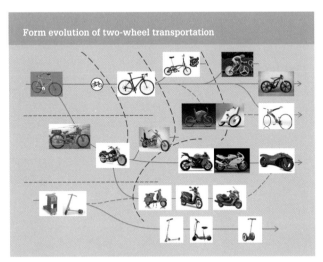

Form evolution of two-wheel transportation

SEE ENLARGED DIAGRAM ON PAGE 153

Highlights

The merging of rider and vehicle bodies into one leads to a strong emotional and cultural attitude towards two-wheel vehicles.

The bicycle, reaching an optimal structure in an early stage, did not change its form over time, despite numerous technological improvements. Folding and electric bikes may initiate a change.

In form archetype terms, the motorcycle was a spin-off of the bicycle. Only when it acquired a substantial outer envelope did significant design variations come about. And outer envelope design variations succeeded only when they did not conceal the core visual traits.

Scooters come from a different structural concept, but the independent family tends to come visually closer to the motorcycle family.

Only the Segway, by creating a paradigm shift, managed to break away from the essential geometry of two-wheel vehicles.

The bicycle

Following a short period of experimental bicycles of Victorian-age England, the Rover Company came out with the first recognizably modern bicycle in 1885. The double triangle diamond frame, pneumatic tires, and pedal-driven chain propulsion evolved into the so-familiar classic form. The British Raleigh bicycles were for many years a fine example of the classic form (fig. 1).

1. THE BICYCLE—OPTIMIZED BY RALEIGH INTO A TIMELESS CLASSIC IN THE EARLY 20TH CENTURY

Social changes occurring in the 20th century affected the way we look at transportation. The bicycle of the western world, for many years a cheap means of transportation, yielded to the motorcar as a main means of transportation (though in the East bicycles are still the more popular means of transportation). The bicycle has changed its role from inexpensive working class transportation to become mostly a leisure and sports vehicle, a coveted and quite expensive object of an affluent but healthy lifestyle. The lifestyle surrounding bicycles sometimes even resembles a cult, if you consider the distinct riding clothes, helmets, team riding, excruciating trekking challenges, and healthy living regimen accompanying the bicycle. Moreover, even the small bike attachments, from brake handles and breaking pads to seats and wire spoke wheels, have become a distinctive bike culture visual language.

2. A SOFTER, FREE-FLOWING VERSION OF BICYCLE ARCHETYPE—GIANT AVAIL COMPOSITE, 2012

Manufacturing technology has greatly changed in time, from the early all-steel frame, to the aluminum frame, to the even lighter-weight alloy frame, and now to the contemporary composite material frame. Mechanical means of power transfer were introduced and ever improved (the derailleur gear). Many bicycles today even have shock absorbers.

Through all these changes, the basic form of the bicycle did not really change. It is one of the most persistent classic form archetypes. If there were form changes here and there, they were not considered to be visually different variations. Even the woman's bicycle, without the top horizontal bar and the doubled, curved bottom bars, was not seen as a different "breed" in spite of the different geometry. The heavier mountain bike and the much slimmer racing bike, though calling for a different riding posture by the geometry of the handlebar, still belong to the same form breed. Composite materials could allow for major changes in the bicycle's structure geometry, but they haven't really done so, yet—at most, only a change from round tubing to oval ones, and some softening of form flow (fig. 2).

Even the ultimate in engineered bicycle form—the Olympic close circuit bike, with disc wheels to enhance aerodynamics—is still very similar to the iconic form (fig. 3).

The folding bicycles are quite a different story. The geometry had to be optimized for both the open and the folded position. There are several methods of folding but the one with the small wheels and the folding main bar is the most common (fig. 4).

3. THE OLYMPIC SPEED BIKE—DEVOID OF ANYTHING SUPERFLUOUS

4. FOLDING REQUIREMENTS LEAD TO DISPROPORTIONATE FORM GEOMETRY

Bicycles have long attracted the attention of product designers. Magazines and the internet are full of unique and ingenious bike design projects—sort of a design initiation ritual or graduation ceremony—maybe because of the urge to prove that the classic form could be radically changed. As such, they are often tour de force design statements, often whimsical (figs. 5 and 6). Most of these concepts do not materialize beyond the concept stage.

Perhaps with so much interest and effort to radicalize the bicycle form, we may someday see some go into production. After all, as I said a moment ago, carbon fiber technology allows for structural geometry that differs from the estab-lished classic Raleigh double diamond. When form innovation is both structurally sound and lightweight, and makes sense both visually and sensually, we will see a new bicycle, maybe along the lines of the design in figure 7. I doubt if we will call that imminent breakthrough a paradigm

7. NULLA IS ITALIAN FOR "NOTHING," WHICH APTLY DESCRIBES THIS CONCEPT MINIMALIST BIKE. DESIGN: BRADFORD WAUGH, 2008

8. GERMAN AUTOMAKER, AUDI, MADE ITS FIRST BIG SPLASH INTO THE E-BIKE WORLD, 2012

shift, as we are already exposed to count-less bike design ideas.

Another trendy direction is the electric assisted bicycle. Using power to assist the bicycle is not an entirely new concept. Many years ago the Solex miniature gasoline motor was an accessory to standard bicycles, used by people riding long distances to work. The recently popu-larity of electric motor bicycles (or e-bikes) initially follows the pattern of minimal intervention in the bicycle's classic form. The electric motor is hidden in the rear wheel axle and the modern battery and electronic pack is attached externally to one of the frame bars. In my opinion what will follow will be quite different from what happened to the hybrid and fully electric cars, where the means of propul-sion changed without a significant change

in external form. In the bicycle family, such change might be more profound in cultural terms—to non-sporty, easy riding. Here we may witness a form paradigm shift. An example of things to come is the new Audi electric bicycle (fig. 8).

The motorcycle

If we look closely at early motorcycles, let's say those of the 1930s, we may see that they have the same structural geometry of the classic bicycle, albeit more robust (fig. 9). Within a decade the tires became much thicker, the motor occupied the previously empty space inside the diamond frame, the streamlined gas tank hugs the horizontal frame bar, and the front wheel's turning geometry is doubled. But it still looks very much like the bicycle (fig. 10).

Eventually, the motor became larger and occupied more space. The fuel tank, seat, passenger seat, and rear mudguard, though of different materials and purpose, were united into one continuous flowing form, and the exhaust pipes, the trumpets that emits the distinctive motorcycle sound, now chrome-covered, became eye-catching. And a windshield could be added. The thin, almost transparent frame of the bicycle disappeared. Altogether, the motorcycle branch became a family of its own. Several famous brand names come to mind: the American Harley-Davidson and Indian; the British Norton and BSA; and the German NSU and BMW. The heavyweight Harley-Davidson motorcycle, with a community of devoted followers, outlasted the family's form upheaval that happened after the Second World War; its current models persistently and lovingly reflect the style of past Harley designs. The Harley is a true motorcycle form classic (fig. 11).

5. A HUMAN FORM BETWEEN THE WHEELS? (COBRA SPECIALIZED VENOM CHILDREN BICYCLE CONCEPT BY BMW, 2006)

6. DESIGNER YUJI FUJIMURA'S ELECTRIC BIKE CONCEPT, 2010

9. THE BRITISH SINGLE CYLINDER NORTON, 1925

12. THE AUSTRIAN MADE KTM 1190 RC8 OF 2008 HAS STRONG ANGULAR LINES

10. GERMAN MADE SACHS PANTHER, 1938

11. THE HARLEY-DAVIDSON FAT BOY OF 2008 ADHERES TO THE CLASSIC MOTORCYCLE FORM

After the Second World War, the motorcycle family changed radically from being an inexpensive means of transportation or a substitute for the car, to being a sporty object of desire and a cult focus. From the moment the motorcycle became visually compressed—almost a monobloc of frame and parts—different visual form rules applied (figs. 12 and 13). The motorcycle turned into a speed sculpture; an

animal, if you wish. The concept of speed is suggested by a free-flowing form, the concept of sports by the exposure of a powerful motor. And riding at high speed often requires that the rider mold his or her body around the motorcycle form. The merging of rider and vehicle bodies into one led to a strong emotional attitude towards the motorcycle. When painted-metal or plastic covers are used, one can play with form as car designers do (actually many motorcycle designers were trained as car designers). Now there is room for brand distinction. New names have emerged, be it a Honda, Kawasaki, Aprilia, or KTM.

The American preoccupation with do-it-yourself design for almost every means of transportation led to countless

13. THE ITALIAN DUCATI SPORT 1000 OF 2006 STILL SHOWS SOME TRADITION IN ITS REAR HALF

varieties of the standard motorcycle form. The Chopper (fig. 14) takes experimentation of form to its extreme. This phenomenon is not limited to form alone. It has wider social ramifications as to what the motorcycle means to people—the cult of freedom of the road.

14. CAPTAIN AMERICA CHOPPER BUILT BY CLIFF VAUGHN FOR USE IN THE MOVIE, *EASY RIDER*, 1969

And what about the future of the motorcycle? As with concept cars, we may glean where things will be going by watching the concept motorcycles made by the manufacturers or free-spirit aficionados. Here the freedom of form experimentation is more apparent than in the car industry, though the animated film *Tron* strongly influenced later motorcycle designers. One designer focuses on expressing brute force (fig. 15), another promotes the feeling of riding on a streamlined animal (fig. 16). Obviously the brute power and speed presented are not for today's roads. I also have hesitations about an enclosed cabin motorcycle. It is a different breed altogether, as the rider is not exposed to the wind. BMW has played for years with production models of closed cabin motorcycles (with small support wheels that come out when stopping at a red light). A recent version of the enclosed cabin motorcycle, made by LIT Motors, is electrically driven and self-balancing (fig. 17). Technically, these are still two wheel transportation devices, but not in spirit. Maybe they belong to the less aggressive motor scooter class.

15. DETONATOR NR.2 FOR COSMIC MOTORS, A CREATOR OF FANTASY VEHICLES. DESIGNER: DANIEL SIMON, 2007

16. FERRARI MOTORBIKE CONCEPT BY DESIGNER AMIR GLINIK

17. LIT MOTORS C1—A FULLY ENCLOSED SELF-BALANCING ELECTRIC MOTORCYCLE

The motor scooter

18. THE ITALIAN VESPA (WASP) WAS MANUFACTURED FROM 1946 BY PIAGGIO & CO., AND STILL IS

The motor scooter's roots come from a very different structural concept than the bicycle. Its origin is in the kick scooter of childhood on which the riding is done standing up or sitting on a base platform. A motor scooter differs from the motorcycle by providing a step-through open frame with a platform for the rider's feet. There were several early models of motorized scooters in the first half of the 20th century; most had an arrangement for seating above the standing platform as kicking was not required for propulsion.

The real breakthrough in motor scooter popularity came about following World War II, when an economic means of urban transportation and ease of parking was in demand. The *Vespa* (fig. 18) and *Lambretta* originated in Italy but became popular the world over. The scooter frame had the advantage over the so-masculine motorcycle because it was suitable for use by women (fig. 19). Their look was therefore by far less aggressive and less concerned with speed. The small, low-power motor was totally concealed under cover below the seat. Vespa's look epitomized this concept, thus becoming, unlike other motor scooter, an icon in itself, similar to the VW Beetle. Even the most recent Vespa bears a strong similarity to the vintage one.

19. VINTAGE VESPA SCOOTER ADVERTISING

20. TAIWANESE-MADE SYM HD2 200 EVO MOTOR SCOOTER, 2013

21. 2008 SUZUKI BURGMAN EXECUTIVE 650 TOURING SCOOTER

As the Eastern hemisphere urban population grew exponentially, many abandoned the pedal driven bicycle in favor of a motor scooter. The eastern version of the motor scooter, manufactured mainly in Japan, South Korea, and Taiwan, had a more dynamic, often aggressive, form (fig. 20). Eventually larger motor versions, sometimes called maxi-scooters, appeared on the market. These have the same frame as

22. A HOMEMADE KICK SCOOTER AND A GERMAN MID-CENTURY VARIATION

23. THE ICONIC RAZOR, A CONTEMPORARY FOLDING ALUMINUM SCOOTER

24. THE RAZOR ELECTRIC SCOOTER E200 HAS A REMOVABLE SEAT

25. SEGWAY'S HT P133 SELF-BALANCING HUMAN TRANSPORTER

the typical motor scooter but, apart from a larger motor, tend to emulate some of the formal features of the mainstream motorcycle (fig. 21). It seems that eventually the boundary line between motorcycles and scooters will be less obvious.

Scooter and power scooter

The kick scooter, usually considered a child's toy (fig. 22, right), and was often built from scrap wood by the child himself (fig. 22, left). It has been around since the early days of the bicycle, but only lately has it became popular again, usually amongst young people (fig. 23), following the popularity of the skateboard. Light aluminum construction and a folding handle allowed it to be taken anywhere, even on busses. It was in the offing that the next step would be to add a power train: a miniature gasoline engine or a miniature battery-powered electric motor.

A folding seat was added in several versions of the power scooter (fig. 24), but it seems to detract from the lightweight collapsing capabilities. So far, the power scooter has not evolved an intrinsic form and so the visual logic of a light, folding scooter may persist.

It is interesting to note that both the power scooter and the motor scooter, though on different evolutionary lines, still carry the same name. If you compare the Vespa (fig. 18) to figure 24 you will notice how similar the form is. The difference is only in scale and road ability.

The self-balancing power scooter

The Segway was invented by Dean Kamen, and on its introduction in 2001, it was hailed as a world- changing means of transportation (fig. 25). In reality, the change was not that dramatic, but it is nice to see more and more tourists and policemen using Segways now. The beauty of the Segway is not in its stationary form but in its dynamics (fig. 26).

I have my doubts whether the Segway should be considered as a "natural" development of the power scooter line. Since the Segway refutes the collective character of all two-wheel vehicles—that balance is achieved only in motion—I can see a rationale for treating it as a new mode of transportation. Therefore, the paradigm shift rule applies here: major formal change as an indicator of a totally new paradigm. Since one cannot see the

clever computer and gyros of the self-balancing mechanism, the outer form should reflect the change. The formal concept of wheel behind wheel, the DNA of two-wheel transportation, was changed to a wheel alongside another wheel configuration. Obviously, this new configuration is an outcome of the self-balancing invention, but it facilitates a radically different form. The two-wheels-on-one-axle form reminds us of the Egyptian or Roman chariot, but without the horses, of course.

26. IT IS ALL ABOUT BODY MOVEMENT

Form evolution of two-wheel transportation

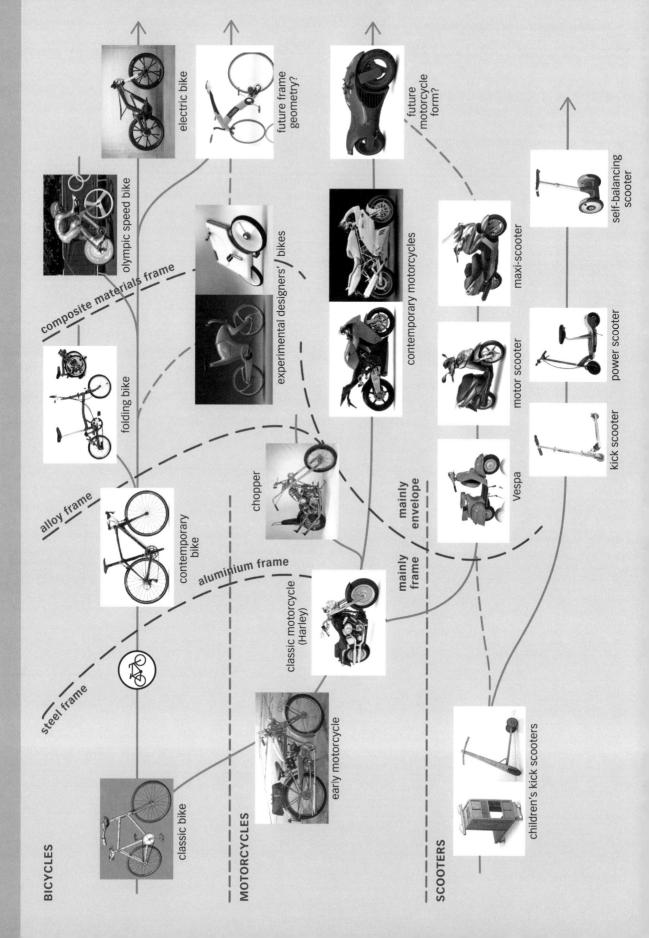

BICYCLES

classic bike

steel frame

contemporary bike

aluminium frame

alloy frame

folding bike

composite materials frame

olympic speed bike

electric bike

future frame geometry?

MOTORCYCLES

early motorcycle

classic motorcycle (Harley)

chopper

experimental designers' bikes

contemporary motorcycles

mainly frame

mainly envelope

future motorcycle form?

SCOOTERS

children's kick scooters

Vespa

motor scooter

maxi-scooter

kick scooter

power scooter

self-balancing scooter

CASE STUDY 8
Vacuum Cleaners

Compared to most product lines' typical visual configurations, vacuum cleaners have many varieties as the technology of dirt suction and collection may be successfully accomplished by rather different engineering component configurations, as Erskin Tjalve pointed out years ago in his book *A Short Course in Industrial Design* (fig. 1). We easily recognize them for what they are, from the small cordless DustBuster, to the much larger size and form of industrial wet-and-dry vacuum cleaners, and to the exposed vortex innards of the Dyson line. We will investigate here why that occurs.

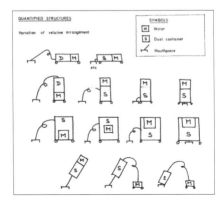

1. TJALVE'S STUDY OF FEASIBLE VACUUM CLEANER CONFIGURATIONS

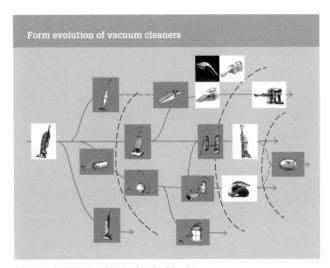

Form evolution of vacuum cleaners

SEE ENLARGED DIAGRAM ON PAGE 161

Highlights

The vacuum cleaner family has a linear functional configuration composed of separate components. Most key components can be rearranged in diverse orders, allowing for considerable flexibility in configuration and easy branching into separate lines.

They present three human-operated branches: upright, canister, and handheld. A separate recent branch is robotics.

Even with a wide breadth of form configuration, vacuum cleaners are easy to recognize visually, less by overall form and more by identifying key visual features: distinctive flexible hose, T-shaped suction tube, dust container, and more. Not all features need to be present in the product in order to facilitate the family identify.

The cordless handheld vacuum cleaner, a late addition to the family, lacks the typical elongated linear arrangement of the family, but here too, in spite of prolific design variations, they are easily recognized.

Contrary to the long-lived tendency of designers to hide engineering complexity from sight, Dyson's emphasis on visually exposing engineering complexity is currently a design leader in the trend to articulating the visual vocabulary of the family.

Robotic vacuum cleaners are not common yet. By eliminating most human involvement, we may anticipate a totally different form archetype.

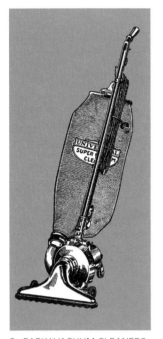

2. EARLY VACUUM CLEANERS HAD THE SAME BASIC FORM. THE LOGO ON THE BAG IDENTIFIED THE MAKER

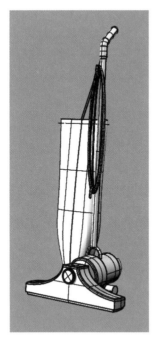

3. PROFESSIONAL, INSTITUTIONAL UPRIGHT VACUUM CLEANER

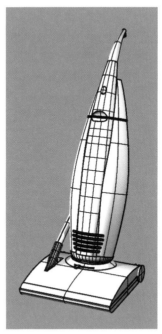

4. A TYPICAL AMERICAN-MADE UPRIGHT VACUUM CLEANER

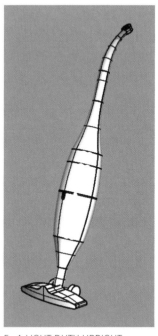

5. A LIGHT-DUTY UPRIGHT DEDICATED TO CLEANING STAIRS

Early vacuum cleaners

In the beginning of the 20th century, inventors in both the United Kingdom and the United States registered patents for early, motorized vacuum cleaners. Their aim was of course to ease manual sweeping chores and replace the broom and dustpan and the manual carpet sweeper. As the cleaning environment did not change—the need being to reach the floor, and nooks and crevices—it was practical to carry on the basic broom structure: a long pole and a short T at its lower end. The suction orifice, made of cast aluminum, hung back to the wooden broom neck shape. Stubbles at the suction end replaced the broom's bristles. The electric suction fan was attached externally behind the suction device. The Inventor of the first practical vacuum cleaner in 1907, James Murray Spangler, turned his wife's pillowcase into a dust

bag, initiating several generations of the dust bag, be it made of fabric or paper, as a sign of dust collection (fig. 2).

The formless bag did not hide the previous broomstick, probably because the bag seemed to be external and insubstantial (consider the grass collector on lawn mowers). In fact, all the new elements were riding on the previous broomstick, now a metal shaft. The added weight of these contraptions dictated wheels to facilitate easy movement on floor or rug. The wheels were quite small and inconspicuous then, but they remained as long lasting cues in the component vocabulary for the family. The slight bending of the broomstick end at the top, though relatively minor, was carried over into future vacuum cleaners.

It is surprising that the components-on-a-pole approach, giving the impression of an archaic engineering prototype stage,

continued for several decades. Even today you may find institutional vacuum cleaners in the hands of hotel cleaning maids that devoutly adhere to that form configuration, including the old-fashioned fabric dust bag and cast aluminum nozzle (fig. 3). That persistent traditional look, which is often acknowledged as timelessly professional, is similar in its lingering aura of the traditional Kitchen-aid professional mixer.

Branching out into separate family subcategories

Home vacuuming requirements were not the same as the commercial ones. Cleaning under beds and wardrobes and vacuuming stairs and couches required different solutions and even different appliances. This is where the different engineering configurations in figure 1 came about, allowing for quite noticeable form (and use) variants: the upright, canister, and handheld varieties.

The classic domestic vacuum cleaner, notably made by Hoover, was characterized as an upright vacuum cleaner, to differentiate it from the floor-hugging canister vacuum cleaner. The upright became lighter in weight by replacing most metal parts with plastics. This also allowed for form modification, integrating the fan motor, dust collecting compartment, accessories storage and pole enclosed by a single, streamlined housing form (fig. 4). Though quite different in its details, you could still recognize a hint of the bent broomstick, puffed fabric bag and suction nozzle of its predecessor.

It should be noted here that the upright vacuum cleaner and its later derivatives are common in the United States, while the canister vacuum cleaner prevails in Europe and the Far East.

A lighter version of the upright vacuum, a light-duty upright was introduced, dedicated to stair cleaning and treatment of accidental spills (fig. 5). Being rather slim and minimal it quite resembled its broom ancestor. It was not really a popular appliance. To me it represents an intermediary state, leading eventually to the future handhelds cordless vacuum cleaner.

The canister vacuum cleaner, introduced in 1921 by Electrolux of Sweden (fig. 6),

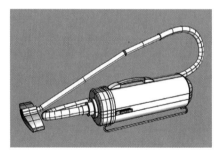

6. THE ELECTROLUX CANISTER VERSION PROMOTED THE VISUAL CUES OF THE TELESCOPIC POLE AND THE FLEXIBLE TUBE

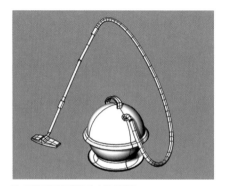

7. THE SPHERICAL HOOVER CONSTELLATION (1952-1975) WAS POPULAR IN BOTH THE US AND THE UK

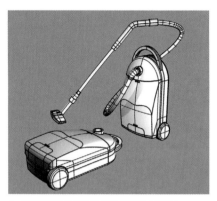

8. CONTEMPORARY CANISTER FORM SHARES HANDLING WITH TROLLEY SUITCASES

solved the need for more freedom in operation of the nozzle by eliminating the burden of carrying around the weight of the motor and the dust bag compartment. The aluminum pole became a telescopic suction tube, returning to the bare essen-

tials of the old broom, but permitting the use of a variety of suction attachments. The Electrolux canister unit took a cylindrical form, as most motor-based tools tend to do. The unit glided on the floor by means of sledge-like skids rather than the more common wheels. Is it a reflection of the Nordic winter heritage?

The key visual element introduced by the canister vacuum was the long flexible "elephant trunk" between the motor unit and the metallic nozzle tube. That flexible tube, with its omnipresent spiral wire spring, became an archetype identifier of the vacuum cleaning action. Its visual iconic role is similar to that of the traditional telephone's spiral cord, or even better: the scuba diver's breathing pipe, as both tubes are similar in shape and also handle air. These separate but distinct identifiers—flexible tube and telescopic T-nozzle—permitted form variations of the motor/dust bag unit without losing the vacuum cleaner's identity. The canister branch started with a cylindrical body form, but later adopted a spherical form as a representation of clean design (fig. 7), and eventually branched into many variations on the ladybug form (fig. 8).

The eventual bulbous form provided storage room for disposable dust bags, vacuuming heads, and electrical cable retractor. Two large wheels, visually indicating mobility, even on deep rugs, gradually replaced skids and hidden rollers. Not surprisingly, it has much in common visually with a small trolley suitcase, as mobility and handling requirements of both are surprisingly similar.

If we can glean a form recognition principle from the evolution of form in both the upright and the canister vacuum cleaners, it may state that we can live with much form flexibility without losing family identification, as long as at least two visually persistent cues identify the product as a vacuum cleaner.

Drum vacuum cleaners

The industrial version of the canister vacuum cleaner has to handle larger volumes of dirt, sometimes even wet materials. This required a different engineering configuration in which the dirt falls into a container before it reaches the fan motor (by releasing suction pressure when passing through the container's input orifice). The image of the industrial drum or shop vacuum (fig. 9) is an expected combination of flexible tube and suction T-nozzle—strong family identifiers—with a typical large industrial liquid drum, including cover lip clips. The wet-and-dry variety looks almost the same: the tube end is usually attached to the top of the drum rather than to its side.

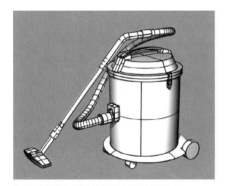

9. THE INDUSTRIAL VERSION USES A STRAIGHTFORWARD INDUSTRIAL LANGUAGE

Cordless handheld vacuum cleaners

Vacuuming suction force requires considerable electrical energy, usually supplied by a power cord. The cord limits free portability to the length of the tether. Thus vacuuming the car required a nearby power outlet; gathering spilled sugar from the kitchen counter required an inexcusable procedure of taking the home vacuum cleaner from its storage place and uncoiling its power cord. In

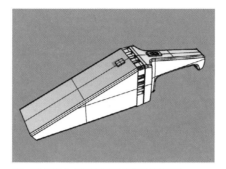

10. BLACK & DECKER'S DUSTBUSTER OPENED THE CORDLESS ERA, TOGETHER WITH A NEW FORM LANGUAGE

11. THE NEXT GENERATION DUSTBUSTER WAS BETTER BALANCED BUT RESEMBLED A STEAM IRON

12. A CONTEMPORARY BLACK & DECKER HAS A SNIFFING SCHNOZZLE

1979 Black & Decker combined an efficient small electric motor and a chargeable battery powerful enough for a short period of vacuuming and enclosed them in a small package.

The popular DustBuster (fig. 10) represented a significant deviation from recognized visual cues of what a vacuum cleaner is. No flexible tube, no stretched proportions and no T-nozzle. The suction head became an integral part of the appliance. Thus the suction lips (a proper

13. ALESSI'S INTERPRETATION BY STEFANO GOVANONI, 2004

analogy) became visually significant, lending credibility to the ability to suck effectively (not to forget the suction sound itself). Since such a small body requires frequent emptying, a second identifying component was soon added: a transparent dust container (fig. 11) that shows the amount of accumulated dirt. Thus, the new handheld vacuum cleaner had some visual affinity to the steam iron. It is the first time that exposed dirt was visually acceptable, eventually becoming a defining convention in most vacuum cleaners.

It should be noted here that rechargeable handheld vacuum cleaners took many sculptural forms. This diversity is a good example of the proximity rule: we do not care much about the form of the industrial drum vacuum cleaner, but the handheld one calls for an emotional attitude. Note the word "handheld" plays a semantic role here, as if it is a toy dog breed. This softer form behavior differs from most kitchen small appliances that tend to stay quite the same in archetypal form and only differ mainly in surface details. This phenomenon is another illustration of the wide form flexibility of the vacuum cleaner family (figs. 12 and 13).

Dual Mode

Since rarely will a family own more than one vacuum cleaner, excluding the handheld cordless one, it was reasonable to combine advantageous attributes from other branches of the vacuum cleaner family into one design. The oldest branch, the upright vacuum cleaner, was the one most likely to borrow from the others. First, a flexible tube was added that allowed vacuuming with a crevice tool and small brushes, borrowed from canister vacuum cleaners. That tube was often exposed in a noticeable loop in order to indicate a dual mode. Eventually the whole power and collection unit was designed to be detached from the main frame and used separately, held by one hand. As a result, the main frame itself took a new, inverted Y-form to hold these accessories. Later, exposing the dust collection in a transparent container was incorporated, dismissing the disposable bags. Following the introduction of cyclone vacuum suction (to be discussed in the next section), the spiraling airflow of dirt within was made visible.

The shape of the "remixed" vacuum held most of the defining cues of the extended family. But on the other hand, the overall form became quite undefined in term of design coherence. With all the parts and attachments, the recent upright vacuum cleaner sometimes looks like an open toolbox (fig. 14).

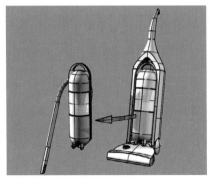

14. BISSEL'S DUAL USE SOLUTION

15. DYSON DC07 EXEMPLIFIES ROCKET ENGINEERING QUALITY AND COMPLEXITY IN EVERYDAY OBJECTS

16. DYSON DC02 SMALL CANISTER VACUUM CLEANER OF 1995. ITS SHAPE ALLOWED IT TO SIT ON STAIRS

17. DYSON'S DC16 HANDHELD HAS UNQUESTIONABLE BRUTAL CONNOTATIONS

Then came Dyson...

It is quite remarkable to follow—it does not happen very often—how an industry's long cherished design models, in both technology and form, may change dramatically by a single entry from an unknown outside innovator. James Dyson, an avid entrepreneur with both engineering and design educations, patented a bagless dust separation process using a cyclonic vortex. In order to underscore that internal process, it was only natural to externally expose that change.

A paradigm change often manifests itself in a radical form shift. If we backtrack through the evolution of the vacuum cleaner family, we realize that it took many years to hide the exposed technology of earlier vacuum cleaners under a clearly designed shell (see figures 4, 5, and 7). In a society more interested in flowing good form rather than the complex engineering behind it, Dyson was definitely swimming against the stream. In the proposition put forward by Malcolm Gladwell in his book, *The Tipping Point*, Dyson's innovation is an example of the unyielding quality of "Early Adopters." Being a perfectionist, with thousands of void prototypes behind him, Dyson eventually came up with the Dyson DC01, in 1993. High aims put the price of the DC01 at almost double that of the conventional vacuum cleaners, but eventually his personal interpretation of quality made him the technology and design leader in the industry. Soon after, transparent dust containers and visible air movement became almost a rule in upright cleaners made by other firms.

The DC01 was a complex visual "contraption," exposing the internals of the vacuum cleaner and fashioning a unique design language. Dyson expanded this design language in following models of his upright vacuum cleaners. This language matured in Dyson's DC07 of 2001 (fig. 15) and still evolves in later models.

Dyson's upright vacuum cleaners were followed by a cyclone canister line (fig. 16), reminiscent of a futuristic astronaut's helmet and life support system, and with a cyclone handle that looked like a science fiction handgun, aptly called Daily Villain (fig. 17).

Dyson's form language is not easy to describe in sculptural terms. It is a conglomeration of elaborate elements that looks like a sophisticated piece of space age or medical engineering. It is a good example of visual storytelling that alludes to the future.

The future of vacuuming: robotics

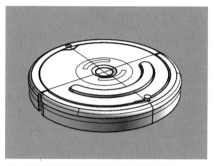

18. ROOMBA'S VERSION OF ROBOTIC VACUUM CLEANING

Around 2000, several companies introduced robotic vacuum cleaners that moved and vacuumed autonomously, crisscrossing the floor following an AI (Artificial Intelligence) plan for mapping the environment. They were cordless, of course, accompanied by a docking station. They could (usually) navigate around furniture and come back to a docking station to charge their batteries; some were able to empty their dust containers into the dock as well. Robotics is an idealization of taking house chores away from the human operator. As there is no longer any relation to the operator's body, there is no commitment to any previous vacuum cleaner form. This is a thorough paradigm shift in both technology and form archetype (fig. 18). Additionally, being cordless and having the ability to go under and around furniture requires a small and low form factor with no external protrusions. The appropriate shape of the vacuuming robot is anonymous and minimal, the unseen and (not so as yet) unheard helper. Vacuuming robots are still uncommon, more related to the gadget family, but they may indicate where the future of vacuuming lies. The low silhouette and bumper car rounded form are operational musts, but it is too early to assume what the mature form of robotic vacuum may be.

Form evolution of vacuum cleaners

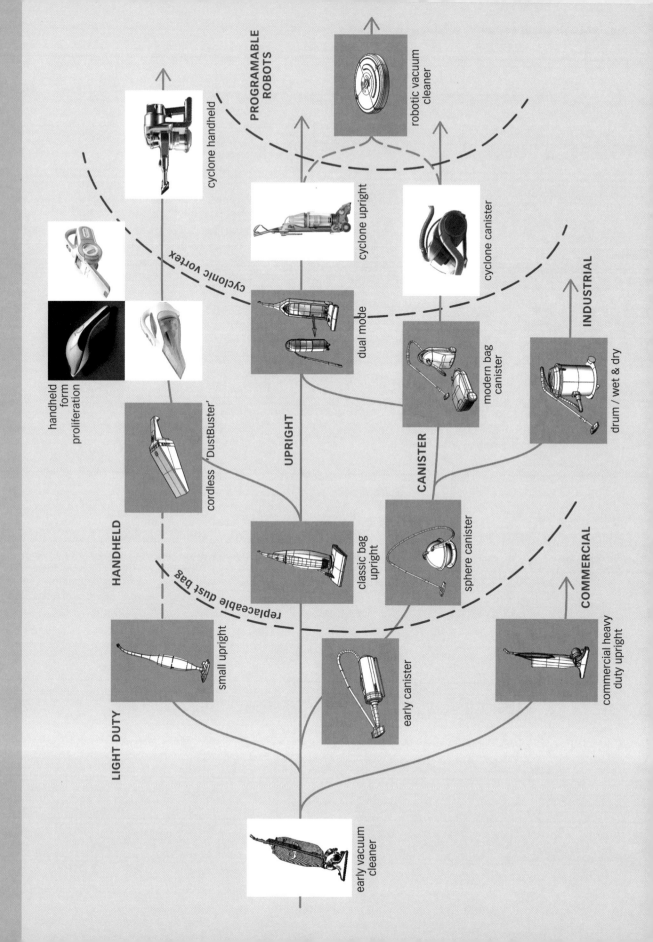

PROGRAMABLE ROBOTS

robotic vacuum cleaner

cyclone handheld

cyclonic vortex

handheld form proliferation

cyclone upright

cyclone canister

dual mode

INDUSTRIAL

cordless "DustBuster"

UPRIGHT

modern bag canister

drum / wet & dry

HANDHELD

CANISTER

replaceable dust bag

classic bag upright

sphere canister

LIGHT DUTY

small upright

early canister

COMMERCIAL

commercial heavy duty upright

early vacuum cleaner

CASE STUDY 9
Home Air-Blowing Devices

I admit that "air-blowing devices" is a somewhat unconventional name for a family of products. If we take the more specific term "fan" we may narrow the family down by ignoring all temperature controlling devices such as heaters and air conditioners, even though they have an internal fan because, in visual terms, we have no clue of that. On the other hand, "heating and air conditioning," the classification used by the Yellow Pages, includes also fireplaces and hot water radiators, which by their visual nature are different form families.

On the other hand, the hair drier was excluded from this discussion, even if it legitimately answers the air-blowing definition. Air-blowing devices are by their nature very physical products. They use electromechanical means to physically move air in the room and we physically feel the air movement. It is logical to assume that we may also see products that say visually, "we blow air."

We will limit our discussion here only to residential equipment. Air moving and control in industry is a much wider playing field, of which we are rarely aware, except in office buildings where central air conditioning grills are visible in the ceiling.

I divided the form development diagram into two separate families: the fan family and the temperature control family.

Highlights

There are two quite different families, both in their origin and in the way they operate. Fans just cool by moving air around while the temperature control family also heats and/or cools the moving air.

There are highly physical expressions in the form of air movement in the fan family. Conversely, there is a low physical expression in temperature control family, thus requiring additional visual indicators.

Both the ceiling fan and the regular electric fan became classic icons that continued to keep the same form for a long time.

A circular form is the main identifier of air blowing fans, while a rectangular form indicates temperature control capabilities.

Lately, as the original fan succumbed to its temperature-controlling relative's advantages, it tended to borrow some of the latter's visual features.

The air conditioner carries only the boxy front face surface design of the large home appliances family.

Dyson's air multiplier conveys homage to the classic fan, even without its predecessors' physical air blowing elements.

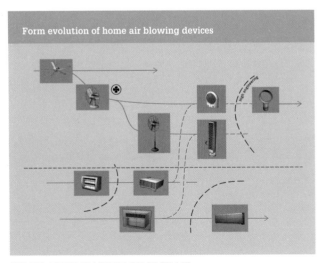

Form evolution of home air blowing devices

SEE ENLARGED DIAGRAM ON PAGE 167

The electric ceiling fan

If we look at the dictionary, the term fan refers to an implement of feathers, leaves, paper, cloth, etc., often in the shape of a long triangle or of a semicircle, for waving lightly in the hand to create a cooling current of air about a person. Fans of that description have been around for thousands of years. Thus it is quite surprising that the same term continued to designate the totally different, both technologically and visually, modern electric fans.

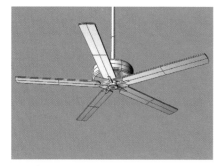

1. A CEILING FAN IS AN INTERIOR FIXTURE WITH A FORM THAT RARELY CHANGES

Early electric fans appeared in the late 1800s, but the first residential fans were the slow moving, six-bladed bedroom ceiling fans introduced in 1910. For some unclear reason, ceiling fans remained as a classic form with barely any change in form, unless you consider a five-bladed ceiling fan variety a major change (fig. 1). Though, overall, ceiling fans have nothing to do with the shape of handheld paper fans, a closer look reveals that at the connecting element between the motor and each blade is reminiscent to the way the handle is attached to the paper half circle of the hand-operated fan. This detail has not changed in time but it appears only in the family's ceiling fan branch.

The free-standing electric fan

The freestanding fan, with its stand, motor, propeller, and protective wire cage, appeared in office and home environments in the 1920s. In the early 1930s, a young interior designer named Jane Evans proposed to Emerson Electric a radical, stylish design for a fan based on the design of a boat propeller. In 1932, Emerson introduced the Silver Swan. The design was a major success, to be copied by everyone else. Soon it became a form icon, a classic (fig. 2). Surprisingly, to epitomize air movement, it was a boat's propeller and not an airplane's blade. Airplane propellers would seem to be the obvious choice because the airplane was a technology front-runner of the time. True, the boat's propeller design moves air more quietly than airplane blades do, but I wonder if the boat design was favored because the wide and overlapping boat propeller blades had a more powerful visual presence when the motor was off. One can find a parallel in automobile design of the 1930s. The automobile's mudguards emulated a fast boat's bow wave. It seems that both design solutions referred to more physical expressions of means of movement.

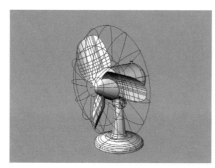

2. THE CLASSIC FREESTANDING FAN ECHOES A BOAT'S PROPELLER

Like freestanding lamps, the classical desktop electric fan diverged into a floor-standing relative, with no change of form besides a lengthened stand (fig. 3).

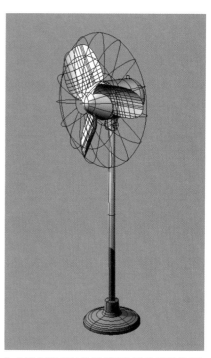

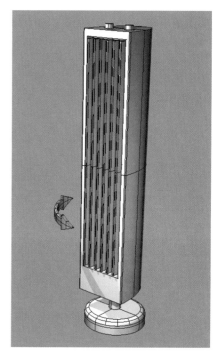

3. A FLOOR FAN IS CLASSIC FAN ATTACHED TO A LONG POLE

4. THE CONTEMPORARY TOWER FAN BORROWS ITS GRILL FROM HEATERS AND AIR CONDITIONERS

5. THE CONTEMPORARY DESKTOP FAN STICKS TO CIRCULAR ROTATION

From here on, most forthcoming fan generations continued these two design versions.

The introduction of the home air conditioner in the 1950s declared the demise of the classic electric fan. The air conditioner had the definite advantage of generating cooled air and later on, heated air. Production of the classic electric fan ceased altogether. Still the electric fan did not entirely die. The need for a cheap means of cooling by flowing air is still vastly in demand in the developing nations, mostly in the tropics and desert areas.

It was time for fan design to radically change its image. This is a common course of action taken in order to revive a dying product line: if you can't beat them join them. Try to borrow from and imitate your successor in order to delay your predicament. Thus, the next generations of electric fans were to hide the obsolete fan blade by replacing the delicate wire protection cage with grill slats, often seen on the air conditioner and the portable heater grill. The outer shell borrowed the rectangular form of the air conditioner as exemplified in the tower fan (fig. 4).

Smaller fans still hinted at the classic fan's circular shape by means of a circular rotating grill (fig. 5).

The temperature control family

Unlike the fan family, which only controls and directs airflow, this product family also controls air temperature. In the past, heating and cooling were separate mechanical concepts with separated deployments. No wonder that two distinct product lines emerged within the temperature control family. Today we bridge that gap with the term "climate control." We are not really interested as to how heating or cooling is achieved. The climate control apparatus is hidden in a black box even if heating is achieved with an entirely different method than cooling. The same black box may emit cold air or warm air as wished; we just have to dial the proper temperature. The single climate control unit is the approach used in modern residences and autos.

As the temperature control family comes from a different heritage than that of the fan family, it is only natural that its physical form manifestation may be quite different. In any case, this family has had to visually set itself apart from the fan family. It took the form a boxy enclosure with air inlet and outlet openings. The internal air-moving fan is a centrifugal fan, looking like a hamster's wheel. Even if it were exposed, it may not be associated with the classic fan propeller. (Interestingly, the air conditioner's cooling radiator fan, located outside of the house, still has the traditional fan form.)

Why do I treat the fan family and the temperature control family in the same case study? Because it is interesting to see how each family creates its own visual identity, distinctive from the other family's identity, and at the same time, how the form of one family influences the other.

Electric Heaters

Electric heaters are the electric descendants of the campfire and the fireplace, and siblings of the home central water heating radiators, the electric infrared heater, the oil heater, and the gas heater. Though of different energy sources, all emit heat by radiation and convection.

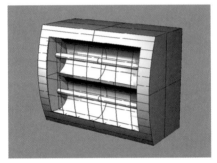

6. A BOX SHAPED RADIATION HEATER

7. A PORTABLE ELECTRIC HEATER

The typical electric radiation heater does not really belong to the family of air-moving devices because it does not have an active means to create airflow. Still, I see it as a stage between the open flame fireplace and the totally hidden heat source of the portable heater. The radiation heater has visible infrared heating rod(s) and a large reflector behind them. The typically rectangular enclosure and the red-glowing rods still remind us of the wood or gas fireplace (fig. 6).

The portable heater was the first heater in which the means of generating heat was hidden (fig. 7). The only visual indicator to suggest air movement was the front grill, probably alluding to automobile dashboard vents. The same type of adjustable slats appeared on the front grill of the home air conditioner, and from then on, any air-cooling and heating device. In form terms, these slats are the visual identifiers of the whole air blowing family. No wonder that later fans borrowed the same slats form.

Domestic air conditioners

The early home air conditioners were usually placed inside a window opening (therefore requiring a rectangular form factor), and the only element seen inside the room was the faceplate. Like most large home appliances, all the other sides of the air conditioner cuboid were faceless, as if non-existent. The faceplate—again, like in most large home

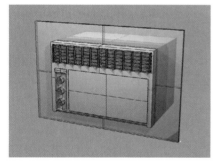

8. THE WALL AIR CONDITIONER RETAINS AN APPLIANCE LOOK (AND SOUND)

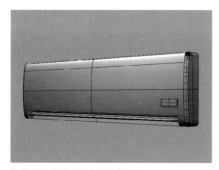

9. THE INTERNAL UNIT OF A CONTEMPORARY AIR CONDITIONER

appliances—is flat and rectangular, with a quite-recognizable air conditioner layout with conspicuous air emitting slats and control knobs (fig. 8).

Only the later separation of the air conditioner into external and internal units, connected by flexible pipes, allowed for an independent form design of the internal unit. As the internal unit became quiet (the noisy compressor was moved to the external unit) the logic was to make the internal unit as inconspicuous as possible (fig. 9).

Air multiplying fans

I have not really made up my mind as to where to place Dyson's Air Multiplier fan. Obviously, as far as function goes, it is a direct heir to the classic fan family. But that family is considered as passé, taken over by climate control devices. So why would a reputable company choose to go down a dead-end alley?

Dyson's research into cyclonic vacuuming bought about several new, highly efficient ways of moving air, in bathroom hand driers, for example. Was Dyson attempting a tour-de-force demonstration in showing that an advanced technology could revive a dying product line? I can only tell from first-hand impressions that people who were introduced to Dyson's air multiplier treated it as an advanced gadget and were willing to pay a high price to own one. Maybe it is the magic of moving air without any of the visible mechanical means of the traditional propeller.

Leaving the marketing question alone, it is exemplary that Dyson chose to refer to the iconic fan form by means of a rotating ring, more or less of the same size of the old fan (fig. 10)—the same approach as hi-tech designers of modern yachts' rigid sails and wind-driven generators.

10. DYSON'S AIR MULTIPLIER PAYS A BLADE-LESS HOMAGE TO THE CLASSIC FAN

As a final note, I feel that the future of air blowing devices, or even climate control devices, is moving away from physical products to environmental stasis: we just rotate that little thermostat knob on the wall. Recall Henry Dreyfuss's iconic 1953 thermostat design for Honeywell, and its 2011 Nest sibling (fig. 11). Nothing else exists, visually.

11. HONEYWELL THERMOSTAT, 1953 (RIGHT) AND NEST LEARNING THERMOSTAT, 2011

Form evolution of home air blowing devices

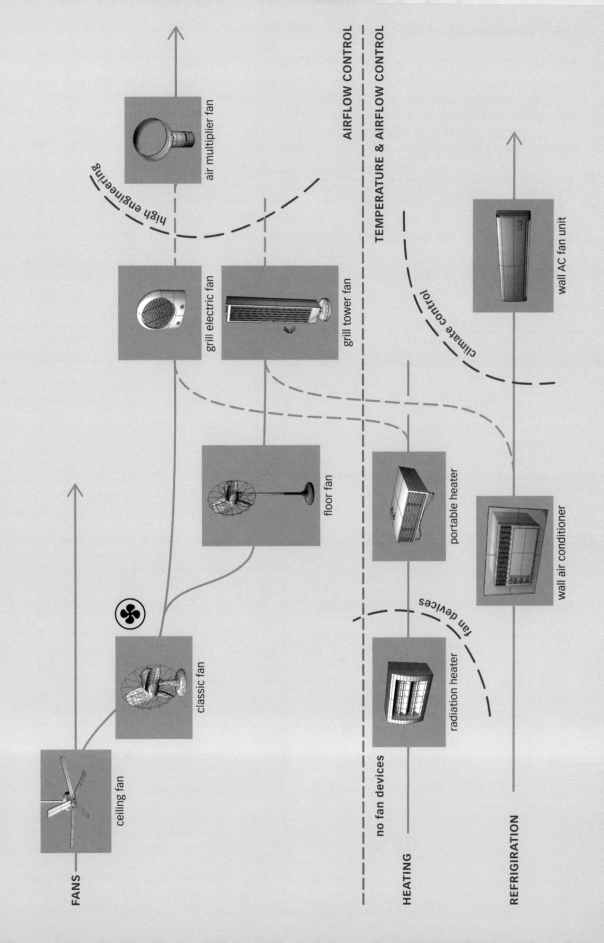

FANS

ceiling fan

classic fan

floor fan

high engineering

grill electric fan

grill tower fan

air multiplier fan

AIRFLOW CONTROL

TEMPERATURE & AIRFLOW CONTROL

climate control

wall AC fan unit

fan devices

no fan devices

HEATING

radiation heater

portable heater

wall air conditioner

REFRIGIRATION

CASE STUDY 10
Major Home Appliances

Major home appliances are distinguished from the vast assortment of household appliances by their size and weight. They are almost fixtures, rarely moved around in the home; thus, becoming a part of the décor in the kitchen or in the laundry area. In these terms, major home appliances are not really different from furniture. Actually, quite often the kitchen is designed and built with appliances in mind, and their dimensions are standardized for such purpose. No wonder that there is some exchange between furniture form and major appliances form. Thinking along these lines, major appliances should be considered as technology-based furniture.

Major home appliances are basically rectilinear boxes, often similar to each other in size and form. What visual clues may add to the identification of a particular appliance?

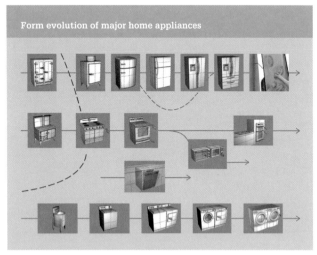

Form evolution of major home appliances

SEE ENLARGED DIAGRAM ON PAGE 175

Highlights

Early pre-electricity appliances were free standing entities and categorically visually recognizable.

As of the 1950s, the kitchen was envisioned as an efficient workplace. Major appliances had to conform to kitchen storage and counter modular layouts, and common dimensions. Modularity tends to become rectangular in shape.

As essentially rectilinear metal boxes, appliances were usually situated with only their front faces showing. Designers had very limited choices in form design. Quite often, design solutions were concentrated in appliance interiors (e.g. the refrigerator).

As all major appliances have large doors, the plane holding the door, the appearance of the door, and the direction it opens is often a clue convention as to the purpose of the appliance. These traits becoming quite consistent. These clues were even carried over to several smaller appliances.

Washing machines and driers, located in less defined areas in the house, have more pronounced archetype designs. Starting as visually separate appliances, they are treated today essentially as identical twins.

Dishwashers, being late arrivals and always built-in, are basically faceless entities.

The refrigerator

Refrigerator is the term given to the electric variety of a device for cooling and preserving food. Its common aliases, fridge or Frigidaire (borrowed from the brand name of one of the early appliance manufacturers), almost have become accepted words (remember Xerox). The refrigerator is functionally, and even visually, a direct descendant of the icebox; therefore, it is worth our time to begin the discussion by investigating the icebox. The icebox from the Victorian Age through most of the first half of the 20th century was a component of ice-cutting and delivery services. It had separate

1. THE ICEBOX OF THE EARLY 20TH CENTURY IMPRINTED THE FEEL AND SOUND OF THE LOCKER MECHANISM

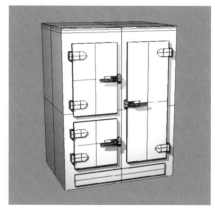

2. THE GE REFRIGERATOR HAD AN EXTERNAL CUE ON TOP

compartments for food, ice block, and the accumulation of melted water. In visual terms, it was a strange combination of substantial locker mechanisms (the ones we see in a butcher's shop) and furniture (often with wood-covered panels and doors, sometimes even furniture legs). Iceboxes came in a wide variety of sizes and arrangements, but always as flat surfaces and rectilinear in general form configurations (fig. 1).

Early landmark refrigerators, such as the General Electric refrigerator, introduced in 1927 (fig. 2), followed closely the rule of Same But Different. The door and legs belonged to the old icebox tradition, but there was only a single door, suggesting "no separate ice and water interiors." Even more noticeable was the electric compressor contraption on top, though meant to allow for heat dissipation, it was almost yelling that it is a new breed of refrigerator. Color was universally enamel white, as were all other appliances in the kitchen.

Refrigerators of the 1940s onwards did not have to publicize the cooling mechanism anymore and so it was made to be hidden within. The addition of the freezer unit with a separate door brought about the classic look of the refrigerator. As almost everything had somewhat stream-lined form at the time, even this rarely-to-be-moved equipment got rounded doors and corners. The old icebox variety handles were still there, somewhat like car door handles of the period (fig. 3).

The international design in vogue in the 1960s flattened the classic refrigerator completely. It was a box with thick doors, fitting well with the entire kitchen cupboards design. All that designers could contribute was by concentrating on the flexible interior arrangement and food tray design. On the exterior, the change was without question limited to new handle orientations (resolved by magnetic

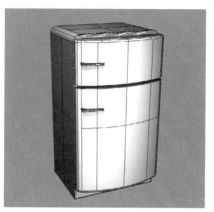

3. 1940S REFRIGERATORS ALREADY HAD THE CLASSICS FREEZER-REFRIGERATOR COMPARTMENT DIVISION

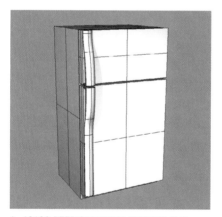

4. 1960S REFRIGERATORS KEPT TO THE SAME CLASSIC FORM, ONLY ADDING HANDLES STYLING

sealing) and, for the first time, options for colors other than white (fig. 4).

The ever-increasing demand for fully frozen food brought about a separate variation on the theme in the form of the deep-freezer. Most deep-freezers were built as simple top-opening chests (not pictured).

The refrigerators of the 1970s and 1980s introduced cold air circulation and ice-free environments. The side-by-side door configuration was the first time that front face division altered the traditional horizontal division (fig. 5). The incorporation of external dispensers for ice and cold water was both a practical and a visual innovation.

The latest line of refrigerators fused into one: the side-by-side concept with a deep freezer. We can tell the freezer side by its drawer-like opening and handle orientation (fig. 6). Certain refrigerators even have more than one drawer. We perceive the influence of the popular (first in Europe, then in the USA) modular kitchen storage systems, where the consumer can choose and arrange almost any combination of cupboards, drawers and door materials. Refrigerators followed suit. There are now more models with different horizontal and vertical subdivisions.

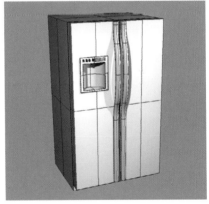

5. SIDE-BY-SIDE REFRIGERATOR

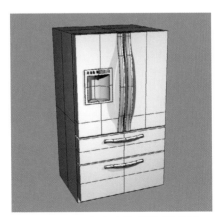

6. THE MODERN REFRIGERATOR ECHOES THE LANGUAGE OF KITCHEN CABINET DOORS AND DRAWERS

Exterior sophistication is expressed by brushed stainless steel, in line with other major appliances.

Looking backwards, we will discover that refrigerator doors always open with a vertical axis. It is not a revelation in itself, but it may make sense when we try to understand the distinctive qualities of each major appliance family.

As for a futuristic outlook, designers show an interest in refrigerators more than in any other appliance. Since the refrigerator is often a major meeting point in the home (recall nightly food cravings), it is also an accepted family posting board. Designers see a future electronic bulletin board as the face of future refrigerators. Others see the food as the main visual element—glazed doors of built-in refrigerators already exist in hi-tech kitchen. This is obviously borrowed from the supermarket frozen food section.

I decided to represent future trends and ideas by a concept illustration of a soft-front gel refrigerator in which you can put food anywhere without even opening a door (fig. 7).

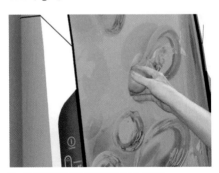

7. ELECTROLUX DESIGN LAB 2010 COMPETITION FINALIST: BIO ROBOT REFRIGERATOR BY RUSSIAN DESIGNER YURIY DMITRIEV

The cooking appliance

Sometimes named a stove, an oven, or a range, the cooking appliance follows a development very similar to that of the refrigerator, and during a nearly identical timeline at that.

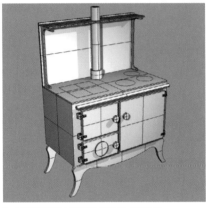

8. VICTORIAN WOOD/COAL STOVE REFLECTS FURNITURE DESIGN

The forefather of the modern stove is the wood or coal burning kitchen stove of the 19th century. Made of cast iron, with a typical stove's chimney, it tried to imitate a piece of furniture, with mock wooden legs and even a top shelf for pots and pans (fig. 8). As a heat and fire-emitting unit, it was understandably designed as a freestanding product, fashioned in many form and size variants.

Its follower, the gas range of the 1930s (fig. 9) had insulated outer walls, thus it could be placed closer and in line with the food preparation counter. It followed the same front subdivision principle of the earlier stove: compartments for baking or roasting, usually side-by-side, and a top surface for cooking. Unlike with the wood-burning stove, the top was not just a hot surface. Now there was a separately placed circular burner element and a gas control knob for each. Eventually the cooking top with four or five black cast iron grates, usually of different sizes,

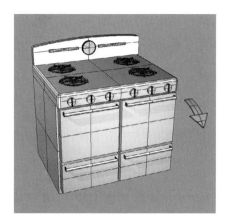

9. 1930S GAS RANGES DEFINED BAKING COMPARTMENT DOOR OPENING

10. THE ESTABLISHED CLASSIC FORM, BE IT AN ELECTRIC OR GAS RANGE

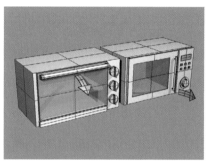

12. THE DOOR-OPENING AXIS INDICATES WHETHER IT IS A HOT OVEN OR A COOL ONE (MICROWAVE)

became a familiar sign, always associated with cooking. Oven door(s) universally opened out and downwards on a horizontal axis. Often there was an additional lower unit, dedicated as a storage drawer for trays and pans.

Surprisingly the electric cooking appliance did not differ or set itself apart from the gas one. I reason that often the oven was electrically heated and the top burners were gas heated, so there was no real distinction between these cooking appliances in term of appearance. Even the visual difference between gas burning tops and electric tops is not that great.

Little was changed in form over the years. Even the oven's pervasive enamel white color persisted. Side-by-side oven doors disappeared. If two oven doors were included, they were placed one above the other. A rectangular viewing glass window was placed in the oven's door. Overall dimensions were standardized to fit the height and depth of the kitchen counter. The control knobs were placed either in front of or behind the burners, depending on which solution was deemed safer (fig. 10).

Matching the refrigerator family line, kitchen modular planning schemes affected the cooking appliance in a similar way, but more in its configuration than in its details. Evidently, we saw a trend of splitting up the cooking appliance into two separate units: the oven and the cooking surface. But unlike the refrigerator these devices are often fully incorporated into the kitchen furniture as built-in units. Surfaces are often of brushed stainless steel (fig. 11).

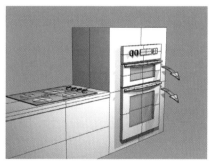

11. THE CONTEMPORARY BUILT-IN APPROACH SEPARATES THE COOKING SURFACE FROM THE OVEN UNIT

So how can you tell a built-in oven from a build-in refrigerator? Externally they turn out to be quite similar (though size is still an identifying factor). Clearly it is important to distinguish the way the doors open in each appliance. Cooling appliances open sideways, cooking doors open downwards. I would like to point out a similar distinction occurring in two countertop appliances in order to point out this convention. The small oven and the microwave oven (fig. 12) are quite similar in form and size, but the electric oven opens downwards similar to the build-in oven and the microwave oven always opens sideways, as the refrigerator, is it because it stays cool?

I do not claim that everything revolves around an intuitive "code" of door direction. You will see additional door distinctions in dishwashers, washers, and driers. In most cases, we recognize which is which in spite of the common box form. And, of course, there are sometimes doors that do not follow the convention, but not often. Still it seems that the convention as to which plane the door is found on, the way the door appears, and the direction in which it opens is often a clue to purpose of the appliance.

As for future trends, it is the cooking surface that keeps developing, though in a two dimensional way, for example: dark glass surfaces with infrared heating areas. No more the ubiquitous circular surfaces.

Dishwashers

I have very little to comment on concerning this appliance. It is a relative latecomer and it doesn't have predecessors to follow visually. In formal terms, the dishwasher is a simple box shape, built-in as a rule, having a flat, nondescript front. Several European manufacturers even attach a laminate front surface, coordinated with the cupboard finish, while others hide the electronic control panel so you cannot tell that a dishwasher exists under the counter. Still, if we search for conventions, the door opens down, like the oven door (both machines use heating), but unlike the accepted oven door it will not have a glazed inspection window in front (fig. 13). It seems that dish cleaning is considered to be a demeaning chore, even for a machine, better to be forgotten.

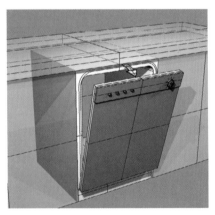

13. A COMMONLY BUILT-IN DISHWASHER IS A FACELESS KITCHEN HELPER

Washing machines and clothes driers

Washing machines and clothes driers, unlike other major appliances discussed earlier, are seldom found in the kitchen. Often they are located in less defined areas in the house, near the bathroom or in a small laundry alcove. Thus, there is a lesser need to incorporate them as built-ins in the architectural environment.

14. AN EARLY MAYTAG UNDERSCORES THE BOILING VAT, REVOLVING AGITATOR, AND ROLLER WRINGER

The idea of the washing machine and the clothes drier as an ever-present pair is a relatively recent one. For a long time washing was the major housewife chore, ripe for a machine-driven labor reducing solution, while clothes drying was easily accomplished by engaging clothing lines and sunrays, quite readily available.

Early washing machines used manually rotated sealed drums, but these were not that common. The first electric washing machine was introduced in 1910 and became prevalent from the 1930s onwards. A typical washing machine of the time, such as Maytag's (fig. 14), well reflected its origins: the cylindrical container was a direct visual descendant of the boiling vat, but it also echoed the existence of a revolving agitator inside. Legs on casters indicated a contemporary,

self-contained, freestanding device. The wringer on top, manually operated at first, but later motor operated, provided a very recognized visual identifier.

In the 1950s, the washing machine took a perplexing visual turn. The technology, though much improved, was basically the same: a top-loading cylindrical boiling water vat and central spinning agitator. The external form (fig. 15) did not represent any of that; it was simply a box built of enameled sheet metal with a rectangular top door. The new washing machine became a totally enigmatic form, a jack-in-the-box that keeps secret what is going on inside.

15. THE 1950S WASHER HAS BARELY ANY VISUAL CUES AS TO WHAT IT DOES

This unexplained formal change is contrary to what this book is dealing with: semantic recognition. I could not find a reason for this mysterious change. Moreover, why did all the appliance manufacturers follow the same trend? Was it for production ease—the same panel technology as other major home appliances? Was a spillover from a Laundromat's rows of washers that dictated cube shapes? Was hiding the laundry a sign of woman's liberation?

With the introduction of the home clothes drier, drying became independent of outside weather. The drying process involved a horizontal drum, in order to flip clothes in the heated air; thus, a front-loading door. Again, no external visual indication exists as to the rotating drums inside. Even the hot air venting pipe was hidden from sight. Washers and driers had the same shape and size; only the door location plane indicated which is which (fig. 16).

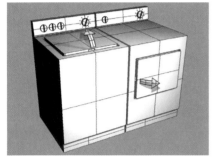

16. AMERICAN WASHER AND DRIER TWINS HAVE PLAIN INDUSTRIAL FORMS, IDENTIFIED ONLY BY DOOR LOCATION

In Europe, space is usually at more of a premium then in the United States. Washer and dryer pairs acquired a smaller footprint by placing the drier over the washer and placing both control panels in front. People do not intuitively consider things like front-loading and horizontal water-filled drums, so, to support in a visual way the washer's function, the door was made round and transparent. This difference in the shape of the door also helped to distinguish between the washer and the drier (fig. 17).

17. EUROPEAN WASHER AND DRIER TWINS

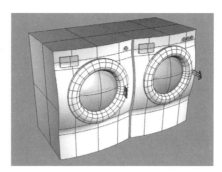

18. CONTEMPORARY WASHER AND DRIER TWINS ARE BARELY DISCERNIBLE

The American market took the twins approach much further. The washer and the dryer became identical twins. Both have a similar round and transparent door, something that was long seen in industrial Laundromats but not at home. Unless you read the labels on the micro-processor controls you may mistakenly wash your dirty clothes in the drier. Visual duality became more important than user interface. Notice that, unlike most major kitchen appliances that became visually flat in time, the tendency in laundry appliances has been to sculpturally enhance the front panel (fig. 18).

As far as door opening "codes" of major appliances, the laundry appliances have a distinct round transparent door; direction of opening is of no importance.

The future of washer and drier design is quite blurred. Much depends on the nature of domestic chores in the future. If the word chore will keep having negative connotations, we may expect to see washers hidden behind walls. Form spec-ulations by young designers tend to put the emphasis on even rounder forms (meaning rotation).

19. MAGNETIC LEVITATION WASHER CONCEPT BY JAKUB LEKES

A concept by designer Jakub Lekes (fig. 19) is notable for its spherical shape, which allows it to spin in all directions. Magnetic levitation, or maglev, holds the ball in place while it spins around, getting clothes cleaner than a circular-spinning drum ever could.

We also may expect that future green technologies, possibly waterless cleaning, may lead to form paradigm changes in washer design.

Form evolution of major home appliances

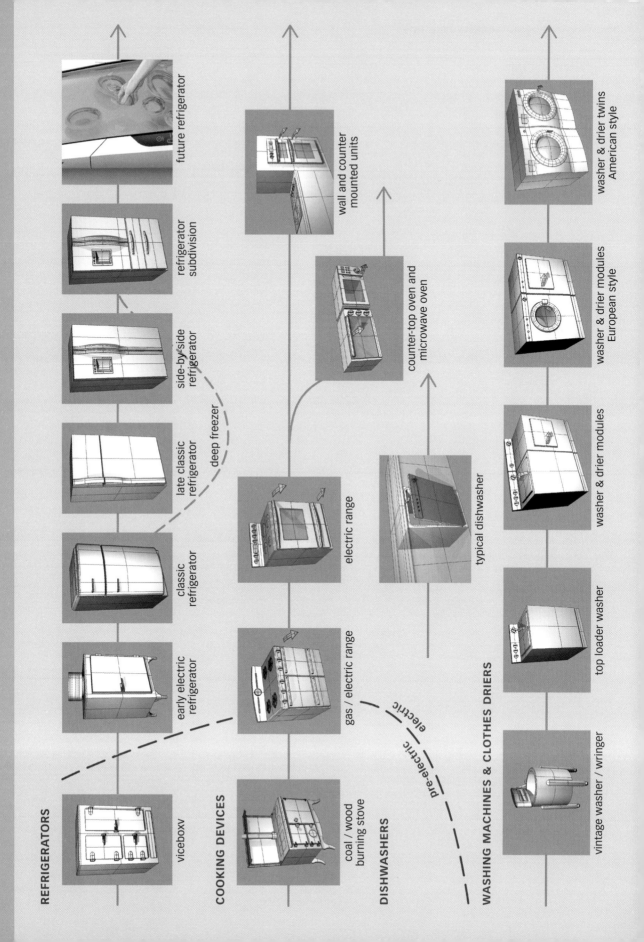

REFRIGERATORS

viceboxv · early electric refrigerator · classic refrigerator · deep freezer · late classic refrigerator · side-by-side refrigerator · refrigerator subdivision · future refrigerator

COOKING DEVICES

coal / wood burning stove · gas / electric range · electric range · counter-top oven and microwave oven · wall and counter mounted units

pre-electric · electric

DISHWASHERS

typical dishwasher

WASHING MACHINES & CLOTHES DRIERS

vintage washer / wringer · top loader washer · washer & drier modules · washer & drier modules European style · washer & drier twins American style

CASE STUDY 11
Food Preparation Appliances

On visiting an appliance retailer, a kitchen supplies retailer, or a department store, we encounter shelves upon shelves of electric kitchen appliances. The variety is stupendous. We may choose from so many brands, so many styles, so many price categories, and so many optional accessories. New lines and new designs appear every year and in holiday seasons. These are the accepted gift material in every price range. No wonder the diversity is extensive and ever expanding.

This raises the first question: can we identify rules that govern the visual form of the large variety of appliances? This question will be treated in detail in the following pages.

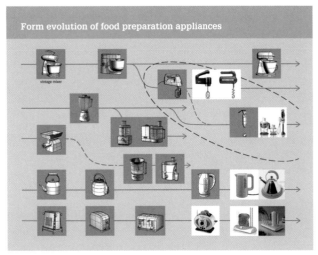

SEE ENLARGED DIAGRAM ON PAGE 185

Highlights

We tend to consider small kitchen appliances as work tools. Each tool has a distinct archetype form that relates to the way it is recognized for what it is and how it operates. Accepted form and handling principles allow concentration on food preparation and not on learning each appliance.

The maker's branding style does not have a strong impact. People rarely buy a "set" of appliances. The archetypal form of each appliance has the visual upper hand.

As long as the archetypal form is easily recognised, designers can play with secondary articulations of form, branding, and details. Thus, there is much room for diversity within set rules.

Food preparation containers should permit a clear view of processed food. As a result, they are fully or partly transparent. Electric and mechanical devices are hidden behind a smooth casing. This often results in a visual distinction between the base unit and the detachable and washable container.

Hybrid appliances (combining two appliances) are more of a gimmick. They usually fail to become established.

Serious cooking is associated with professional, old-style equipment; therefore the recent popularity of retro style appliances. Cast metal and brushed stainless steel finishes are considered to be professional.

Portable appliances have become central to today's lifestyle. Portable tools have distinct contemporary forms, with sufficient cues as to what they do. They exist concurrent with traditional, professional appliances.

The second dilemma is of taxonomy: what is the appropriate classification of small electric kitchen appliances? We are already aware that major appliances, such as refrigerators and ovens, belong to an entirely separate breed. We should remember that not every appliance that resides in the kitchen, such as a hand vacuum cleaner or an iron is functionally related to the kitchen workplace, even if they are grouped together on the same shelf at the store. It seems that the proper family name should be electric food preparation appliances. If I refer from here on to appliances, it is shorthand for electric food preparation appliances.

Furthermore, as familiarity promotes a distinct visual image, we should distinguish between well-established food preparation tools such as mixers and toasters and less well-known and recently introduced appliances, such as bread makers, deep fryers, ice cream makers, rice cookers, slow cookers, electric can openers, and meat carvers (Amazon's site lists about 30 categories of small food preparation appliances). There are even less-familiar products that you will not identify unless cooking is a hobby of yours. So we may skimp on quite a few of them since they did not make a lasting archetypal image, and instead we will concentrate on only the well-known archetypes.

And finally, several of these appliances—coffeemakers, small ovens, and microwave ovens—are discussed in other case studies in this book.

Early non-electric appliances

Kitchen tools have been with us for a long time; actually, we still use many non-electric kitchen tool s with designs originating centuries ago, though often made in plastics rather than wood or metal. Tradition clearly influences the kitchen environment. If you are a real French-cooking aficionado you will use wooden spoons and wire eggbeaters.

The early kitchen appliances were mechanical, operated by hand and quite similar in form to tools used by other professions. The first eggbeater with rotating parts was patented in 1856. Mechanically, it employed the same principles as the manual carpenter's drill, except is pun faster and had a pair of loops for whisking at the end (fig. 1). That foretold the emergence of the rotating pair of whisking loops as the archetypal identifier of the future mixer.

1. THE CLASSIC MANUAL MIXER FORM COMES FROM A LONG TRADITION OF TOOLS

The meat grinder, or mincer, was used for the fine mincing of raw or cooked meat, fish, or vegetables and replaced the knife in many jobs. The grinder has a distinct funnel on top, a manually operated horizontal screw and an endplate with holes acting as a mechanical extruder. The manual handle, the top funnel, and the resulting ground meet ribbons were conspicuous visual elements of the grinder (fig. 2, top). Its electric successor (fig. 2, bottom) just added a motor box

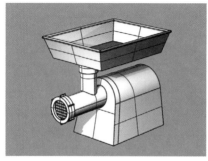

2. WE EASILY RECALL THE MANUAL MEAT GRINDER, BUT WHO REMEMBERS THE ELECTRIC ONE?

and enlarged the intake funnel. It did not imprint any lasting image in our mind since it did not have a defined form yet, but mostly because we do not prepare ground meat at home anymore. To the homemaker it faded into oblivion.

Heat-based tools, such as the traditional kettle, were placed on a heated surface. The kettle form continued a long tradition of pottery, and later metal, cylindrical container forms. The form rested on a long tradition of the tea-making ceremony; the Russian samovar is an example. Therefore, I have dedicated a separate case study for coffee and tea preparation. Once the kettle became portable, its handle and spout, located opposite each other, confirmed what the container was for.

Most mechanized appliances, and eventually the early electrical successors, were made for industrial high-capacity food preparation in restaurants; only decades later were they adapted for domestic use. This stimulated the prevalent industrial look of early household electrical appliance.

Different inventors separately invented the early electrical kitchen appliances. Each inventor started his own production shop bearing his name. In time, most expanded their original invention lines to fabricate complete ranges of appliances. Thus, you may find that many of the current appliance companies bear the original inventor's name (Waring, Oster, Hamilton Beach), or the name of their first product (Electrolux, KitchenAid).

Food mixers

The first mixer with an electric motor was invented in the United States in 1885. The Hobart Manufacturing Company was an early manufacturer of large commercial mixers. It introduced a relatively small model called Hobart KitchenAid. Another concurrent patent for the Sunbeam Mixmaster (fig. 3) made the two companies the forerunners of famous American brands of electric mixers. The early use of the electric mixer was limited to industrial and restaurant use. Domestic electric mixers were rare before the 1920s, when they were adopted for home use.

3. SUNBEAM'S EARLY UNIQUE FORM DETAILS CONTINUED TO APPEAR IN LATER MODELS

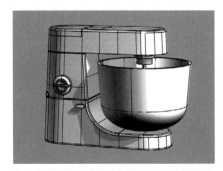

4. A CONTEMPORARY COUNTERTOP MIXER RETAINS THE C FORM IN ONE MONOBLOCK MASS

The structural "C" principle of the stationary, or countertop (as opposed to portable), electric mixer is similar to that of the industrial band saw or the domestic sewing machine: you have to operate on the work area (the mixing bowl) from above (with the rotating tool) and from below (a sturdy base and sometimes mixing bowel rotator) in order to have access to the bowl (by turning the top on a pivot). Consequent heavy-duty power demands for mixing dough kept the countertop mixer on the larger size of the appliance family, this in spite of the always-inadequate counter area in the kitchen. Even today, the countertop mixer is still a big and heavy (cast aluminum) machine (fig. 4); the "C" form still exists without any obvious styling fanfare (for easy cleaning). The tendency then to add a blender and a meat mincer accessory was probably to justify the space demands and equipment cost. One company offered an under-the-counter universal motor for any mixing and blending purpose, but it did not last for long. No one wants to spend valuable time on daily assembly and disassembly of parts.

The mobility lifestyle eventually reached the kitchen. The introduction of lightweight, easy to assemble, use, clean, and store hand mixers were in step with the fast pace of modern life. In archetypal terms, hand mixers formed a new breed. Hand mixers do not look at all

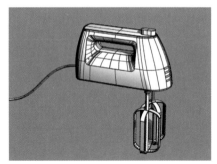

5. THE HANDHELD MIXER ARCHETYPES SHARE THE SAME FORM CONFIGURATION WITH THE IRON AND JIGSAW

like their stationary equivalents. If there is any association to be found for the hand mixer, it is with the clothes iron: a rounded plastic casing with an integral handle, control buttons at its front end, and a cord extended from behind. So how can we tell that it is a mixer and not an iron? Obviously, it is possible to do so by noticing the pair of whisking tools (fig. 5). As the whisking heads are so prominent, they act as the sole family identifiers; therefore, the hand mixer can take a wide range of shapes (figs. 6 and 7).

FIGS. 6 (LEFT) AND 7. AS LONG AS WHISKING HEADS ARE THERE AS A CUE, FORM GEOMETRY MAY CHANGE

With the advent of the portable mixer, we may ask, who needs a heavy countertop mixer? It seems we have taken a cue from the past as the demand for the traditional countertop mixer thrives again. Possibly the trend to return to fresh, healthy, organic food and to invest in home cooking is behind it. Mixing bread dough is the domain of the stationary mixer. Consequently, the mixer's return to popularity means that the proper stationary mixer should look like the one of years ago. In the cooking environment, the professional tool is rather traditional in form since it emulates tools found in the chef's kitchen. KitchenAid successfully capitalized on this retro trend (fig. 8). All in all, the countertop mixer's form differences are just about styling. So, today, we often have both the backward-looking form of the countertop mixer and the modern looking form of the hand mixer coexisting in the same kitchen.

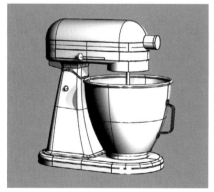

8. THE KITCHENAID COUNTERTOP MIXER SUBMITS THAT RETRO IS PROFESSIONAL

Blenders

9. THE BLENDER'S GLASS CONTAINER FORM IS ARCHETYPAL

Stephen Poplawski was the first person to put a spinning blade at the bottom of a glass container that could chop, grind, and puree foods and beverages, thus inventing the first blender in 1922. He used his invention to make soda fountain drinks. Using his design, Hamilton Beach Manufacturing Company and the famous Waring blender dominated the early USA market.

Blenders are probably the most conservative of appliances in terms of form development. The basic soda fountain form still rules as an archetype form; check at any diner or coffee counter. All the blenders have a removable tapered glass container, often rectangular in cross section. The conical tapering of the glass container is often reflected in an opposing taper of the motor enclosure to define where they detach. The two form elements will always align on the same vertical motor axis (fig. 9).

A late newcomer to the blender family is the hand blender (fig. 10). Although it can't totally replace the full-size blender, the hand blender (also called stick or immersion blender) is handy for puréeing soups or frothing milk, whipping cream, and blending smoothies. The hand blender has become an appliance family of its own.

The hand blender still reflects in its form the configuration of two cones connected at their tips, albeit very slim in form and with a long neck. Ergonomic consideration allowed carving into the motor unit to prevent the blender from slipping in one's hand. Lately, another visual canon—the symmetrical axial form—was broken by bending the top for easier handling. The portability and elimination blender's glass container were so successful that the hand blender is used now as a low-power chopper and mixer, even coffee grinder, depending on which accessory is attached to the motor shaft (fig. 11).

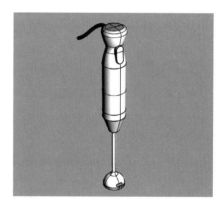

10. AXIAL SYMMETRY PERSISTS IN THE HAND BLENDER

11. WE MAY ACCEPT A VARIETY OF ATTACHMENTS IF THEY DO NOT OCCUPY MUCH SPACE

Juicers

People used to squeeze juice by hand until the electric juicer was introduced around 1930. It had two distinct versions. One was for squeezing juice out of halved citrus fruits, ever equipped with the tell-tale fluted cone of the leverage press, but with an action of rotation rather than compression (fig. 12). The other version was used for extracting juice from vege-tables and non-citrus fruits. This juicer entailed a feed, not unlike that of the meat grinder, and the squeezed juice was poured into a separate container. We can still recognize in the juicer something of the earlier meat grinder's form: feed at the top, output in front. Almost as a rule,

12. THE CITRUS JUICER IS RECOGNIZED BY THE TRADITIONAL JUICE-EXTRACTING CONE

13. THE FRUIT AND VEGETABLE JUICER IS RECOGNIZED BY BOTH THE SPOUT IN FRONT AND THE FEED TUBE OPENING AT THE TOP

liquid handling calls for a transparent container. The unused fruit pulp collects in another container, usually less prominent and made to look as though belonging to the juicer's main body, probably to signify that only the output juice container is worth any attention (fig. 13). Though of quite a complex form configuration, the juicer, sans the detachable juice container, is clearly visually related to contemporary food processors.

Food processors

The food processor we are so familiar with today is a latecomer to the food preparation appliance family. In 1971, Carl Sontheimer, an engineer devoted to cooking, adapted a French industrial blender for kitchen use, naming it Cuisinart. It took several years before the Cuisinart became an essential tool in domestic and restaurant kitchens. The food processor bears a clear resem-blance to its predecessor, the blender (the rule of continuation but differentiation). Since it has a more powerful motor and much larger cutting heads it assumed a low and squat build. A visual addition, non-existent in the blender, was the cap feed tube for inserting fruits and vegeta-bles, an element borrowed from the juicer. The slightly conical transparent container and the somewhat rounded motor housing, still recalling the blender, evolved eventually into distinct geometric forms: a cylinder sitting on top of a cube (fig. 14). An alternative configuration, more preva-lent in Europe, placed the motor housing cube next to the food cylinder (fig. 15).

14. THE FOOD PROCESSOR—A CYLINDER ON TOP OF A CUBE, SEPARATING THE STATIONARY FROM THE REMOVABLE

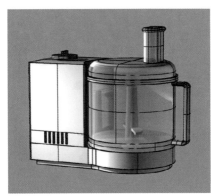

15. THE EUROPEAN VERSION OF THE FOOD PROCESSOR, INTRODUCED BY BRAUN

Electric kettles

Kettles have a lengthy form tradition. The history of the electric kettle is linked with that of the historical iron, pewter, or copper pots used for cooking. Cooking pots eventually evolved into teakettles, which often took a form specific to various regions and countries. In western countries the traditional spout and insulated top handle of the teapot were always the recognition cues (fig. 16).

16. THE TRADITIONAL STOVE-HEATED KETTLE

Various experimental designs for heating kettles with their own electric element, in lieu of an external flame, were tested from 1880 onwards. General Electric introduced an electric kettle in 1930. The credit for creating the first automatic electric kettle goes to Russell Hobbs, a company established in the United Kingdom in the early 1950s. Due to the deeply entrenched ritual quality of the old kettle, the electric kettle form did not change much. Electrifying the kettle also introduced the addition of a power socket, an on-off switch, and a Bakelite handle. Visually the early electric kettle was a somewhat strange hybrid (fig. 17).

17. THE ELECTRIC KETTLE HAS AN UNGAINLY APPENDIX

Only with the introduction of the cordless kettle in the 1980s, with its detachable power supply base, and with the increasingly popular use of high temperature plastics did the form of the electric kettle mature, and immediately a wealth of sculptural variations followed. Almost any conceivable form, from the highly geometric to the sculptured, and even the bizarre, were available. Today's spout is quite minimal in comparison to past ones, and the body-to-handle connection has many variations. Also, newly available were water level viewing windows, and even internal lighting. As in other popular object names, we see that the well established name of the product, kettle, allows for a wide latitude in form variations (figs. 18, 19, and 20).

In Case Study 14: Coffee and Tea Preparation, the kettle's form will be explored again, though from a somewhat different angle related to teapots and hot drink preparation.

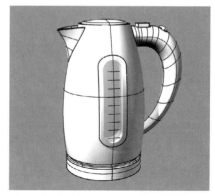

18. THE CORDLESS KETTLE'S INJECTION-MOLDED PLASTICS PERMIT SCULPTURAL FORMS

19. BODUM'S BISTRO KETTLE HAS HIGHLY GEOMETRIC FORM AND STRONG COLORS

20. ALESSI'S ELECTRIC KETTLE BY POSTMODERN ARCHITECT MICHAEL GRAVES, 2002

Toasters

Toasting bread over fire began in Roman times as a method of prolonging the life of bread. In modern times, General Electric submitted its first patent application for an electric toaster in 1909. The early electric toaster had a completely different shape than the toasters we are all familiar with today. Its vertical heating element had a spring-loaded sheet metal plate

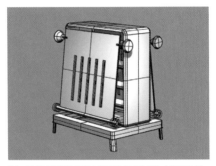

21. THE EARLY TOASTER IS IN ITS ARCHAIC STATE OF DISTINCT FORM DEVELOPMENT

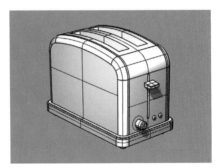

22. THE CLASSIC FORM ARCHETYPE OF THE TOASTER

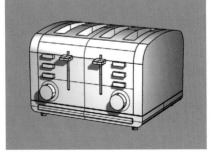

23. THE FOUR-SLICE TOASTER HAS THE SAME CLASSIC FORM

24. THE GLIDE TOASTER CONCEPT BY GEORGE WATSON, 2007

on each side. Closing the plate brought the slice of bread close to the heating element. As the plates were hot to the touch, Bakelite handles were added at the top (fig. 21).

The automatic pop-up toaster, which ejects the toast on its own after toasting it to the right doneness, was introduced only in 1925—the first well-known Toastmaster. Since the introduction of the Toastmaster, little has changed over the years in the form configuration of the two-slice toaster: the same boxy form (slightly more rounded in later models), the same shiny metal surface, the same control knobs, and the same two feeding slots at the top (fig. 22). The toaster has acquired its classic archetypal from. A four-slice toaster was almost the only variation, still adhering almost religiously to the same classic form (fig. 23).

I find it astonishing that the toaster adhered to the same classic form for such a long time, since it is almost the only kitchen appliance in which you cannot see the food while it is being processed, to say nothing about incidents of poking a spoon inside in the effort to retrieve a stuck slice. As a reaction to this

phenomenon, proposed designs for future toasters, seemingly using other heating technologies, have focused on exposing the slices of toast (figs. 24 and 25).

It was not the only way to "rebel" against the boring classic toaster form. I had at home a toaster-radio (fig. 26). The idea makes sense—to have a complete breakfast experience—toasts, coffee, fried eggs, and the morning news in one place, but the results seem strange. Personally I never turned on the radio. Eventually it found its way to the top kitchen cupboard.

25. SEE-THROUGH TOASTER CONCEPT BY INVENTABLES CONCEPT STUDIO, 2012

26. KENWOOD/DELONGHI RETRO TOASTER AND RADIO, 1940'S STYLE

27. TEM500 EGG-AND-MUFFIN 2-SLICE TOASTER AND EGG POACHER BY BACK TO BASICS

What do food preparation appliances have in common?

In spite of a seemingly large assortment on store shelves, we consider small kitchen appliances as essential work tools, so we come to an understanding that each tool has a distinctive archetypal form that not only identifies that particular tool but also relays to us what it does and how. With safety in mind, most of these appliances are quite intuitive to operate. We should focus on what happens to the food and not with where the controls are and how to stop the motor. This is why hybrid appliances (i.e. two or more combined functions) are largely unacceptable, not only because they are not professional enough to our mind but also because they infringe on clear archetype identity (figs. 26 and 27). And so they regularly fail. Every Christmas you may find new combination appliances, splendid gift ideas but doomed to remain in the rear of the kitchen drawer.

To keep with distinct archetypal forms, design changes are accepted as long as they will not confuse our tool recognition cues. As we see, there are many styling and branding variations but they adhere to archetype differentiation. Following these limitations, designers can play as much as they like with secondary articulations of form, brand recognition, and details.

As a rule, technical parts such as motors, electronic controls, and internal mechanisms are always hidden, covered by enclosed, double-insulating surfaces. On the other hand, the food containers are fully transparent. If not transparent, as in the mixer bowl or the electric kettle, there is still ample view of the food contents. The toaster is probably the only exception. This separation of food domain and machine domain leads to another char-

29. PHILIPS' ALESSI LINE SUGGESTS EMOTIONALLY SOFTER FORMS. DESIGN: STEFANO MARZANO

acteristic of food preparation appliances: the clear physical and visual distinction between the base unit and the detachable container.

The abundance of companies in small kitchen appliances, with their brands and their tendency to refresh the design of these fashionable product lines every few years, creates a competitive arena for design and branding. In spite of the effort invested by companies in creating brand recognition for a whole line of appliances (Bodum, fig. 28), it seems that most home makers perceive each appliance they purchase as an individual item and not necessarily as part of a whole.

28. BODUM'S HIGHLY DISTINCT BISTRO LINE OF ELECTRIC APPLIANCES, 2010

Several decades ago, the Japanese concern Panasonic developed an experimental concept of a totally altered group of appliance forms that differ from any accepted convention. It never materialized in the marketplace as it disregarded any of the tenets discussed here. On the better side, the Dutch concern Philips consistently experiments with pushing the form borders, adding emotion to its appliances but without losing any semantic recognition (Philips' Alessi line, fig. 29).

In spite of the almost universality of kitchen appliance archetype forms and the shared global markets, there seems to be a regional style variation of appliances. The European firms prefer modern designers' appliances; the Americans prefer traditional designs. Cooking is often regarded as a highly creative but traditional art. Serious cooks always use professional appliances seen in restaurants' kitchen. Traditional, proven appliances are taken as an indication of professionalism. No wonder then, that the retro look of KitchenAid is ever popular nowadays, as is the use of external cast aluminum and sheet stainless steel.

On the other hand, portability is a currently popular trend: no-nonsense, small appliances, all likely to be cordless in the near future. Easy handling means swift, hurried use, out of the cupboard and back in again.

Form evolution of food preparation appliances

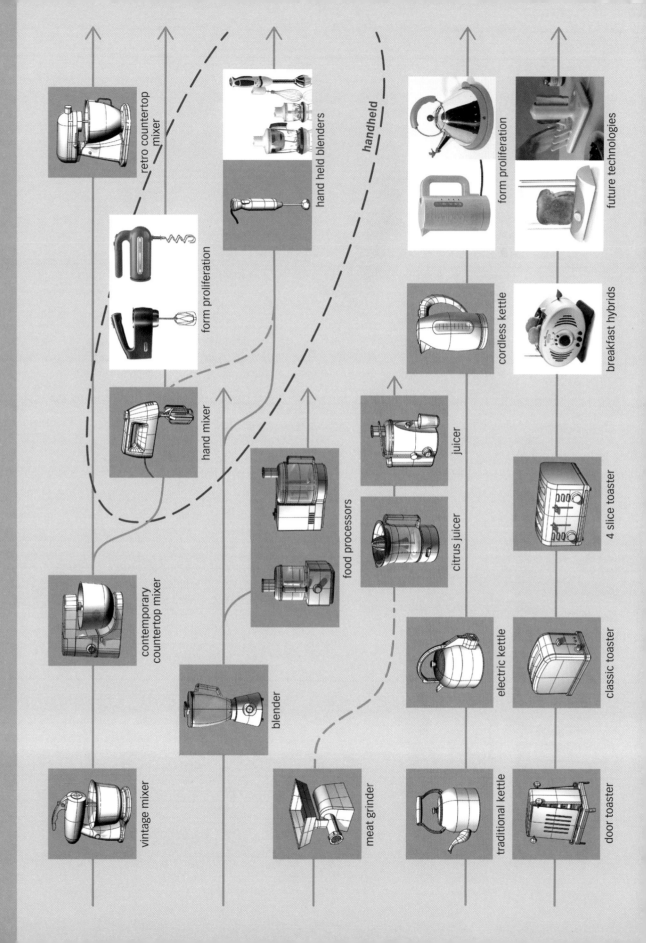

retro countertop mixer

form proliferation

hand held blenders

handheld

form proliferation

future technologies

hand mixer

cordless kettle

breakfast hybrids

contemporary countertop mixer

food processors

juicer

4 slice toaster

citrus juicer

blender

electric kettle

classic toaster

vintage mixer

meat grinder

traditional kettle

door toaster

CASE STUDY 12
Hand Power Tools

Most readers may recall grandpa's hobby workshop in the garage. On the wall hung a tool board—a sheet of plywood on which his hand tools, then mostly carpenter's tools, were neatly suspended on nails. No problem in returning a tool to its place, as the tool's image was painted on the tool board. Hand tools were always easily recognized by their silhouette—handsaw, hammer, hand drill, pincers, and monkey wrench, amongst others (fig. 1). Thinking about it, most hand tools—in wood-working, gardening, and machining—are basically two dimen-sional, having a well-recognized silhouette. Not much changed over the years.

Electric hand tools are visually in a different breed, with no resemblance to their hand tool predecessors and by far more three dimensional and sculptural in form. In spite of these differ-ences, each power tool has a unique form imprint in our brain. We will not reach by mistake to grab the electric drill when we intend to use the circular saw.

1. HAND TOOLS HAVE IDENTIFYING SILHOUETTES

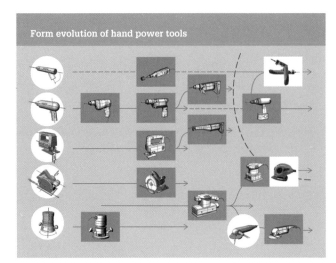

Form evolution of hand power tools

SEE ENLARGED DIAGRAM ON PAGE 193

Highlights

Power tool form is all about form fixation—minimal changes in form over time. Therefore, there is little to discuss in terms of historical visual development.

Each tool has a unique configuration based on component geometry—axial arrangement of features in space. In most cases, there is one conclusive, visually identifiable view.

Power tools are defined by three main components: the motor, handgrips, and work head arrangement. Their spatial geometry and axis define the tool's visual archetype.

Due to form fixation, companies limit themselves to superficial brand identification with persistent brand color or color combination, texture, and logo. In addition, there are only minor sculptural design details.

The battery case is intentionally prominent in cordless tools.

I will point out in this case study that hand power tools are defined by differentiating form fixations and that these key differentiating elements did not really change over time in spite of significant advances in tool technology. Some may say that this is a pure outcome of function: the way the tool works as well as ergonomic considerations (the component geometry tenet). I agree, but I claim that functionality is not the only reason. The tool families, from gardening tools, to jeweler's tools, and to dentist's tools, are in linguistic terms highly taxonomic families. Each tool variant is distinguished by a unique name-word and size identifier: tongue-and-groove pliers, slip joint pliers, eight-inch diagonal pliers, lineman pliers, and long nose pliers, just to name a few. Here, lingual taxonomy has a strong visual expression. A different name makes a different visual image (the professional tool classification tenet). And that image is an identifier that does not change much over time. I call it form fixation. I do not mean it in a derogative way as it allows for visual imprinting.

The moment we label hand power tools as tools they follow the same rigidity of visual language taxonomy as other tool families. Naturally, there are few deviations from the form fixation rule.

There are quite a few hand power tools around; some are only used by professional journeymen, not familiar to the general public. I will deal here with the most common ones, the ones we may see in almost every home toolbox. Here and there I will refer to heavy duty and professional "cousins" in order to emphasize a point.

Power tool history

There is not much to tell as far as timeline methodology goes. Compared to other product families discussed in this book, the form of power tools underwent surprisingly few changes during the last century. It is not that technology did not change and improve over time; power tools are getting lighter in weight. Electric motors became smaller in size and by far more efficient. Electronic controls and drive train designs allow the operator to change tool speed and motion when required. On the downside, unlike some outdoor gardening power tools that have gasoline engines, the portability of home power tools still depends on the length of its power cord and availability of a nearby power outlet. The hand drill, screwdriver, and some sanders are the only ones in which the power requirements tolerate a rechargeable battery.

I mentioned before that hand tools have unique silhouettes. Can we see these shapes in power tools doing the same kind of work? As figure 2 shows, the answer is, not at all. The reason for it is that power tools' ancestors were in most cases the large, heavy-duty, and stationary workshop power equipment.

2. UNLIKE HAND TOOLS, POWER TOOLS' SILHOUETTES ARE SOMEWHAT CONFUSING

We may divide the power tool's form history into three stages on the basis of casing materials. Early power tools were encased in heavy (compared to today's) cast aluminum casing, using steel parts only where necessary (chucks, guiding plates etc.). In the second stage, several elements, typically motor casings and grip handles were replaced by durable ABS plastics, greatly reducing the tool's weight. As a result, design concentrated on the visual subdivision of form based on materials, often using colors. In the last stage, almost the whole casing was injected plastics (except tool heads and some high-wear parts), providing more freedom in form development, as long as form fixation rules were not violated. It was easier to deal with colors and textures, such as rubberlike elastomers, in order to expedite a subdivision of form. Overall, power hand tools became much lighter, less bulky, somewhat smaller, and more sculptural over time.

3. SKIL—COMPLEX RED AND BLACK SURFACE SUBDIVISION

It should be noted that exterior application of corporate branding features is the accepted rule in hand power tools. This strategy was long seen in farm machinery. Each brand is identified by a particular color—blue for Bosch, Green for Makita, yellow for DeWalt, red for Skil, etc. (figs. 3 and 4). There are manufacturers that even differentiate their different groups of professional tools by color. Almost all play with color accents and decorative accents unique to their line of tools. Most

4. DEWALT—ASSOCIATION OF YELLOW WITH PROFESSIONAL TOOLS

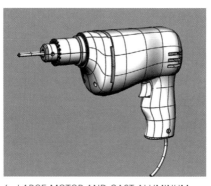

6. LARGE MOTOR AND CAST ALUMINUM CASING MAKES BOTH HANDLING AND VISUAL IMAGE HEAVY

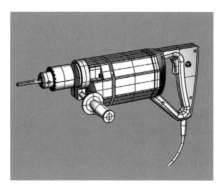

8. THE HEAVY-DUTY POWER DRILL IS RECOGNIZED BY ITS GRIPS

of the design play is concentrated in the softer elements—grips and handles—but not in anything that should interfere with observing the cutting head. Still, recent power tools look fairly softer than before.

The power drill

The Power drill defining form is its single governing axis; the motor, chuck, and drill bit are all in line, or almost in line, with a slight axis shift at the gearbox. This shift is often eliminated in late drill models. The grip and trigger handle, similar to the handgun grip, is an integral flowing extension of the main body. The grip angle is shared by many hand tools. The linear axis flow is enhanced by the tapering in of the chuck towards the drill bit, adding the bit as an integral visual element of the drill (fig. 5). Heavy-duty drilling requires two-handed operation, necessitating a closed pushing handle, located at the end

5. HAND DRILL AXIAL CONFIGURATION

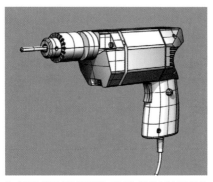

7. MODERN ELECTRIC CORD DRILLS HAVE A MORE PRONOUNCED MAIN AXIS, REMINISCENT OF HANDGUNS

of the main axis and a visually separate additional stabilizing hand grip perpendicular to the main axis (fig. 8).

The power drill family is relatively unique in this case study as we can see a direct visual expression of advancement in technology. It started with a one-speed motor in a bulky cast aluminum body (fig. 6). Then plastic casing and a compact, elongated motor gave the power drill a more directional handgun look (fig. 7). Then drilling speed control and hammering capabilities were incorporated by adding a pronounced speed control ring in line with the main axis. Then the standard Jacobs chuck was replaced by a variety of fast-locking grip heads, making the revolving part of the drill visually a part of the main body (fig. 9).

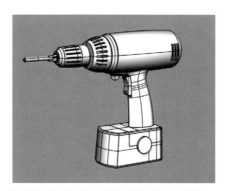

9. THE RECHARGEABLE BATTERY ASSISTS IN BALANCING A COMBINATION DRILL AND SCREWDRIVER

Freedom from the electric umbilical cord, by introducing a rechargeable battery power source, and the capability to reverse-drive screws, were such a significant development that it had to have a distinct visual expression. In visual form it was a paradigm shift. Rather than to hide the battery somewhere inside, like the magazine of a gun inside the grip, it was added as a prominent bulge, almost perpendicular to the grip, now located much forward (fig. 9). Surprisingly, the added weight of the battery and the grip location added to holding stability.

The power screwdriver

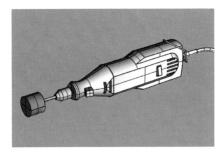

10. A HOBBYIST DREMEL MULTI-TOOL

A slow-speed, high-torque option and motor-reversal control added a screw driving option to drilling. As handling screws requires a much more slender tool body in order to access hard to reach places and does not require as much pushing force as drilling, it was only logical for the electric screwdriver to branch out into a fresh sub-family. A simplified cylindrical form came about, probably borrowing something from the shape of the long-existing hobbyists Dremel tool (fig. 10).

The cordless screwdriver is the ultimate single axis tool. It seems that the well-established gun-form tradition did not disappear completely, and we may find several banana shaped screwdrivers or even a folding screwdriver with two operating modes (fig. 11).

11. A RECHARGEABLE, FOLDING, TWO-MODES SCREWDRIVER ALLOWS ACCESS TO CONFINED SPACES

Almost all run-of-the-mill electric drills now acquire screw-driving capabilities. The drywall screwdriver (not shown here) is an odd bird, it is a heavy-duty screwdriver used by professional builders, but it fully retains the identifying shape of a power drill.

The router

The form of the router (fig. 12), and even its casing material, did not change much with time. Like the power drill and the electric screwdriver, the router is also a one-axis tool. Still, it cannot be mistaken for the other two. Its main features are a chubby high power motor, a motor casing cylinder, and, opposed to the power drill form factor, a tool-end cover that tapers

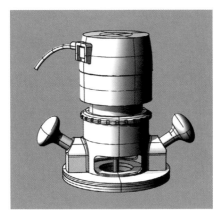

12. A TYPICAL ROUTER DEFINED BY ITS TWO DISTINCT HANDLING KNOBS

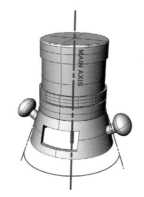

13. ROUTER AXIAL CONFIGURATION

out rather than in, in order to provide a gliding surface plane. X-Y handling of the cutting tool calls for two-hand control delivered by two very distinct round knob handles. The handles in different routers may differ somewhat in form, but they are always visually separated from the main cylindrical body. The router's natural axis orientation is always vertical (fig. 13).

The jigsaw

14. JIGSAW AXIAL CONFIGURATION

The jigsaw tool does not revolve like most other power tools. It has a reciprocal motion. Therefore it is not surprising that everything circular in its form is downplayed. A closed grip at top is almost as a rule an integral part of the main body; it has an overall rectangular, boxy form with an addition of a rectangular tilt and skid plate at the bottom (fig. 14).

As we may expect from the boxy image, in some cases even the motor housing does not reflect the cylindrical form of the motor as seen in most hand power tools. The prominent feature of the jigsaw is that the cutting tool moves up and down in perpendicular to the motor's axis. In a way, working with a jigsaw is not unlike moving a laundry iron. Therefore it is not surprising that the jigsaw's handle was the part most treated by designers, while the rest of the casing did not change much over time (fig. 15).

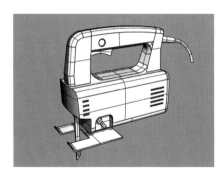

15. A TYPICALLY BOXY JIGSAW FORM FACTOR

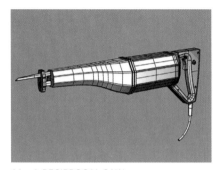

16. A RECIPROCAL SAW

The reciprocal saw, less visually familiar in the domestic scene (fig. 16), is a professional power tool, used mainly in wood housing construction. It may be considered a close-work relative of the jigsaw since it has the same reciprocal cutting head. I included the reciprocal saw here because it draws its form factor, probably not intentionally, from the traditional handsaw. Unlike the jigsaw, the cutting head here follows the motor axis and the grip is quite related to the good old handsaw wooden handle. This is almost the only case of an electric tool drawing on the old hand tool form.

The circular saw

Power tools are visual manifestations of their specific component geometry. In this family the circular saw has the most compound configuration. It is a combination of a powerful motor, a bulging handle with a knob extension for holding and pushing, a rectangular tilt and skid plate, and a prominent tool guard. The cutting disc itself is the largest and most conspicuous of all the replaceable tools in the power tool family, if we overlook the chain saw (too professional to be included here). Such a form complexity requires a well-defined, intuitively understood form organization that works together with the way one operates the tool. This is done by parallel axis placement of most physical elements and unifying the movement directions accordingly; the cutting direction, tool movement direction, grips axis, safety cover direction, and skid plate plane, are all placed in agreement with that basic axis. Only the motor and the disc rotation axis are unavoidably perpen-

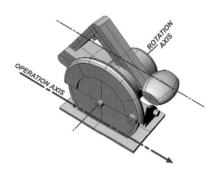

17. CIRCULAR SAW AXIAL CONFIGURATION

18. A TYPICAL PORTABLE CIRCULAR SAW

dicular to the rest of the group, but the motor housing is comparatively short and almost hidden below the bulging handle. No wonder that this "agreement" tends to remain unchanging and to last persistently (fig. 17).

The circular saw has a unique form configuration, setting it apart from the rest of hand power tools. Unlike most power tools, the circular saw has several dissimilar faces, each viewed from different angles. But in advertising you may find only one viewpoint, as it features the large saw disc (fig. 18).

Sanders

The sanders are the odd members of the power tool family. It seems that the principle of differentiation by form fixation does not apply here. What muddles the building of an identifying form is the fact that sanders employ three different mechanical methods of sanding: vibration, belt rotation, and spinning. This is why you will not find an axial configuration diagram associated with this group. As I have mentioned previously, tool name differentiation tends to influence the visual language form and that adds to the confusion. The vibrating sander, the most common in domestic hobby use, did not develop a clearly defined uniform form. It is sometimes compact and cylindrical in form (fig. 19), sometimes quite boxy with an elongated sanding pad and a separate grip and knob handles (fig. 20).

Not surprisingly, the most innovative form change happened here, with the introduction of the Black & Decker Mouse sander in 1998 (fig. 21). The Mouse sander, used for finishing work, combines the images of both the laundry iron and the computer mouse, tail included. When there are no "linguistic obstructions," designers have ample form design leeway.

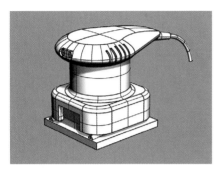

19. SMALL SANDER WITH PEBBLE SHAPED TOP TO FIT THE PALM OF THE HAND

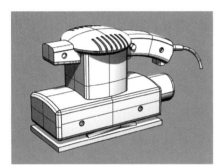

20. A LARGER SANDER REQUIRES TWO-HANDED OPERATION

21. BLACK & DECKER MOUSE SANDER

The belt sander (not shown here) is an uncommon domestic hand power tool. You will find it only in a professional shop. Like the portable power planer (a relative of the router), it is a mechanical translation of its larger stationary carpentry workshop tool.

Circular sanders and angle grinders

In usage terms, the circular sander belongs to the sanders family discussed earlier. I placed it under a separate heading since it becomes a distinct form archetype for a separate tool family, this time with a distinctive well-defined form configuration. A replacement of disc and safety cover converts it from polishing buffer (fig. 22) to a disc sander, or to a metal grinder, now an indispensable tool of the metal and welding trades (fig. 23).

22. A POLISHING BUFFER

The circular sander took over the sanding disc head used on power hand drills since holding the drill vertically over the work surface was awkward. It made sense to bend the sanding head axis at 90 degrees to the motor axis. This was accomplished in a gearbox attached to the front of the motor. Holding the tool close and parallel to the work surface instigated a tapered extension of the motor casing—which then performs as one handle—and also a second control handle butting out perpendicularly from the gearbox (fig. 24).

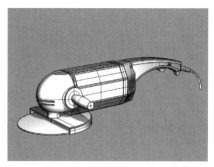

23. THE ANGLE GRINDER IS A COMMON FINISHING TOOL USED BY WELDERS

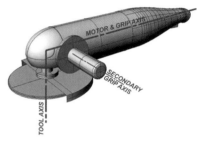

24. AXIAL CONFIGURATION OF AXIAL SANDERS, BUFFERS, AND GRINDERS

Form evolution of hand power tools

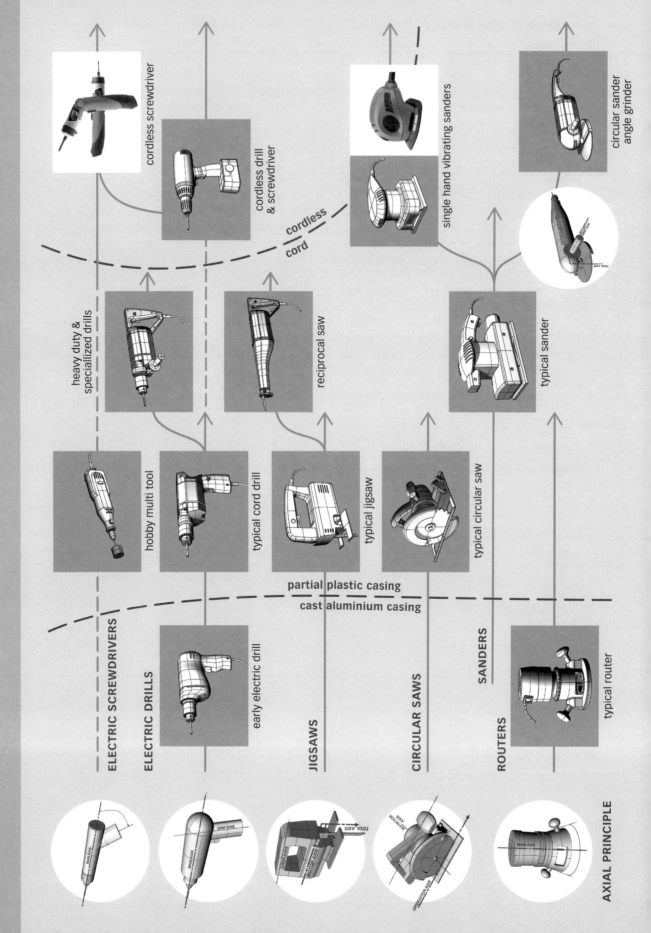

cordless screwdriver

cordless drill & screwdriver

single hand vibrating sanders

circular sander
angle grinder

cordless
cord

heavy duty & specialized drills

reciprocal saw

typical sander

hobby multi tool

typical cord drill

typical jigsaw

typical circular saw

partial plastic casing
cast aluminium casing

ELECTRIC SCREWDRIVERS

ELECTRIC DRILLS

early electric drill

JIGSAWS

CIRCULAR SAWS

typical router

SANDERS

ROUTERS

AXIAL PRINCIPLE

CASE STUDY 13
Chairs

I once came across an estimate that there are about 10,000 different chair models in production around the world. I am not sure how serious this estimation is, but there is no doubt that, outside the fashion industry, chairs are the most prolific in variety of all products. What is really amazing is that, except for a few very highly experimental chairs, we easily recognize chairs for what they are.

The chair case study is a specific example of furniture. It seems that almost all furniture has a narrow vocabulary to describe them—indeed, few new words for furniture forms were added in the last century, and still these few words allow for so many visual varieties.

Another fascinating observation is that in spite of a long existence—spanning several thousands of years—chairs did not change much over time. True, many new materials and technologies were introduced, especially in the last century, but as an archetype, the chair hardly evolved over time. Of course, different fashions and styles arose and faded away, but they were just skin-deep. By and large, chairs constitute a phenomenon worth looking at.

The chair is probably the ultimate design product. Almost every industrial designer tries to show his virtuosity by providing a unique functional and visual solution while pushing structure and material to their limits. It is obvious why; a chair is almost one hundred percent design. Unique chairs usually carry the name of the designer or architect who designed it.

Highlights

Though several millennia old, chairs acquired a basic archetypal form very early, most changes since were superficial.

Chairs are highly structural products, if built by craftsmen or if built with materials and production techniques tested in advance.

Chairs embody a paradox: a huge form variety "controlled" by minimal tolerance for linguistic semantic variety.

The chair reflects our body in form and terminology—legs, seat, back, arms, skin, vertebra, and lumbar support.

The proximity law encourages many form solutions, but cultural disposition and advancement in technology set the stage for last century's proliferation in varieties.

Since form change is by far more lateral than temporal, there is less importance placed in establishing chair classifications.

The classification suggested here is based on form: a matrix using three-dimensional basic design form definitions in one axis, and on Roger's diffusion of innovation divisions in the other axis.

The chair is the ultimate challenge for a designer's virtuosity, and it also enjoys additional, direct, hands-on attention from the designer during prototyping. The chair also lends itself to "one-off" production.

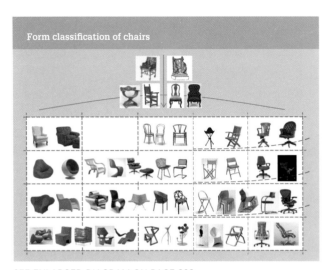

Form classification of chairs

SEE ENLARGED DIAGRAM ON PAGE 203

What's in a name?

Let us begin by investigating the semantics of the word "chair." A thesaurus will suggest a few synonyms: seat, pew, stool, couch, recliner, rocker, settee, and more. More often you will find the noun, "chair," combined with a second word: *armchair, folding chair, lounge chair, dining chair, office chair, director's chair, chaise-lounge* (French for long chair). It will not come as a surprise that another meaning for chair—as a title of office (chairperson, chairman, etc.)—offers by far more variations. Centuries ago, chairs were quite scarce and were commonly a sign of office for kings (*throne*), noblemen, ministers, judges (*bench*), and the likes.

On hearing the word "chair," people will momentarily envision in their mind's eye a simplified image of a chair (fig. 1). Personally, I tend to envision the Vincent Van Gough chair (fig. 2), which is basically the same icon. I take it that this common image was set by childhood memories, the way children draw chairs: square seat, straight back, four legs, and no armrests.

1. CHAIR ICON

When we pay attention to basic chair parts we notice that they are inanimate reflections of our bodies: seat, back, arms, legs, though the more stable four-leg base is borrowed from the animal kingdom. That is probably why we do not see many 3-legged chairs (except in African stools). Most ancient throne legs had literal sculptured lion paws and heads.

We should notice in general that most furniture, in spite of their imposing presence and large size compared to the human body, traditionally have a very

2. *VINCENT'S CHAIR* BY VINCENT VAN GOGH, 1888

limited vocabulary: *chair*, *table*, *bed*, *sofa*, *bench*, *wardrobe*, *cabinet*, *cupboard*, and *chest*. Table, chair, and bed are probably the oldest of the group. There is a particularly limited vocabulary for storage furniture. Several centuries ago a trunk carried our ancestors' meager belongings (leading to the strange combination a chest of drawers or book case). To overcome such limitations we add to most furniture a second, more descriptive word: folding table, dining table, three-seat sofa, love seat, or TV stand, to name a few. More recent furniture names are combinations of two or more separate entities: sofa bed, coffee table, park bench, car seat, kitchen cabinets, children's room furniture, and so on. Quite a limited verbal vocabulary may lead to a larger visual vocabulary, and also to many visual and functional variations.

The noun "chair" also appears in quite unusual word combinations: wheelchair, electric chair, and dentist chair. They look quite different from our iconic chair, but the chair within is still easy for us to visualize. Our mind's visual dictionary is pretty efficient in that.

What makes a chair visually identifiable?

Chairs, the piece of furniture most intimately in contact with the human body, almost religiously adheres to the proximity rule—the closer the object is in contact with your body the more the variety. If a chair may take so many different forms, how can we tell it to be a chair? There must be something in common to all chairs and their form boundaries that should not be crossed. Let me try to propose a few:

■ Size: Watch people resting while on a hike or in a park, they may sit on anything suitable and available: a large rock, a fallen tree, a camping container. They will look for things that will bring their legs to about a right angle. This is the comfortable posture we are used to. So size of whatever we sit on has to relate to our body's proportions. We will not sit on a child's or giant's chair even if it looks a chair (fig. 3).

3. NOT FOR SITTING—GIANT'S CHAIR, HENRY BRUDENELL-BRUCE'S ENVIRONMENTAL SCULPTURE, UK

■ Chair-body visual interface (visual compliance): We look for cues to suggest that we can successfully sit (fig. 4). To achieve this, chairs have functional restrictions. These are barred zones which the form cannot occupy, just as, for example, the hollowed space within a shoe cannot be obstructed in any way, it is reserved for the foot. In the same way, a chair matches in negative space the contour of the sitting posture. Body compliance has also much to do with gut feeling—that we can get into this strange thing comfortably and that the chair is stable

4. COMPLIANCE: INTERFACE WITH THE BODY—BOULOUM CHAISE LOUNGE BY DESIGNER OLIVIER MOURGUE, 1969

5. CONFORMITY: CHAIRS BY LUIGI COLANI—CHAIRS OR ABSTRACT SCULPTURES?

6. CONTESTING SYMMETRY: CHAIR BY KENJIRO YAMAKAWA AND LOREN KULESUS, 2011

7. PROPORTIONS CHANGE WITH POSTURE

and will carry our weight. No wonder a bean bag or a large rubber ball may suggest a lesser acceptance as seats. There are experimental chairs that, due to lack of visual compliance, may not easily be accepted as chairs (fig. 5).

■ Symmetry: Chairs are, as a rule, symmetrical. It makes sense since our body is symmetrical. There are, of course, marginally asymmetric chair designs, but not very many (fig. 6).

■ Customary proportions: This category is somewhat more complex. Preferably an ideal chair takes the proportion of the body (fig. 7). In our mind, beauty has often to do with ideal proportions. Not absolutely so; several physiological and cultural consideration may affect such proportions. On the physiological side, a relaxed posture (which is also culturally accepted) requires a tilt of the chair's back and a lower seat height. At a deeper recline, the legs require support (as in an ottoman). A purely cultural consideration is the height of the chair's back; the taller it is the more commanding your position—the idea behind the throne. This feature is common in office chairs. Chair width is probably less important as far as proportions go, but at a certain point a couch becomes a two-seater sofa or a love seat. There are many exceptions to "correct" proportions: a stool does not reflect body proportions at all and a bar stool does not adhere even to leg proportions.

■ Chairs should refrain from being other products: As the chair form has wide visual latitude, it may easily lose its chair identity by masquerading as something else. And yet, naturally, designers will continue to explore these recognition boundaries, often in whimsical ways (fig. 8).

8. A CHAIR, A COAT HANGER, OR A HAT RACK?

The chair in historical perspective

The chair was not the first furniture made by man. The bed probably preceded it, in forms from the primate's nighttime leaf nest, to the indigenous hammock, to the sleeping shelf of antiquity. Humans can rest well by squatting, sitting cross-legged on the ground, or even leaning on a cane. You can find these traditional postures common in many third world countries. The chair was, for a long time, the sole domain of kings, noblemen, priests and office holders. Ordinary people sat on benches (check Pieter Brueghel the Elder's 1567 painting *The Peasant Wedding*).

As chairs were uncommon and custom-crafted for the very few, it is startling to realize that the tomb furniture of the 1300 BC Pharaoh, Tutankhamen, is so structurally and visually close to today's furniture, especially the chairs (fig. 9). Roman chairs and 15th century Renaissance chairs (fig. 10) were progressive enough to be copied by 19th Century Victorian craftsmen as practical "retro" chairs.

Visually, these examples may reveal their antiquity, but if we remove all the finials and surface embellishments, the bare archetype will be practically modern. Through the ages, chairs reflected changes of style and fashion, sometime austere, sometimes opulent, but the structures were basically alike.
Let me propose an explanation. Chairs are fundamentally structural products; a chair has to support an adult using no excess of materials. Thus, a sound structural solution may hold for a long time. The structural materials and workmanship did not change much over several millennia, remaining mainly woodwork (though forged iron chairs existed) so the craftsmen concentrated on craftsmanship of work and artistic details.

Structural products did change with the introduction of new materials and technologies. The evolution from crafts to industrial carpentry tended to simplify form. Use of steam to bend wood brought about round curves (as by Thonet) and later bent plywood (Alvar Aalto, Charles Eames, Frank Gehry). Modernism saw the use of materials hitherto not seen in furniture: bent steel tubes (Marcel Breuer) and reinforced fiberglass shells allowed for intricate round forms, and one-piece

9. KING TUT EGYPTIAN ROYALTY CHAIRS

10. RENAISSANCE STYLE CHAIRS

plastic-molded chairs followed suit. Office chairs became sophisticated machines. What used to be largely one material chair with the addition of fabric upholstery gave way to numerous combinations of materials in one chair. The availability of a wide range of materials, some rigid, some soft, some textured, some smooth, some transparent, opened endless possibilities of setting them together, structurally or expressively, as long as the human body was sufficiently supported. Designers still try to come up with ever-innovative chair designs. No other product challenges designers as much as the chair (an adjustable lamp is a far second; cars are a separate sphere of design). Virtuosity is the rule. The nice thing about chair design is that you have to prove that it works structurally, so prototyping is imperative, though not all ideas become marketable products.

Chair classification

The chair's evolution had barely any archetypal change for a long time even considering a sudden burst of new possibilities within a short span of time brought about by both technology and cultural acceleration. The chair's evolution is hardly temporal, and is rather mostly lateral—quite a few concurrent principles. The problem stemming from this situation has to do with the classification of these tracks in a way that makes sense in terms of form analysis.

As I mentioned in an earlier chapter, there is a human tendency to find order in things. Since the word "chair" is so all encompassing, we cannot use a traditional verbal terminology as in other product families. There are several alternatives to classify chairs. Interior designers classify furniture according to location: living room, dining room, kitchen, bedroom, and so on. This makes sense when you plan, coordinate, and purchase your furniture in complete sets. Ikea's catalogue is arranged that way. Or you can classify by materials: wooden chairs, metal chairs, plastic chairs, upholstered chairs, and so on. That doesn't apply anymore because there are combinations of materials in most chairs. Historians and the public often prefer classification based on style: antique, traditional, contemporary, and modern are commonly used terms.

Since we are dealing with form, I propose looking at chair classification from a formal point of view. When designers learn three-dimensional design, they use a vocabulary of mass, surface, and line structural approaches to form. Relating this terminology to chairs, I prefer the terms "volume," "sheet" and "frame." The terms range from maximal space occupation to minimal. Naturally, there are chairs that are somewhere in between these categories: a frame with a seat shell, for example. This range looks fine but it does

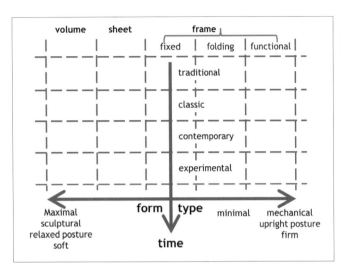

11. CHAIR CLASSIFICATION MATRIX

12. A TYPICAL COUCH AND OTTOMAN

13. DANIEL MICHALIK RECYCLED CORK CHILDREN CHAIR (2004); AND RON ARAD BIG SOFT EASY CHAIR (2001)

not take into account three variants of chair structure: the static (fixed) frame chair, the folding frame chair and the adjustable frame chair. The latter is ubiquitous in the office environment, so I prefer to use the term "functional" rather than "adjustable." Now, the proposed range is not just from the maximal to the minimal, it also ranges from the sculptural to the functional and from the relaxed posture to the upright posture.

So far I was quite technical and did not take into account any cultural variables in this classification. So I will base the cultural range on Roger's diffusion of innovation theory, ranging from the traditional, through the classical, the modern, and to the avant-garde (I prefer the use of the term "experimental"). The grouping of the form and function classification axis and the cultural acceptance axis creates a classification matrix (fig. 11).

Looking at the diagram at the end of this chapter you will notice that there is a usually smooth form transition in the horizontal rows. I placed representative chair images more as indicative visual images and not as a collection of best design icons. This is particularly noticed in the classic row since I placed there very common (literally) chairs next to icons of

design. Certain chairs cannot be pigeon-holed in one specific classification. They may belong to two categories. Admittedly, there will be certain chair designs that will resist any classification at all, especially the experimental ones. The design world is not and should not be strictly rational.

Now let me delve into the visual characteristic of each form type category.

Volume chairs

Chairs in this category are by definition massive, as they fill the space between the floor and the human body and even more. Massive chairs came about early in Homo sapiens' evolution: a suitable rock or tree stump. In historical times, the volume component was usually ancillary to structure, mainly to cushion the chair's seat and armrests. From the Victorian era onwards, increasingly informal and comfortable living prodded upholstery to eventually cover the whole chair. The reclining posture called for an ottoman (fig. 12).

Volume chairs usually hide an internal support structure; most couches are built around a rough wooden frame, others may have rigid foam fillings, and some,

like beanbags, have no support at all. As the internal structure or filling is not visually apparent, we deal in visual terms with a volume—a mass—even if we are aware that the cover fabric is only skin-deep. An egg looks like a rock until the eggshell is ruptured to reveal a shell. Lacking a structural form commitment, volume chairs may take almost any shape design. Most tend to overstate their volume by surrounding the body. Volume chairs are large, sculptural, and soft, at least in visual terms, and less portable (fig. 13).

Sheet chairs

Chair-as-skin as a design concept is a relative newcomer. Structural strength based on bending and folding sheet material was realized only when technology was ready. The Charles Eames 1955 lounge chair reveals a bent plywood sheet structure but it is conceptually still a frame type chair. Alvar Aalto, Charles Eames, and Frank Gehry are renowned for their exploration in forming sheets of plywood (fig. 14).

Ron Arad dropped the pre-forming of material to shape, and instead experimented in twisting and riveting exposed sheet metal. Ana Linares suggests a sheet metal folding approach (fig. 15).

Even earlier, in the 1960s, fiberglass shells and, later, plastic heat-forming and molding allowed for a wide range of soft-curved chair shells, but most of them were externally supported by a metal frame—somewhere between sheet and frame classifications. In these cases, the frame tends to be visually minimal as in the handkerchief type chairs here (fig. 16).

Ron Arad also carried out several innovative experiments with rigid, preformed plastic skins. I chose to show his lacquered plywood three-skin chair, which has a convincing formed-plastic feeling. The purest sheet plastic chair is probably the iconic molded chair by Verner Panton, produced in 1960 (fig. 17).

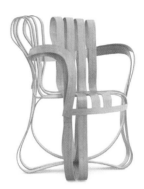

14. EARLY BENT PLYWOOD CHAIRS BY ALVAR AALTO (1943); AND A CONTEMPORARY CROSS CHECK CHAIR BY FRANK GEHRY

16. THOMAS PEDERSEN STINGRAY CHAIR; AND ARMCHAIR BY JASON LIU BASED ON HANDKERCHIEF CHAIR BY MASSIMO & LELLA VIGNELLI

15. RON ARAD'S WELL TEMPERED CHAIR (1986); AND ANA LINARES' CONVERSATION CHAIR

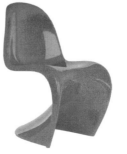

17. MOLDED PLASTIC CHAIR BY VERNER PANTON (1967); AND RON ARAD'S THREE SKIN CHAIR

Static frame chairs

Static frame chairs follow the time-honored historic chairs tradition in many refreshing ways. Static chairs offer the right balance between form design and structural design in one. In most cases the static frame chair returns to a structural honesty, without excesses. That is why most of these chairs have four legs; few have just three since thee-point supports tend to tip over.

Structural honesty is a mainstay of Modernism. Since structural honesty conflicts conceptually with sculptural excesses, interested designers were inclined to investigate minimal designs (fig. 18) and the allocation of proper materials for each part of the chair. It seems that the visual sensibility and lack of excesses of this classification lent themselves to many successfully marketed chairs; quite a few of them became well-known classics (fig. 19).

Contemporary frame chairs tend to be bolder in form and even whimsical, but they still tend to adhere to the clean design spirit (fig. 20).

Folding/stacking chairs

Folding chairs are a variety of frame chairs. They are quite ancient. They followed kings and generals to battle in ancient Egypt and Rome. The basic folding principles and the incorporation of fabric or leather are still in use today (fig. 21).

Folding chairs are like a puzzle to be solved and, therefore, a challenge in chair design. They have to be lightweight, flat, and minimal when folded, but sturdy when open. And the act of unfolding should be something dazzling. Folding chairs are often exercises in design ingenuity (fig. 22).

The stacking chair (fig. 23) is a relatively recent space-saving design used mainly in mass-populated venues, offices, and restaurants. They are actually straightforward, fixed-frame chairs cleverly designed to fit each other.

Functional chairs

Functional chairs are frame chairs designed for specific human work requirements. They are adjustable and usually movable in order to fit the user to his workspace. This is quite a prolific category as it includes dentist's chairs, car and airplane seats, standing machine-tool operator seats, and a few others. I will concentrate here on office functional chairs since they are the most popular of this category. The others are niche specialty chairs, or are considered as parts of cars and airplanes.

The office chair developed both mechanically and visually into a well-recognized breed associated with the functional and formal office environment. You cannot mistake them to be house chairs (though the advent of the home office and the student computer desk brought office chairs into the home environment too).

The office chair has two identifying features: the prerequisite to turn the chair around and move along the work surface required a swivel pedestal and castors, giving the chair a characteristic look. The second feature comes from office hierarchy; a manager's position within the organization should be reflected in his chair (figs. 24 and 25). So chair's back height, opulence, and number adjusting levers (and price, of course) are the visible signs of the office hierarchy.

Better ergonomic qualities gradually transformed a worthy office chair into a sophisticated machine. The mechanism is hidden behind and under the chair's seat, but you could (and should) notice the controls. The language of the office chair is quite elaborate. Jonathan Olivares book, *A Taxonomy of Office Chairs* (2011), is a recent bible of office chair visual language.

18. EXAMPLES OF MINIMAL FRAMES FOR THEIR TIMES:
THONET CHAIR (1859); BERTOIA CHAIR (1950)

22. FLAT-FOLDING CHAIRS

19. CHAIR CLASSICS: CESCA CANE SIDE CHAIR BY
MARCEL BREUER (1925); AND THE WISHBONE CHAIR
BY HANS WEGNER (1949)

23. STACKING CHAIRS

20. CHAIR ONE BY KONSTANTIN GRCIC (2003);
AND SARAPIS BAR STOOL BY PHILIPPE STARCK (1986)

24. TRADITIONAL OFFICE SWIVEL CHAIR DESIGNS ARE
STILL SEEN IN AMERICAN OFFICES

21. POPULAR FOLDING CHAIRS

25. OFFICE HIERARCHY IS DEFINED BY CHAIR BACK HEIGHT

26. FLEXIBLE FABRIC SKINS—AERON CHAIR (1994); EMBODY CHAIR (2009)

27. POSTURE FOLLOWING VERTEBRA CHAIRS: A CHAIR CONCEPT (LEFT);
AND A DETAIL OF SETU CHAIR (RIGHT), BOTH BY HERMAN MILLER

Don Chadwick and Bill Stumpf's Aeron chair of 1994 (fig. 26, left) heralded a new design language of office chairs. A fabric mesh replaced the upholstered shell. Not surprisingly, the Aeron chair is in the collection of the Museum of Modern Art. The next stage was the adjustable lumbar support replicating the spine (fig. 27). The modern office chair became a living thing.

Other inhabitants of the office environment are visitors' chairs, usually the stacking variety. There are also several types of unusual office sitting devices, not exactly chairs. The kneeing office chair is the most familiar.

Where to next?

After thousands of years of hardly any form evolution to the archetype (mostly just changes limited to decorations and surface style changes superficial to the form archetype), the 20th century finally brought about an exponential growth of the chair population. So much variety is now covered by the word "chair." The expansion is likely to continue in spite of designers' growing awareness of sustainability issues. There are several interlocking reasons:

- As suggested before, designers, from school projects onwards, see the chair as a design challenge. It is a chance to play with structural and sculptural possibilities and novel uses of materials.

- The chair is the ultimate design product—one of the few products where the designer's name is adequately publicized. The internet provides an added living museum.

- Culture opened up to accept a variety of sitting postures and to cater to many tastes. Eclecticism is the established rule.

- Many chair designs are particularly suitable for small shops and limited production series, allowing designers to enjoy hands-on, do-it-yourself, and one-off production.

- And let's not forget the proximity law: the human propensity for many varieties in objects in close touch with the body.

Form classification of chairs

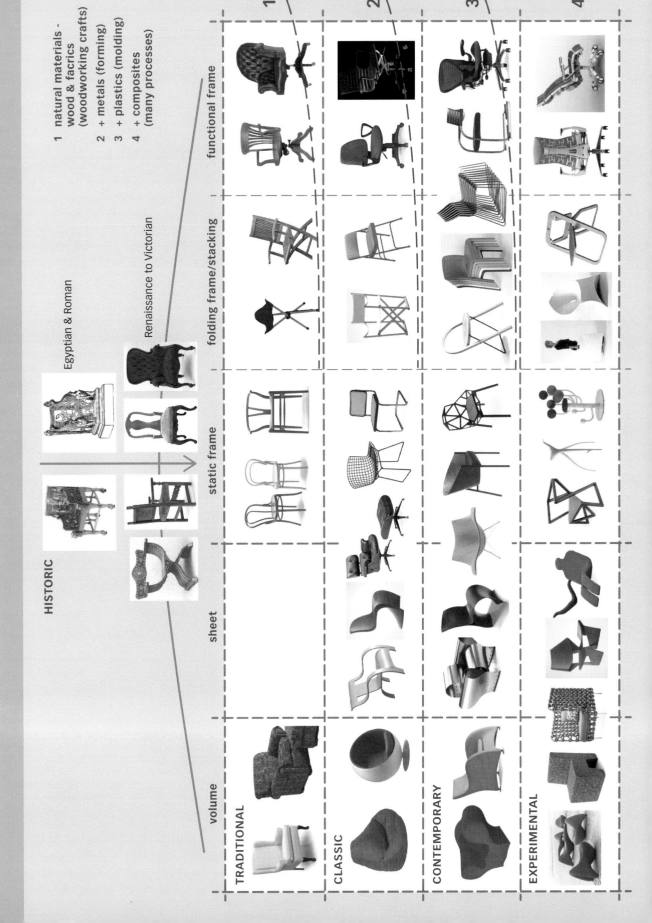

HISTORIC

Egyptian & Roman

Renaissance to Victorian

1 natural materials - wood & fabrics (woodworking crafts)
2 + metals (forming)
3 + plastics (molding)
4 + composites (many processes)

	volume	sheet	static frame	folding frame/stacking	functional frame
TRADITIONAL 1					
CLASSIC 2					
CONTEMPORARY 3					
EXPERIMENTAL 4					

CASE STUDY 14
Coffee and Tea Preparation

My aim here is to examine a representative example of predominantly culture-based products, in order to probe whether objects laden with cultural symbolism follow the same evolutionary route as most products investigated in the previous case studies (and yes, in this case they do!). The title of this chapter could have been a generic description, as it was in previous chapters, something like "Hot Beverages Preparation." But I feel that such a title is too sterile, since the word "coffee" brings about a smell, a tradition, and a ceremony of both preparation and drinking. The phrase "hot beverages" carries the connotations of a vending machine. There are of course other hot drinks, such as hot chocolate (or hot cocoa) and hot cider, but they are esoteric. Coffee and tea have by far the more distinct visual product family vocabulary.

Coffee and tea are immersed with ritual and tradition, sometimes to the point of being religious. The Japanese tea ceremony comes immediately to mind, but try to argue with an Italian about the proper way to prepare a cup of espresso, or with an Englishman about the proper way to serve afternoon tea (with milk, of course), and you will find that we are dealing here with well-established national and cultural rituals.

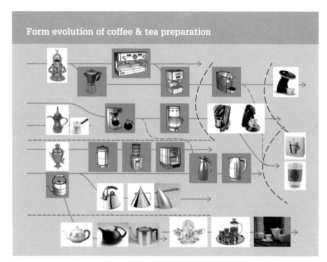

Form evolution of coffee & tea preparation

SEE ENLARGED DIAGRAM ON PAGE 215

Highlights

Coffee and tea preparation products evolved from different cultural traditions. Since late 20th century globalization brought cross-cultural exchange, they reflect social habits rather than cultural rituals.

Coffee and tea preparation products have shown in the last century a distinct evolution from localized cultural sculptures to global contemporary appliances.

There are two distinct groups of products: the communal (seen in coffee houses etc.) and the domestic (usually of the smaller, single-cup variety).

Product differences are usually defined by the preparation process: espresso and ready-made capsule coffee focus on the brewing stage; filter coffee on the serving pot; and tea on serving and drinking.

Coffee brewing products (especially espresso), even domestic ones, were considered to be machines for experts. In recent times (with the introduction of ready-made capsules, for example), they changed from "machines" to consumer friendly coffee-makers, eventually progressing to one-button gadgets.

Serving products—teapots and coffee pots—adhere to the traditional kettle form, though with a latitude for variation as long as they remains recognizable.

Hot water dispensing machines are plain, practical products without any cultural overtones. In an age of on-the-run disposable products, this practicality has influenced the democratization of tea and coffee making by being "indifferent" to prior traditions.

Paper cups, instant coffee, coffee capsules, and teabags created a disposables culture, leading away from past traditions.

The contemporary coffee house chain culture, typified by Starbucks, is less about coffee and more about working and mingling in leisure environments.

Two future trends emerge: one will continue to advocate the physical presence of coffeemakers, maybe as cultural gadgets; the other will continue to dematerialize both processes and objects.

1. COFFEE CEREMONY IN ETHIOPIA, THECRADLE OF COFFEE GROWING AND DRINKING

Apart from the visual aspects of form evolution, this case study is concerned with the ritual layer that lies on top of product archetypes. Food preparation is generally highly ritualistic, particularly when it comes to drinking (recall alcoholic beverages). The products involved in preparing tea and coffee in the past had strong cultural and traditional aspects that could not be ignored. To remember just a few: the Russian tea *samovar*, the Arab coffee *finjan*, and the English quilted teapot cover (or "tea cozy"). Even Starbucks, as young as it is in comparison, became a center for a sort of modern ritual, a place of devotion, admittedly, very American in spirit. At the same time, the

objects of ritual are diminishing, unless you consider the paper cup with the Starbucks logo (a mermaid!) a ceremonial object.

Coffee & tea preparation processes

Methods and procedures are important in food preparation in general. The products we deal with here are mere tools in a process of preparing "the perfect cup of coffee." The procedure is covered with layers of personal taste and preference, national tradition, and ongoing cultural trends.

I will ignore here all aspects of agriculture, plant growing, harvesting, the roasting of coffee beans, the drying of tealeaves, and their packing, exporting, and distribution. I will concentrate only on the last stages of preparation, something with which the public is universally familiar (fig. 2). I will explore the products associated with these final stages and analyze the evolution of their visual languages.
The preparation process of hot beverages is typically divided into three distinct

stages: brewing, serving, and drinking. To clarify these terms, brewing has to do with the equipment and tools for heating water and applying coffee or tea into that hot water. Serving has to do with vessels and other objects used to carry the beverage to the table. Drinking has to do with the personal drinking vessel, be it a coffee mug, espresso cup, teacup, or the likes. These stages are not of equal significance in the process. Coffee is more about brewing; tea is almost exclusively about serving. A stage may even be totally omitted in some processes—for example, in espresso making, there is not any serving intermediary; coffee is brewed directly into the drinking cup.

3. THE COFFEEHOUSE AS A VENUE FOR CULTURAL ENGAGEMENT AND LEISURE

Both coffee and tea preparation products may be grouped according to two different venues: the communal group, present in public places—coffee houses and tea houses which often remind us of previous eras of opulence and leisure (fig. 3); and the domestic or personal group of products, which is an outcome of our ever-increasing pace of life and need for instant gratification. Obviously, communal venues will have commercial, high capacity, and industrial strength equipment.

The developing instant culture brought about another category of preparation tools: the hot water machine, always there, ready to pour, but totally indifferent to whether you prepare a cup of coffee

2. THE PUBLIC STAGES OF COFFEE MAKING

or tea or soup. Since this indifference reflects upon other preparation products, I will devote a later section to hot water makers.

Because I will focus my discussion on the evolution of key preparation tools, I will ignore most of the auxiliary paraphernalia involved in the process, such as coffee roasters, grinders, milk foam makers, and tea strainers.

Coffee preparation

> **Coffee is a language in itself.**
>
> **Jackie Chan**, a Chinese film actor and martial artist/comedian

Coffee preparation is the process of turning coffee beans into a beverage. In the process, raw coffee beans are roasted, the roasted coffee beans are ground, the ground coffee is mixed with hot water for a certain time (brewing), and finally the liquid coffee is separated from the used grounds. Coffee is usually brewed immediately before drinking.

There are four ways of brewing coffee which greatly affect the coffee preparation product: boiling, gravitational feed (drip brewing, filter brewing), pressurized percolation (espresso), and infusion (steeping, French press).

4. TRADITIONAL TURKISH IBRIK AND CONTEMPORARY MIDDLE EASTERN FINJAN

Boiling was the universal method used for brewing coffee until the 1930s and is still used in some places, notably Middle Eastern countries, where the ground coffee is purposefully not separated from the water and remains in the drinking cup. This method, named "Turkish coffee," uses a kettle called *ibrik* or *finjan* that is heated over a stove. The traditional *ibrik* has an elaborately sculptured Middle Eastern image (fig. 4). Its contemporary version looks almost like a regular cooking pot, the ritual is in the pouring gesture.
In the infusion or steeping method of coffee brewing, a plunger inside the pot is pushed down several minutes after the hot water was poured in, separating the coffee from the grind. This method was common in France, named *Cafetière* or "French press." The traditional *Cafetière* and its Bodum modern design version are quite the same (fig. 5).

5. A TRADITIONAL FRENCH PRESS; AND A MODERN BODUM *CAFETIÈRE*

6. THE ORIGINAL BEZZERA ESPRESSO MACHINE, 1905 (LEFT); AND A RETRO-INSPIRED, LEVER-OPERATED MACHINE (RIGHT), 2014

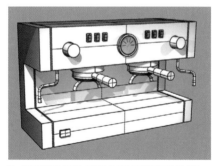

7. ARCHETYPAL FORM OF COFFEEHOUSE ESPRESSO MACHINE

Boiling pots and infusion pots owe their form to traditional jugs. The infusion pot looks modern as its plunger action entails a clean cylindrical form. Boiling and infusion had a limited form evolution, while other brewing methods—pressurized percolation (to simplify I will use the term espresso) and drip-filter coffee makers—evolved significantly.

Espresso originated in Italy, but since the 1950s, it has become popular all over the world. It is made by forcing boiling hot water under high pressure through a lightly packed matrix, called a "puck," of finely ground coffee. It is one of the most concentrated forms of coffee regularly consumed, with a distinctive flavor provided by crema, a layer of foam floating on the surface, which is produced by the high pressure. Espresso is the basis for many coffee drinks. The traditional communal steam espresso machine of 1905, invented by the Italian inventor Luigi Bezzera, was really an awesome machine in the tradition of Victorian era steam engines, with many dials and levers (fig. 6). Note the sculpture's "helmet" top, which represents the presence of pressurized steam. The successors of the Bezzera machine from the 1940s onwards, the ones we are most familiar with in coffee houses, changed form from a vertical axis sculpture to an efficient, horizontal design (with a top balcony for storing cups, and featuring a control panel, an intermediate consumables handling tier, portafilter

8. MOKA POT, ITALIAN HOME ESPRESSO MAKER

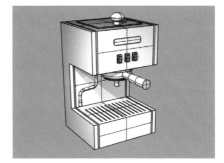

9. THE ARCHETYPAL FORM RELEGATED TO DOMESTIC USE

handles, foam tubes, and a base that doubles as a drip collector). This rectilinear, horizontally extruded "C" design represents the classic espresso machine (fig. 7). Some models may have a rounded version of the basic form. Aside from technological improvements that eliminated long pressure levers, the basic form hardly changed over time. Interestingly, the machine's blank rear panel is all customers see in a coffeehouse environment, perhaps with a distinct logo and the telltale cups on top. Still, our recognition lies with the form always facing the barista.

The moka pot, the domestic Italian stovetop espresso maker (fig. 8), has a form absolutely unrelated to the commercial machine. Its form is based on traditional pots and jugs. Its hourglass form hints at how it works, the bottom cone is a pressure cooker, the waist is the coffee puck location, and the top collects the

coffee forced up by pressure. In spite of the hourglass body form, the traditional faceted octagonal shape and muscular handle are masculine, hinting at pent up pressure inside.

As expected, the next version of home espresso machines adopted a compact form of the commercial one, with only one brewing station and a topmost water compartment (fig. 9). As in most home appliances, brands (almost all Italian) tried to differentiate their designs, but principles of form did not change much from the classic archetype form. In fact, the home espresso machines adhered adamantly to the complex "machine" look, as if espresso brewing were a secret, macho art that relates somehow to operating a steam locomotive.

10. DELONGHI HIGH-END ESPRESSO MACHINES

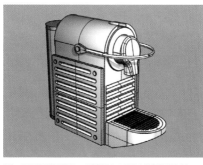

11. NESPRESSO—FORM AND LIFESTYLE PROMOTER

Only with the spread of electronic controls did espresso brewing progress into the realm of pushbutton operation. The high-end DeLonghi espresso machines (fig. 10) are a good example. In it, mechanical brewing operations are hidden, including the brave omission of the portafilter and its signifier handle: the language of all past espresso machines. Still, it manages to retain the "expert" aura. The rule of continuation but differentiation applies here with the machine proportions based on a cube. The traditional three-tier horizontal division of form is still present, but a new vertical division into three segments is introduced. The central intersection of the horizontal and vertical is carved in, signifying the place for the coffee cup, a cue taken from coin operated automats. But in order not to be confused with similar designs of hot water dispensers, a milk container is added to the form. The increased prominence of the vertical arrangement will be echoed in many later automated coffee makers.

The next form evolution came with the introduction of coffee capsules that eliminated once and for all the cleaning of spent coffee grinds. In my opinion, the Nespresso brand line (fig. 11) epitomizes the modern cultural image of espresso machines: elegance replacing what was formerly complex. Controls, even push buttons, are reduced to a minimum. Turning one lever to start the process commemorates past pressure levers. Even that single reminder disappeared from subsequent models.

The Nespresso models incorporate several formal changes. The cube form came to be narrow, tall, and deep, providing a smaller footprint on the kitchen counter. Two previously hidden internal elements are exposed: a transparent cylindrical water container at the back and a horizontal barrel top that suggests an internal pressure piston. The coffee spout reflecting past portafilters is placed prominently in front. This transformed language vocabulary is almost a paradigm change of a very persistent cultural tradition. To facilitate the impression of highest quality, Nespresso created a refined lifestyle and design culture around its products, in a similar way to what Apple did in the computer market.

While pressurized percolation (espresso), in concurrence with the spread of chain espresso houses and gourmet coffee blends, replaced coffee boiling methods in most of Europe, the United States (always the top consumer of coffee) maintained its allegiance to drip brewing. Drip brewing or filter brewing is a straightforward way of keeping the coffee sediment away. Boiling water is poured through a paper funnel filled with ground coffee and the dripping coffee collects in a mug or a coffeepot. A brewed coffeepot is ready for dozens of servings and can be kept warm on a hot plate. Ready-made coffee perfectly befits a culture that depends on consuming

FIGS. 14, 15, AND 16 COFFEE CAPSULE-BASED COFFEE MAKERS BY KEURIG, PHILIPS, AND NESTLÉ

12. A DINER FILTER COFFEE MAKER AND THE UNFORGETTABLE SERVING POT

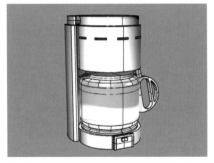

13. BRAUN AROMASTER FILTER COFFEE MAKER

quantities of coffee at work. Compared to espresso, the process is simple. But unlike espresso, where brewing is the key stage of the process, in filter brewing the serving is the part we remember. Recall movie scenes where morning breakfast in a diner is about coffee served by a tired waitress from a Curtis glass coffee decanter—the globular one with a black Bakelite handle. That globular coffeepot design embodies the image and form of filter brewing: the brewing machine, with a visual language of commercial stainless steel equipment, plays by far a lesser visual role (fig. 12).

Subsequent American domestic coffeemakers have not acquired a conclusively recognizable form. The glass coffeepot shape (and the black liquid inside) was adequate. The European appliance manufacturers, most likely less familiar with diner coffee, had better success with integrating the forms of the glass coffeepot and the plastic body of the drip brewer into one geometric entity. The essentially cylindrical Braun Aromaster, designed in 1972 and still in use today, is a well-recognized modern classic (fig. 13). There were other good designs on the market but with no lasting image to be regarded as a form archetype. It seems that filter brewing, like the diner of the 1950s, gradually lost its place to Starbucks and coffee capsules.

And then came the ready-made capsule—almost as easy as inserting your bankcard into the ATM and getting your money (coffee) out in no time. Many flavors and combinations of coffee existed in sealed individual portion pods, with no sediments exposed. Several machines even can prepare cocoa and tea. Nespresso, Keurig, Tassimo, and Lavazza are several names that come to mind and, as Nespresso's patent expired in 2012, more players may arrive. Nespresso decided to strictly adhere to the espresso process tradition, but most capsule-based coffeemakers are somewhere on the murky spectrum between high-pressure espresso and filter coffee. The brewing method is less important here. In terms of product form evolution, they all belong to the same product family: capsule-based coffeemakers. As a new family, with less established tradition, there is a proliferation of coffeemaker forms (figs. 14, 15, and 16); some are quite experimental and often highly sculptural. Vertical proportions and visual aggregation of external elements, characteristics mentioned when discussing Nespresso earlier, are more profound. Note that in most photographs, a coffee cup is required in order to complete the image in order to identify what it is. I propose that gradually we will synthesize a visual archetype for this family. That will depend much on the word(s) we will use to call that family of coffee makers (could it be *one-cup-maker*?).

Tea preparation

If you are cold, tea will
warm you;
If you are too heated, it
will cool you;
If you are depressed, it
will cheer you;
If you are excited, it
will calm you.

William Ewart Gladstone, British
prime minister 1860s–1890s

Tea, originally from China, is the second
most consumed beverage on Earth after
water. Tea drinking is an older tradition
then coffee drinking; thus, tea ceremonies
are long established in several cultures,
notably the Chinese and Japanese tea
ceremonies, each of which employs traditional techniques and ritualized protocol
for brewing and serving tea for consumption in a cultured setting. In western
cultures, especially in Britain and Russia,
tea is the center of social events, such as
the famous British afternoon tea and the
tea party.

In terms of tea preparation processes,
brewing is straightforward – just pour
hot water over crushed tealeaves kept
in a strainer or a paper bag. Yes, there
exist tea-brewing products, but most of
us will recall none. As a result, in terms
of products and tools, the serving and
drinking phases are the ones that carry
the burden of visually representing tea.
No wonder that *drinking* tea is inherently
more social and ritual than it is for
coffee. To some, the world stops for a five
o'clock tea (fig. 17).

The traditional Western ceramic teapot
form has been long-established as iconic
in form (fig. 19). It probably embodies
everything about tea drinking. Its charac-

17. A LEISURELY AFTERNOON TEA SETTING

18. CHINESE TRADITIONAL CAST IRON
KETTLE AND TEAPOT BY DAOLI

19. DESERT ROSE CERAMIC TEAPOT BY
FRANCISCAN, 1941—THE LARGEST SELLING
PATTERN IN THE HISTORY OF AMERICAN
DINNERWARE

teristic form is taken from the traditional
pewter or steel kettle or the Chinese
cast iron teapot (fig. 18) with the handle
moving from top (away from stove fire) to
the side and the base ends with a smaller
diameter.

Please note that from here on I intentionally do not use archetypal computer
generated images. Artistic form details
and surface decoration are just as intrinsic
parts of the tea culture as aroma and
ritual are. You cannot separate them.

Teapots are, first and foremost, cultural
objects. The word "product" seems out
of place here. As cultural products, they
are objects of desire and collector items.

Thus, the diversity of personal interpretations of the teapot form is enormous.
Artists, craftsmen, designers, and architects try anything imaginable, from a stern
design to designs of pure extravagance,
from strictly traditional to bold experimentation. And we still recognize them.

I chose to represent two classic designs,
and a whimsical one (figs. 20, 21, and 22).
Our semantic mind will readily recognize
them for what they are.

20. TAC TEAPOT, WALTER GROPIUS FOR
ROSENTHAL, 1969

21. CILINDA TEAPOT BY ARNE JACOBSEN
FOR STELTON, 1967

22. AMPERSAND TEAPOT BY ADRIAN SAXE,
1988

23. AN ENGLISH TRADITIONAL CHINA TEA SET BY WEDGEWOOD

24. A GLASS AND METAL TEA SET

25. A MODERN TEA SET IN THE MEMPHIS TRADITION. UNKNOWN DESIGNER, 1980S

26. A PORCELAIN TEA SET BY HEINRICH WANG FOR NEWCHI, 2012

Teapots may have free spirits, sometimes removed from the tea drinking ritual. A traditional Western tea event requires a full tea serving set, where the teapot is just one player, albeit a major one, akin to chess sets. The teapot is accompanied by a hot water pot, sugar and cream bowls, and a set of teacups, saucers, and cake plates. Traditional tea sets were made by far Eastern or European manufacturers of bone china (fig. 23). You will also find in Europe a variety of tea serving sets made of glasses placed in a silvered holder. Modern examples of glass and metal tea serving sets follow the style of the art deco period onwards (fig. 24).

Designing a set of visually associated products is always a challenge and, like modern teapots described earlier, there exists a large variety of tea serving sets (figs. 25 and 26).

Hot water dispensers

The term hot water dispenser includes traditional kettles drawing heat from stoves, hot water vessels, electric kettles, and hot and cold public water dispensers. I have already discussed kettles in Case Study 11: Food Preparation Appliances, where they rightfully belong. To most people, boiling water for human consumption, time-honored as it is, is purely practical and does not carry the social aura of coffee and tea preparation. This impression may not be entirely true.. Since tea preparation necessitates a kettle, there is a strong visual affinity between kettles and teapots. On the other hand, the office hot water dispenser has a significant role in removing ritual from coffee making.

27. AN ORNATE ELECTRIC *SAMOVAR* REPLICATING VINTAGE COAL-HEATED RUSSIAN *SAMOVARS*

When discussing bygone communal water heaters, the traditional Russian hot water heater, the *samovar* (fig. 27), comes to mind as an extravagantly ornate cultural object. Hot coal placed at a central core brought water to boil. The *samovar* and several Middle Eastern equivalents were then strongly associated with never-ending tea drinking. In contrast, the common electric hot water boiler (fig. 28), which is still around, is as devoid of any self-conscious qualities as one can be. The water level indicator tube and tap are plain engineering solutions.

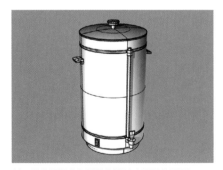

28. ELECTRIC COMMUNAL HOT WATER BOILER

29. A SPARKLETTS BOTTLED WATER DISPENSER

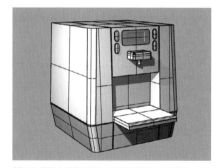

30. A COUNTERTOP HOT/COLD WATER DISPENSER

Sparkletts, the most popular bottled water provider, and itself an icon of bottled water, introduced a dispenser of hot and cold water (fig. 29). The dispenser had plain institutional form qualities, and identity was retained by the blue bottle. A closer examination will find this dispenser to be the form origin of recent coffee-makers: three vertical divisions with a set-in tap opening. Subsequently purified tap water, using an internal filter, replaced bottled water. Devoid of the bottle, the lackluster lower part of its predecessor turned into a countertop product with basically the same form. With some changes in proportions and the addition of electronic controls it turned out to be an appreciated appliance, thus finding its way to the domestic environment (fig. 30).

31. CLASSIC STOVE-HEATED METAL KETTLE

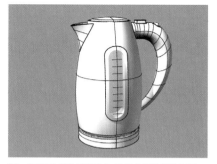

32. CORDLESS KETTLE. THE DETACHABLE BASE ACTS AS AN ELECTRIC PLUG

The ever-present kettle (fig. 31) is a classic and age-old archetype. As I pointed out previously, teapots share the same arche-typal form as the kettle. The handle may have changed location, but the spout and lid remain the same. Eventually, an electric heating coil was added inside, but the archetypal form persisted with just an addition of an electric socket opposite the spout. The next development was the introduction of the cordless kettle (fig. 32), which permitted the kettle to be used as a serving pot. Lightweight, heat-tolerant plastics offered new freedom in design. Subsequently, the formal changes were quite pronounced. The overall form became taller, and the handle, lid, and spout were visually grouped together with button controls on the handle's top for easy reach. The most noticeable visual element was the integrated window revealing the water level, often with a blue internal light. The diagram at the end of this chapter suggests a possible form influence from the coffee (or hot water) thermos.

The traditional stove-heated kettle did not disappear in spite of the electric kettle. A familiar modern version is the whistle kettle that also allows filling through the wide spout (fig. 33). There is a continual interest in it as an art form, and as in most declining products, designers take form investigation to the extreme. One can hardly tell by form a kettle from a teapot. It seems to me that modern teapot designs took hold of the traditional kettle (figs. 34 and 35).

33. A MODERN WHISTLE KETTLE—UPLIFT KETTLE BY MARK NADEN FOR OXO, 2008

34. IL CONICO KETTLE, DESIGNED BY ALDO ROSSI FOR ALESSI

35. PHILIPPE STARCK'S HOT BERTAA KETTLE FOR ALESSI, 1989

Cultural gadgets or dematerialization?

> Starbucks was founded around the experience and the environment of their stores. Starbucks was about a space with comfortable chairs, lots of power outlets, tables and desks at which we could work and the option to spend as much time in their stores as we wanted without any pressure to buy. The coffee was incidental.
>
> **Simon Sinek**, author, commentator, motivational speaker, popular TED speaker

Since the last quarter of the 20th century, many traditional cultural expectations relating to the proper way to brew and serve tea and coffee have been abandoned. Cultural globalism introduced green and herbal teas to western society's taste; ever-present coffeehouse chains made Italian espresso terms such as *cappuccino* and *macchiato* accepted in languages other than Italian. We tend to forget how fast (and getting even faster due to globalization) cultural changes take place. The common knowledge is that Italian espresso culture is centuries old. Actually it did not exist a century ago and in the 1960s it already proliferated in Britain, but still under Italian-named coffeehouses like "Costa" and "Nero." Today, Starbucks is sufficient to represent Italian coffee. Many assume that coffee with milk is Spanish or Mexican in origin (Café Ole), not being aware of the French

spelling (café au lait). The chart (fig. 36) shows how readily coffee combinations cater to many tastes.

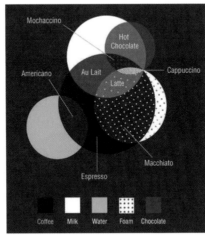

36. "THAT'S WHAT'S IN A CAPPUCCINO" VENN DIAGRAM BY GRAPHJAM.COM

As globalization becomes widespread, today's products and tools used in preparing hot beverages have become quite similar. Local cultural tea and coffee objects evaporate. The on-the-run lifestyle leaves less time for leisurely social coffee drinking. Who can afford to leave work for an afternoon tea? Even the personal mug may soon disappear; more and more, people habitually drink tea or coffee out of disposable cups, with complementary insulation grips (fig. 37). Is this the path to the total dematerialization of coffee and tea preparation culture?

The instant coffee and tea trend is not recent at all. One instant coffee process was invented in Germany in 1901 and became commercial in 1938. Then came freeze-dried instant coffee, and later ready-made coffee capsules. Americans abandoned teaspoons long ago in favor of plastic stirring sticks. Nothing about preparation is revered anymore. Teabags were commercialized in 1904, leading to the gradual exclusion of brewing teapots and the rituals associated with it. Today, the wooden assorted teabag box

embodies what is left of ceremony. I am not sure how many families still keep in the cupboard, let alone use, a full bone-china tea serving set.

The Starbucks phenomena, as mentioned in the quote from Simon Sinek, is about a new way of socializing, where, if you prefer, you may plug you ears with music and concentrate on your laptop, oblivious to others who prefer social drinking and loud conversation on nearby couches. There is still a display of various coffee products around you, but the art of coffee making is characterized in a few words abbreviated as hieroglyphs on a paper cup (fig. 38)—*Steve, Grande caramel macchiato*. In terms of this book's theme, the spoken and written language replaces the visual language of the product. Dematerialization!

37. THE ULTIMATE HOT DRINK PRODUCT

38. STARBUCKS HIEROGLYPHS

Dematerialization can still exist in visual terms, for example, as a purely graphic icon of a cup of coffee. The WMF1 Single Serve Coffee Maker (fig. 39) could not be any simpler in terms of design or functionality. It features a single button and a mug-shaped hole—a mug that fits perfectly right inside. The rest of the brewing operation is intentionally eliminated.

39. WMF1 ONE-CUP COFFEE MAKER CONCEPT BY WMF DESIGN TEAM

40. PIAMO MICROWAVE COFFEE MAKER

41. ELECTROLUX DESIGN LAB CONTEST 2012 FINALIST COFFEEMAKER BY WENYAO CAI

Dematerialization is just one future scenario. I doubt if culture will take such an extreme course in the domestic coffee-making market. After all, we tend to enjoy physical gadgets we can touch, play with, and brag about to friends. So maybe we don't face absolute dematerialization, but rather substantial simplification.

Piamo is also a one-cup espresso maker, perhaps a sophisticated version of the old moka pot. Invented by the German firm Gemodo Coffee, designed by studio Lunar Europe (fig. 40), it consists of a cup, water chamber, filter inlay, and filter cap. Brewing is done in thirty seconds in a microwave oven.

More gadget-like is a design concept by Wenyao Cai presented in a 2012 Electrolux design competition. It combines visually a coffee maker and a tablet. It recognizes your palm print and prepares your coffee to your personal taste. In this future trend-speculation, coffee ultimately becomes a highly personal experience rather than a social one, by nature.

Form evolution of coffee & tea preparation

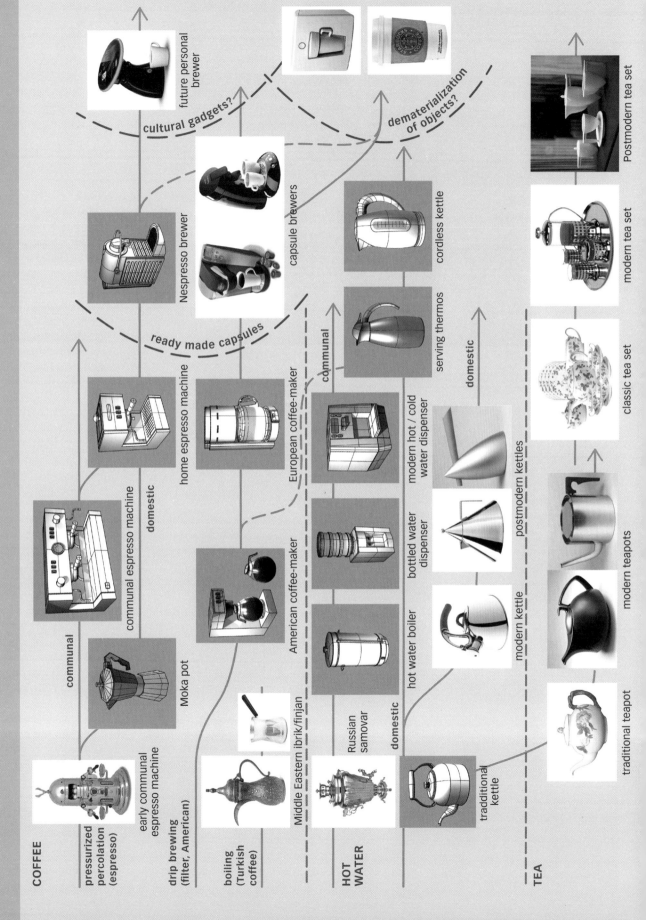

COFFEE

pressurized percolation (espresso)

early communal espresso machine · communal · communal espresso machine · domestic · home espresso machine · Nespresso brewer · capsule brewers

Moka pot

ready made capsules

cultural gadgets? · future personal brewer

drip brewing (filter, American)

American coffee-maker · European coffee-maker · communal · serving thermos · cordless kettle · domestic

dematerialization of objects?

boiling (Turkish coffee)

Middle Eastern ibrik/finjan

HOT WATER

Russian samovar · domestic · hot water boiler · bottled water dispenser · modern hot / cold water dispenser

traditional kettle · modern kettle · postmodern kettles

TEA

traditional teapot · modern teapots · classic tea set · modern tea set · Postmodern tea set

POSTSCRIPT
...but what is it?

But after having examined the subject more closely here, we have found that, in truth, technology takes the major role in defining how a product looks, with concerns for fitting the task to the user playing the next most important role (as reflected in the notion of "form follows function"). And then, finally, the corporation and the designers have their chance to influence form. Gradually we find out that that form follows form, or to be more precise—form follows the language of form.

It is inspiring to observe the many parallels between the form language of man-made objects and what we usually call language, the way we communicate with each other. Designers often refer to the language of form but rarely in concrete linguistics terms. Sign language is probably the most visual full-fledged language; it has its own grammar, syntax, and semantics. The language of form is different; it has meaning (product semantics) and even morphology. The way words are assembled is analogous to the way formal elements are assembled into something coherent. But I am not sure what parallels the rules of grammar and syntax in the visual language. There is still much to be researched and learned.

To be less speculative, we can assume that our minds hold a comprehensive dictionary that translates images into words; that a recognized form has an explicit noun assigned to it; sometimes a description (e.g. a flat-bed truck) will perform the proper translation. But meaning is evidently more complex than basic recognition; the form of the object declares something to us, sometimes emotionally.

As both language and man-made objects are major participants in defining our culture, we may also assume that the dictionary is not the same in different languages (even sign languages may differ). And as the spoken and written languages continually evolve over time, so does the language of form, maybe even more so since the causative technology evolves almost exponentially. And any change requires an implicit relationship to previous knowledge of the visual world; the development of form is evolutionary, considering the past and present when constructing the future. Designers take the role of arbiters between technology and culture, between the future and the past.

Innovative forms are more acceptable to designers. Being proficient in the language of design, they are the innovators and early adopters of cutting-edge design language. As creative people, they try to push the boundaries of design language even at the risk of their latest creation not being understood and accepted, and thus not becoming a part of the time-honored design language. In any spoken language new words abound, but only some take hold. Form language does not differ.

Now, when inexpensive 3D printers are moving from the realm of the professionals into the domain of any computer-savvy layperson, we may see more and more experimentations in the language of form. Most may not gain acceptance, but some will lead into unexpected directions.

> **I can imagine the following dialogue:**
>
> *Mom, look what I designed and built...*
>
> *What a beautiful thing you have made,* but what is it?

That is when we should backtrack to probe the semantic building blocks of the language of form!

Bibliography & References

Adams, James L., *Good Products, Bad Products: Essential Elements to Achieving Superior Quality*, McGraw Hill, 2012.

Bannert, Michael M. & Bartels, Andreas, *Decoding the Yellow of a Gray Banana,* in Current Biology 23, 2013.

Baxter, Mike, *Product Design: Practical Methods for the Systematic Development of New Products,* Chapman & Hall, London 1995.

Butler, Samuel, "Darwin among the Machines," *The Press*, Christchurch, New Zealand, 1863.

Bayley, Stephen, *Cars: Freedom, Style, Sex, Power, Motion, Colour, Everything*, Conran Octopus, 2008.

Bejan, A. and Zane, J.P., *Design in Nature*, Doubleday, 2012.

Boradkar, Prasad, *Designing Things: A Critical Introduction to the Culture of Objects*, Berg Publishing 2010.

Carsetti, Arturo (ed.), *Seeing, Thinking and Knowing: Meaning and Self-Organization in Visual Cognition and Thought*, Springer, 2004.

Chung-Hung Lin, "Research in the Use of Product Semantics to Communicate Product Design Information," in *Proceedings of HCD 2011—Human Centered Design: Second International Conference*, Springer, 2011.

Cila, Nazli, *Metaphors We Design By: The Use of Metaphors in Product Design*, PhD thesis, TUDelft 2013.

Cila, Nazli, Ozcan, E., and Hekkert, Paul, "Product Metaphor Generation: Mapping Strategies of Designers," *Proceedings of the 8th International Conference on Design and Emotion*, London, UK, 2012.

Cila, Nazli, Hekkert, Paul, and Visch, Valentijn, "Source Selection in Product Metaphor Generation: The Effects of Salience and Relatedness," *International Journal of Design*, Vol 8, No 1 (2014).

Company, Pedro, Vergara, Margarita, and Mondragón, Salvador, "Contributions to Product Semantics Taxonomy," in *Proceedings of VIII Congreso Internacional de Ingeniería de Proyectos*, 2004, Bilbao Spain, pp 872-879.

Corn, Josef J. and Horrigan, Brian, *Yesterday's Tomorrows: Past Visions of the American Future*, Johns Hopkins University Press, 1996.

Crow, David, *Left to Right: The Cultural Shift From Words to Pictures*, AVA Publ., 2006.

Dehaene, Stanislas, *Reading in the Brain*, Viking, 2009.

Dennett, Daniel C., *The Evolution of Culture*, in *Culture*, editor John Brockman, Harper Perennial, 2011.

Desmet, Pieter, and Hekkert, Paul, *Framework of Product Experience*, International Journal of Design, 2007.

Dyson, George, *Darwin Among the Machines*, Basic Books, 1997.

Henry Dreyfuss, *The Measure of Man: Human Factors in Design*, Whitney Library of Design, 1967.

Editors of Phaidon Press, *Phaidon Design Classics*, Phaidon Press, 2006.

Edsal, Larry, *Concept Cars: From the 1930 to the Present*, VMB Publ. 2009.

Edson, John, *Design Like Apple*, Willey, 2012.

Elam, Kimberly, *Geometry of Design: Studies in Proportion and Composition*, Princeton Architectural Press, 2001.

Embacher, Michael (editor), *Cyclepedia, A Tour of Iconic Bicycle Designs*, Thames & Hudson, 2011.

Eijs, Loe et al (ed) "Design and Semantics of Form and Movement" (digital conference proceedings), *DeSForM* 2008.

Fenko, Anna, Schifferstein, H.N.J., & Hekkert, Paul, "Shifts in Sensory Dominance Between Various Stages of User-Product Interactions," *Applied Ergonomics*, 41, 34-40, 2010.

Folkmann, Mads Nygaard, *The Aesthetics of Imagination in Design*, The MIT Press (Design Thinking, Design Theory Series), 2013.

Gladwell, Malcolm, *The Tipping Point: How Little Things Can Make a Big Difference*, Little, Brown & Co., 2000.

Guffey, Elizabeth E., *Retro: The Culture of Revival*, Reaktion Books—Focus on Contemporary Issues Series, 2006.

Hekkert, Paul, "Design Aesthetics: Principles of Pleasure in Product Design," *Psychology Science*, 48, 157-172 (2006).

Hjelm, Sara Ilstedt, *Semiotics in Product Design* (report), CID, Centre for User Oriented IT Design Universitat Stokholm, 2002.

Holland, Gray, "A Periodic Table of Form: The secret language of surface and meaning in product design," in *Core77* (online design magazine), 2009.

Holland, Steve, *Sci-Fi Art: A Graphic History*, Collins design, 2009.

Hosey, lance, *The Shape of Green: Aesthetics, Ecology, and Design*, Island Press, 2012.

The International Journal of Design (accessible at www.ijdesign.org).

Jackson, Gifford, "Trends in Styling of Industrially Designed Products," in *Industrial Design Magazine*, September 1962 issue.

Kenneally, Christine, *The First Word: The search for the origin of language*, Viking, 2007.

Krippendorff, Klaus & Butter, Reinhart, *Exploring the Symbolic Qualities of Form*, Innovations 3, 2 pp. 4–9, 1984.

Krippendorff, Klaus, *The Semantic Turn; A New Foundation for Design*, Taylor & Francis, CRC Press, 2006.

Kunkel, Paul, *Digital Dreams: The Work of the Sony Design Center*, Universe Publishing, 1999.

Kurzweil, Ray, *The Singularity is Near*, Penguin Group, 2005.

Leder, Helmuth, "Thinking by Design: The Science of Everyday Beauty Reveals What People Really Like—And Why," *Scientific American Mind*, July 2011.

Lévy, Pierre, "Beyond Kansei Engineering: The Emancipation of Kansei Design," *International Journal of Design*, Vol. 7 No. 2 2013.

Li, Yangyan, et al, "GlobFit: Consistently Fitting Primitives by Discovering Global Relations," *ACM Transactions on Graphics* (TOG), volume 30, issue 4, 2011.

Lidwell, William & Manacsa, Gerry, *Deconstructing Product Design*, Rockport, 2009.

Loewy, Reymond, *Industrial Design*, Overlook, 1979.

Lokman, Anitawati Mohd, "Design and Emotion: The Kansei Engineering Methodology," *The Malaysian Journal of Computing*, 2010.

Lupyan, Gary and Ward, Emily J., "Language Can Boost Otherwise Unseen Objects into Visual Awareness," *Proceedings of the National Academy of Sciences of the USA* (PNAS), 2013.

Maeda, John, *The Laws of Simplicity*, MIT Press, 2006.

Mau, Bruce and Leonard, Jennifer, *Massive Change*, Phaidon, 2004.

Marr, D. and Nishihara, H.K. (1978), "Representation and Recognition of the Spatial Organization of Three Dimensional Shapes," *Proceedings of the Royal Society of London*, B, 200, 269-294.

McMullin, Jess, "A Rough Design Maturity Continuum," *Design + Business*, 2005. www.bplusd.org

Mitchell, W. J. T., "Word and Image," in Robert Nelson and Richard Shiff, *Critical Terms for Art History*, U of Chicago Press 1996.

Mokhtarian, Farzin, & Abbasi, Sadegh, "Automatic Selection of Optimal Views in Multi-view Object Recognition," *Proceedings of the British Machine Conference*, BMVA Press, 2000.

National Science Foundation (NSF), Language and linguistics, *A Special Report—Language Change*: www.nsf.gov/news/special_reports/linguistics/change.jsp

Norman, Donald A., *The Design of Everyday Things*, MIT Press, 1998.

Norman, Donald A., *Emotional Design: Why We Love (Or Hate) Everyday Things*, Basic Books, 2004.

Norman, Donald A., *Living with Complexity*, MIT Press, 2011.

Olivares, Jonathan, *A Taxonomy of Office Chairs*, Phaidon Press, 2011.

Palmer SE, "The Effects of Contextual Scenes on the Identification of Objects," *Memory & Cognition*, 3(5): 519-26, 1975.

Petroski, Henry, *The Evolution of Useful Things*, Random House. 1994.

Phaidon Press (ed.), *Phaidon Design Classics* (3 Volume Set), Phaidon Press, 2006.

Pinker, Steven, *How the Mind Works*, Norton, 1997.

Pinker, Steven, *The Stuff of Thought: Language as a Window into Human Nature*, Penguin, 2008.

Polster, Bernd, *BRAUN: Fifty Years of Design and Innovation*, Edition Axel Menges, 2010.

Postrel, Virginia, *The Substance of Style: How the Rise of Aesthetic Value is Remaking Commerce, Culture, and Consciousness*, Harper Collins, 2003.

Pye, David, *The Nature of Design*, Studio Vista, 1964.

Reed, Stephen K., *Cognition: Theory and Applications*, Thomson Wadsworth, 2007.

Risku, Juhani, *Future of Design and Technology*, (PDF of slide presentation), 2012 http://interestmachine.files.wordpress.com/2012/10/12_juhani-risku-cloud-2017-keynote-future-of-design-computing-science-technology-5-10-2012-helsinki-university2.pdf.

Rogers, Everett M., *Diffusion of Innovations*, 5th Edition, the Free Press, 2003.

Rose, David, *Enchanted Objects: Design, Human Desire, and the Internet of Things*, Scribner, 2014.

Sacks, Oliver, *The Man who Mistook his Wife for a Hat*, Picador, 1986.

Sacks, Oliver, *The Mind's Eye*, Knopf, 2010.

Sanderson, Paul, "Why Do All New Cars Look Alike," 2012, in his blog: http://5thcolor.wordpress.com/2012/03/14/why-do-all-new-cars-look-alike.

Schmittel, Wolfgang *Design, Concept, Realisation: Braun, Citroen,* Miller, Olivetti, Sony, Swissair, ABC Editions, 1975.

Schwind, Valentin, *The Golden Ratio in 3D Human Face Modeling*, 2011, www.vali.de/wp-content/uploads/The-Golden-Ratio-in-3D-Face-Modelling.pdf

Shih-Wen Hsiao, Fu-Yuan Chiu, Shu-Hong Lu, "Product-Form Design Model Based on Genetic Algorithms," *International Journal of Industrial Ergonomics* 40 (2010).

Sjöström, Jonas & Donnellan, Brian, "Design Research Practice: A Product Semantics Interpretation," International workshop on *IT Artefact Design & Workpractice Intervention*, Barcelona, 2012.

Smith, Pamela Jaye, *Symbols, Images, Codes: The Secret Language of Meaning in Film, TV, Games, and Visual Media*, Michael Wiese productions, 2010.

Steadman, Philip, *The Evolution of Designs: Biological Analogy in Architecture and the Applied Arts*, Cambridge University Press, 1979, revised edition: Routledge, 2008.

Sterling, Bruce, *Shaping Things*, MIT press, 2005.

Storkerson, Peter, *Designing Theory in Communication*, (PDF) www.communicationcognition.com/Publications/Des_Theo_Com.pdf

Sudjic, Deyan, *The Language of Things: Understanding the World of Desirable Objects*, Norton & co., 2008.

Takamura, John H. Jr. *Product Teleosemantics: The Next Stage in the Evolution of Product Semantics*, in ISDR07 proceedings 2007.

Taylor, Nick, *Golden Mean Calipers*, in his blog: www.goldenmeancalipers.com

Tjalve, Eskild, *A Short Course in Industrial Design*, Hodder Arnold, 1979.

Tomasello, Michael, *The Cultural Origins of Human Cognition*, Harvard University Press, 1999.

Tse, P. U. and Hughes, H. C., "Visual Form Perception," *The Encyclopedia of Neuroscience* Adelman, G. and Smith, B. (Eds.). Elsevier, 2004.

Verganti, Roberto, *Design-Driven Innovation*, Harvard Business Press, 2009.

Wardley, Simon, *On Mapping and the Evolution Axis*, 2014, in his blog http://blog.gardeviance.org/2014/03/on-mapping-and-evolution-axis.html

Ware, Colin, *Information Visualization: Perception for Design*, 3rd ed. Morgan Kaufmann, 2012.

Ware, Colin, *Visual Thinking for Design*, Morgan Kaufmann, 2008.

Weinschenk, Susan M., *100 Things Every Designer Needs to Know About People*, New Rider, 2011.

Wu, Chun Ting & Johnston, Malcolm, "The Use of Images and Descriptive Words in the Development of an Image Database for Product Designers," in *Design and Semantics of Form and Movement* (conference proceedings) 2005 p. 68.

Xu, Kai, et al, "Fit and Diverse: Set Evolution for Inspiring 3D Shape Galleries," in *ACM Transactions on Graphics (TOG)*, SIGGRAPH 2012 Conference Proceedings, Volume 31 Issue 4, July 2012.

Image credits

Images not credited in the following list are copyrighted by Josiah Kahane.

Introduction: What we "read" between the lines: 1-Yacht Island Design, 2-Frankie Flood, 3-Yacht Island Design, 4-Jean Pierre Lepine, 5-Vivien Muller, 6-Dexsil, 7-HJX, 8-Plantronix, 9-Lothar Windels Industrial Design, 10-unknown source, 11-Hiromi Kiriki, 12-courtesy of ASKA, 13-Jai Ho Yoo and Lukas Vanek, 14-Hiromi Kiriki, 15-unknown source.

The mind's eye: 1-Flip Schulke, 2a-Snooty Peacock, 2b-Mind That Works, 3a-Gaetano Kanizsa, 3b-WWF, World Wildlife Fund, 3c-Unilever Corporation, 4-Josiah Kahane, 5-unknown source, 6-based on Marr & Nishihara, 7-Marr & Nishihara, 8a-Josiah Kahane, 8b-Radu Horaud, 9-Aaron Diaz, 10a-unknown source, 10b-Stylo Design, 11a-University of Oxford, 11b-FMRIB Centre, 12-AIGA, the Professional Association for Design, 13-Stanislas Dehaene, based on Ishai and Puce, 14-The Lighthouse, Glasgow, 15-Universal Studios, 16-Mozainuddin, 17-Mokhtarian, Farzin, & Abbasi, Sadegh, 18-Suzuki Corporation, 19-Shutterstock, 20-BIS Publishers, 21-unknown source, 22-Help Remedies Inc., 23-based on Bejan & Zane, 24-Shutterstock.

Reviewing the designed form: 1-miniature room by Tim Sidford, 2-Jerom M. Eisenberg inc., 3-members.iinet.net.au, 4-Don Mammoser / Shutterstock, 5-Raymond Loewy, 6-Gifford Jackson, 7-Wired Magazine, 8-Jesus Diaz, Gizmodo, 9-Cranbrook Academy, 10-IDEO, 11-Illuminated Mirrors, 12-Jan van Es, 13-unknown source, 14-unknown source, 15-Vladimir Rachev, 16a-Enjoy Dive, 16b-Liquid Image Co., 16c-Hanok Electronic Co., 17-Art Lebedev Studio, 18-Gray Holland, 19-Gray Holland, 20-Gray Holland, 21-NASA, 22-Josiah Kahane, 23-Buy Costumes, 24-unknown source, 25-USAF, 26-Li, Yangyan, et al, 27-Xu, Kai, et al 28-Xu, Kai, et al, 29-Xu, Kai, et al.

In context 1: Aesthetics of Form: 1-Discover Digital Photo, 2-Figure7 / Meritt Thomas, 3-Braun AG, 4-Brandon Hollingshead, The Fountain Pen Network, 5-Princeton Architectural Press, 6-Chris Boardman, 7-Desmet, Pieter, & Hekkert, Paul, 8-Josiah Kahane, 9-unknown source, 10-Nick Taylor, 11-Juhani Risku.

A conjectural framework: 1-Jess McMullin, 2-Josiah Kahane, 3-unknown source, 4-Josiah Kahane, 5-Josiah Kahane, 6-Michael Gudo & Manfred Grasshoff, 7-Peter Storkerson, 8-Thinkmap Visual Thesaurus, 9-The English Duden, 10-Shih-Wen Hsiao, Fu-Yuan Chiu, Shu-Hong Lu, 11-Glennz Tees.

Temporal aspects of form evolution: 1-based on Simon Wardley, 2-Josiah Kahane, 3-Josiah Kahane, 4-Josiah Kahane, 5-Adapted from Paul Kunkel, 6-Herman Miller, Inc., 7-Reza Akhmad, 8-Coca Cola Company, 9-unknown source, 10a-Conair Corporation, 10b-Fiat, 12a-unknown source, 12b-Kata Music, 12c-Kata Music, 13-unknown source, 14-Shutterstock, 15-Public domain, 16-Sonny Ericsson, 17-Segway.

Spatial aspects of form evolution: 1-Fred Butler, 2-Josiah Kahane, 3-Josiah Kahane, 4-Josiah Kahane, 5a-Nikodem Nijaki, 5b-Singer Sewing Company, 6-Erskin Tijalve, 7-Aim Surgical, 8-Shutterstock, 9-Daniel Abendroth & Andreas Meinhardt.

External catalysts of form evolution: 1a-Kate Spade New York, 1b-MagicSky, 1c-Mosnovo, 2-Swatch Ltd., 3-Jaguar Land Rover North America, LLC., 4-Muji, 5-Boskke.

In Context 2 – Technology Leaders: 1-Josiah Kahane, 2-Public domain, 3-Universum Film (UFA), 4-Hugh Ferriss Architectural Drawings and Papers Collection, Columbia University. 5-Bauhaus-Archiv Berlin, 6-unknown source, 7-Jean-Noël Cabanettes, 8-Ransom Center's Bel Geddes archive, University of Texas, 9-Christer Johansson, 10-unknown source, 11-Daniel Laon Design, 12-Kyle Bean, 13-Amblin Entertainment, 14-Adidas Originals & Lucas Film, 15-20th Century Fox, 16-Island Press, 17-Kellar Autumn, 18-Next Home Collection, 19-Josiah Kahane.

Case Study 1 – The Camera Family: 1-Public domain, 9-Minolta Corporation, 25-Tasco.

Case Study 2 – Personal Media Communicators: 15-Sony Corporation, 26-unknown source, 27-Johnny Chung Lee, 29-Tommaso Gecchelin.

Case Study 3 – Faxes, Printers, and Copiers: 7a-unknown source, 7b-Creative Commons license,., 10-Xerox Corporation, 15-Xerox Corporation, 19-Canon Inc., 21-MakerBot Industries, 22-Stratasys.

Case Study 4 – Television Screens: 4-Patti Schlutz Design Studio, 5-teddy@.t3d.be, 9-Vintage Italy, 12-Plus Minus Zero Co., 13-Sharp Corporation, 14-Panasonic Corporation.

Case Study 5 – Home Entertainment: 5a-Shutterstock, 5b-Shutterstock, 7-Denon Electronics, 11-JVC-Kenwood Corp., 14-Samsung Corp., 17-Bang & Olufsen A/S, 18-Bang & Olufsen A/S, 19-Bang & Olufsen A/S.

Case Study 6 – The Automobile: 1-Rohit Seth / Shutterstock, 2-Ugur Sahin, 3-Toyota Motor Corporation, 4-Paul Sanderson, 5-Toyota Motor Corporation, 6-Jeep, 7-unknown source, 8-unknown source, 9-unknown source, 10-unknown source, 11-unknown source, 12-Ford Motor Company, 13-Daimler AG, 14-Chrysler GEM, 15-Public domain, 16-unknown source, 17-unknown source, 18-Toyota Motor Corporation, 19-GM Holden Ltd, 20-Bayerische Motoren Werke AG, 21-Citroën S.A, 22-Alfa Romeo Automobiles S.p.A., 23-IFCAR, 24-Chrysler Group LLC, 25-Christer Johansson, 26-Cadillac Division GMC, 27-Jaguar Land Rover, 28-unknown source, 29-unknown source, 30- unknown source, 31-Daimler AG, 32-unknown source, 33-Citroën S.A, 34-Citroën S.A, 35-Ransom Center's Bel Geddes Archive, 36-High Museum of Art, Atlanta, 37-unknown source, 38-Ondrej Jirec, 39-Bayerische Motoren Werke AG, 40-Fernando Faria, 41-Columbia Pictures, 42-DeLorean Motor Company, 43-Jai Ho Yoo and Lukas Vanek, 44-Pineapple Fez, 45-Toyota Motor Corporation, 46-Fiat S.p.A.

Case Study 7 – Two-Wheel Transportation: 1-Josiah Kahane, 2-Giant Bicycle Inc., 3-David Iliff. License: CC-BY-SA 3.0, 4-Brompton Bicycle Ltd., 5-Bayerische Motoren Werke AG, 6-Yuji Fujimura, 7-Bradford Waugh, 8-AUDI AG, 9-unknown source, 10-unknown source, 11-Harley Davidson USA, 12-KTM Sportmotorcycle GmbH, 13-Ducati Motor Holding S.p.A, 14-replica following Cliff Vaughn, 15-Daniel Simon / Cosmic Motors LLC, 16-Amir Glinik, 17-Lit Motors, 18-Vespa Nation, 19-unknown source, 20-Sanyang Industry Co., 21-Suzuki Motor Corporation, 22-American Girl, 23-unknown source, 24-Razor USA LLC, 25-Segway Inc., 26-Segway Inc.

Case Study 8 – Vacuum Cleaners: 1-Eskild Tjalve, 2-public domain, 11-Black & Decker Inc., 12-Black & Decker Inc., 13-Alessi SPA, 15-Dyson Ltd., 16-Dyson Ltd., 17-Dyson Ltd.

Case Study 9 – Home Air Blowing Devices: 11a-Honeywell International Inc. 11b-Nest Labs.

Case Study 10 – Major Home Appliances: 7-Electrolux Design Lab/ Yuriy Dmitriev, 18-Jakub Lekeš.

Case Study 11 – Food Preparation Appliances: 1-Levi Szekeres (public domain), 2a-LEM Products Inc., 6-Dualit Limited, 7-Koninklijke Philips N.V., 11-Braun GmbH, 19-Bodum (Schweiz) AG, 20-Alessi SPA, 24-George Watson, 25-Inventables Concept Studio, 26-Kenwood Limited, 27-West Bend Housewares/Back to Basics Products, 28-Bodum (Schweiz) AG, 29-Koninklijke Philips N.V.

Case Study 12 – Hand Power Tools: 1-Shutterstock, 2-Shutterstock, 3-Robert Bosch Tool Corporation, 4-DEWALT Industrial Tool Co., 11-Robert Bosch Tool Corporation, 21-Black & Decker Inc., 22-Makita Corporation.

Case Study 13 – Chairs: 1-Icons etc., 2-a detail from Vincent Van Gogh painting, The National Gallery, London, 3-Henry Brudenell-Bruce, 4-Arconas, Canada, 5-Colani Collection by Kusch+Co, 6-Kenjiro Yamakawa and Loren Kulesus, 7- Shutterstock, 8-Peter Opsvik, 9a-unknown source, 9b-unknown source, 10a-unknown source, 10b-unknown source, 11-Josiah Kahane, 12- American Signature Furniture, 13a-Daniel Michalik, 13b-Morosco, 14a-public domain, 14b-Knoll, 15a-Vitra, 15b-Ana Linares Design, 16a-Fredericia, 16b-Jason Liu / Vignelli Archive, 17a-Vitra, 17b-Morosco, 18a-Thonet, 18b-Knoll, 19a-public domain, 20a-Magis, 20b-Driade, 21a-public domain, 21b-unknown source, 22a-Ambivalenz, 22b-Vange, 23a-Magis, 23b-Plycollection Ltd. Latvia, 24a-American Country Home Store, 24b-Boss Office Products, 25a-unknown source, 25b-Commodore, 26a-Herman Miller, Inc., 26b-Herman Miller, Inc., 27a-Herman Miller, Inc., 27b-Herman Miller, Inc.

Case Study 14 – Coffee and Tea Preparation: 1-Tadesse Wolde Aregay, 2-Shutterstock, 3-Antonio Milena (public domain), 4a-unknown source, 4b-unknown source, 5a-Yongbin (Free Documentation license), 5b-Bodum (Schweiz) AG, 6a-public domain, 6b-La Pavoni S.p.A., 10-De'Longhi Appliances S.r.l., 14-Keurig Green Mountain, Inc., 15-Philips Electronics N.V., 16-Nestlé S.A., 17-Armathwaite Hall Hotel, 18-Daoli, China, 19-Waterford Wedgewood USA, 20-Rosenthal GMBH, 21-Stelton A/S, 22-Adrian Saxe, 23-Waterford Wedgewood UK, 24-shop3ds, 25-Brice Hudson, 26-NewChi Company, LTD, 27-BEEM, Blitz-Elektro-Erzeugnisse, Manufaktur Handels-GmbH, 33-Oxo, 34-Alessi S.p.A., 35-Alessi S.p.A., 37-unknown source, 38-unknown source, 39-WMF Württembergische Metallwarenfabrik AG, 40-Piamo-Espresso, 41-Electrolux Design Lab/ WenYao Cai.

Index